Being in the news business, I have a front-row seat to the ugly side of life. But never have I seen our country so divided. It is sick, miserable, and evil, and that is why Brigitte Gabriel and her message are so needed in this hour. I hope her new book, *Rise*, can alert people to the attacks on religious freedoms. I believe it is our responsibility to recognize and confront evil in the world—and I'm convinced that if we fail in that mission, it will lead us to disaster. That's why I applaud Brigitte for writing *Rise* and fearlessly speaking the truth once again about the real threats to our country. If you're a concerned American who wants to know the truth, you need to read this book!

—SEAN HANNITY
NEW YORK TIMES BEST-SELLING AUTHOR; POLITICAL COMMENTATOR;
AND HOST, HANNITY AND THE SEAN HANNITY SHOW

As a former prosecutor and judge, I've seen firsthand the evil in our world and the toughness it takes to keep that evil at bay. As the host of a Fox News show, I've also witnessed the sinister agenda of the radical Left that is determined to erode the foundations of our great nation and change America as we know it. Amid the liberals, liars, and lunatics, I'm grateful there are still voices of sanity out there willing to stand up and speak the truth no matter the cost. Brigitte Gabriel is such a voice. Like me, she has seen evil and she isn't afraid to tell it like it is. Her first book, *Because They Hate*, was a wake-up call about the agenda of radical Islamic terrorism, and I believe her new book, *Rise*, will have a similar impact on the new and increasing threats to our nation today. *Rise* is a must-read for every American who senses the perilous path we're on and wants to do their part to change the course of our country.

—JUDGE JEANINE PIRRO
HOST, JUSTICE WITH JUDGE JEANINE ON FOX NEWS

Brigitte Gabriel's new book, *Rise*, is a searing, truth-telling exposé of the growing threat to the values of Judeo-Christian civilization and a recipe for what concerned Americans can do to save this country in the time we have left.

—DINESH D'SOUZA
AUTHOR AND FILMMAKER

My friend Brigitte Gabriel is a fierce and fearless patriot who fights every day to defend America and the West from civilizational threats at home and abroad. Heed her warnings. Follow her lead. Support her work. Brigitte is an invaluable beacon for freedom!

—Michelle Malkin
Author and Political Commentator
Senior Editor, Conservative Review

Brigitte Gabriel has it right. Radical Islamists do for the world what the Ku Klux Klan did for African Americans in the South. Their apologists are particularly distasteful; their ideology would set us back to the Middle Ages. Brigitte shines truth like a tenfold beacon at night.

—Bill Cunningham
Nationally Syndicated Talk Show Host, Conservative
Commentator, Attorney, and Entrepreneur

I love the principles I was raised with and saw in action growing up in southern Missouri. I know that Brigitte Gabriel shares my passion for defending these same principles. That's why I encourage you to read her book *Rise: In Defense of Judeo-Christian Values and Freedom*. It's an eye-opener that will inform the way you think, but more importantly it will empower what you do!

—Dana Loesch
Activist, Host of the Nationally Syndicated Daily Radio Show
The Dana Show, and Best-Selling Author

Brigitte Gabriel is the epitome of an American patriot, a resolute and courageous woman who has seen evil firsthand and survived. When she speaks, she articulates why America is indeed the exceptional "shining city on a hill." In her new book, *Rise: In Defense of Judeo-Christian Values and Freedom*, Lady Gabriel issues a resounding, stentorian call to action for those who love this great country, the constitutional republic we call home, these United States of America. No one is more passionate. No one is more clear. No one is more fearless when it comes to the defense of our Judeo-Christian values and freedom than my dear friend and fellow warrior Brigitte Gabriel. If you seek her strength, then read *Rise* and, in the words of the motto of my hometown Atlanta Falcons, "Rise up."

—Lt. Col. Allen B. West, US Army, Ret.
Former Member, 112th US Congress

Brigitte is not only an inspirational picture of courage and female empowerment, she is the perfect example of the American Dream. I am honored to call her a friend. *Rise* is not just a book—it is a rallying cry for Americans. If we don't rise up and come together to protect and defend the American way of life, we will lose it forever. This book serves as the perfect reminder of what we have and what we have to lose.

—Tomi Lahren
"Final Thoughts" Commentator, *Fox News Insider*

During a time in our country when the phrase *American exceptionalism* is deemed exclusionary by the Left, when the idea that America is the land of opportunity has been labeled as a racist microaggression on college campuses, and when Democratic senators choose to ask presidential nominees about gay sex in an effort to label all Christians as bigots and extremists, Brigitte Gabriel is unafraid to defend the principles on which our nation was founded: the universal truths that all men are endowed by their Creator with the unalienable rights to life, liberty, and the pursuit of happiness. Only in America have these truths been protected for as many men, women, and children, for as long and as wholly as they have for the past 241 years, and if we don't continue to defend the Judeo-Christian values on which our idea of justice was built, our grandchildren won't be able to look at their country and say the same thing. Brigitte Gabriel in *Rise* is fighting the good fight.

—Liz Wheeler
Host, *Tipping Point With Liz Wheeler*
on One America News Network

In an era of fake news and an unabashed agenda of the Left to confuse and misinform the American people, it is now more important than ever that the voices of truth rise up and make themselves heard. Brigitte Gabriel is one of those voices and in her new book, *Rise*, she exposes the true state of our nation and the very real threats to our national way of life. She boldly exposes the biases, hatred, and lies being spread about conservative principles in the name of "tolerance" and "justice." Like Brigitte, I believe there are critical times in the life of every nation when taking a passive stance leads to irreversible destruction. If we choose the passive route in this crucial time, our grandchildren will not know the same America that has been our privilege to experience. If we remain silent, the forces that seek to destroy America will win. Brigitte's new book is a clarion call to everyone who holds our freedoms dear. No longer can we remain inactive. No longer can we ignore the truth. No longer can we sit silently while radicals advance their plans to erode our nation's foundation. It's time to stand strong in defense of our values and freedoms. It's time to rise.

—L. Brent Bozell III
President, Media Research Center
Chairman, ForAmerica

We live in a world where it's much easier to be offended than to take responsibility for the problems in culture and use our unique, individual voices to become part of the solution. That's why when I find someone willing to take an honest, politically incorrect approach to discussing the complex issues facing our country today and empowering people to get involved, I pay attention. Brigitte Gabriel is an unfiltered, unapologetic voice of truth exposing the threats to free speech and other rights that Western countries are built upon. The driving force behind her new book, *Rise*, is her belief that "we never really own freedom. It's something we preserve and pass on to the next generation." *Rise* is a call to action, challenging and equipping Americans to stand up and preserve the values that made our country great. Brigitte is someone who cares about preserving our freedoms. That's what *The Rubin Report* is all about, and that's why I highly recommend Brigitte and her new book, *Rise*.

—Dave Rubin
Comedian and Host, *The Rubin Report*

Lady Brigitte Gabriel has been a frequent guest on my show, *Rose Unplugged*. I am always inspired by her commitment to our sovereign nation and the protection of the freedoms that guarantee our security. She is one of the bravest women I know. Unafraid to speak out in the face of threats from the enemies of freedom, undaunted she fights!

This book is a must-read. It must never be forgotten that it was God who established this nation, and it is those Judeo-Christian values that have kept us afloat for over two hundred years.

—Rose Somma Tennent
Host, *Rose Unplugged*

Brigitte Gabriel is an icon of American bravery. Her courageous stands in the face of corruption stiffen the spines of American patriots who want to see their beloved country excel and advance in the best ways possible.

—Imam Tawhidi
Australian Muslim Scholar, Educator, Speaker,
Leading Voice in the Global Movement of Islamic Reform

Brigitte Gabriel has so much in common with America: they're both incredibly inspirational; they've both struggled and thrived in the face of overwhelming odds; and they're both warriors for the cause of freedom.

—Joe Piscopo
Radio Host, *The Joe Piscopo Show*

Brigitte Gabriel has taught the masses—me included—so much about our great land, freedom and liberty, our value system, and what it truly takes from all of us to retain and protect what it is we take for granted. In *Rise* she reminds us why America is much more than a place on a map. It's a value system and mind-set constantly under siege by those who want to force their own ideology upon her and control the population. This is a very important must-read for all who love freedom!

—Joe "Pags" Pagliarulo
Host, *The Joe Pags Show*

RISE

BRIGITTE GABRIEL

Most CHARISMA HOUSE BOOK GROUP products are available at special quantity discounts for bulk purchase for sales promotions, premiums, fundraising, and educational needs. For details, write Charisma House Book Group, 600 Rinehart Road, Lake Mary, Florida 32746, or telephone (407) 333-0600.

RISE by Brigitte Gabriel
Published by FrontLine
Charisma Media/Charisma House Book Group
600 Rinehart Road
Lake Mary, Florida 32746
www.charismahouse.com

Unless otherwise noted, all Scripture quotations are taken from the Holy Bible, New International Version®, NIV®. Copyright © 1973, 1978, 1984, 2011 by Biblica, Inc.™ Used by permission of Zondervan. All rights reserved worldwide. www.zondervan.com. The "NIV" and "New International Version" are trademarks registered in the United States Patent and Trademark Office by Biblica, Inc.™

Scripture quotations marked NKJV are taken from the New King James Version®. Copyright © 1982 by Thomas Nelson. Used by permission. All rights reserved.

Visit the author's websites at www.actforamerica.org and www.risebybrigittegabriel.com.

Library of Congress Cataloging-in-Publication Data:
Names: Gabriel, Brigitte, author.
Title: Rise / Brigitte Gabriel.
Description: Lake Mary, FL : FrontLine, 2018.
Identifiers: LCCN 2018029512 (print) | LCCN 2018032920 (ebook) | ISBN

9781629995489 (ebook) | ISBN 9781629995472 (hardcover)

Subjects: LCSH: Christianity--Influence. | Christianity and culture--United States. | United States--Social conditions--21st century. | United States--Politics and government--21st century. | United States--Forecasting.

Classification: LCC BR517 (ebook) | LCC BR517 .G28 2018 (print) | DDC 277.3/083--dc23

LC record available at https://lccn.loc.gov/2018029512

18 19 20 21 22 — 987654321

Printed in the United States of America

Dedicated to my mother and father who devoted their lives to honoring God, giving to charity, and showing me how to live a meaningful life. They loved America and everything it represented. Though they never lived to reach its shores, as my way of honoring them and their legacy, I fight to protect and promote the Judeo-Christian values that shaped their lives and America's freedoms and rights, which they admired and respected. I dedicate this book and all my efforts to honor them.

CONTENTS

INTRODUCTION

MY EYES SLOWLY opened, and I found myself staring once more at the mildew-covered cement wall just inches from my face. Strange as it sounds, those gray blocks were as beautiful as the Sistine Chapel to me. The sight of them meant I had survived another night in the dingy underground bomb shelter in Lebanon that I called home.

Despite the circumstances, I glowed from ear to ear every morning, because I knew that by waking up, it meant at least one more day that I could hug and kiss my parents. Having air in my lungs meant I still had a chance to survive and that one day things would go back to the way they were before the war.

I was forced to live in that eighty-by-ten-foot bomb shelter for seven years, from the age of ten to seventeen, robbing me of my childhood. Instead of playing games with friends, I spent years in that shelter lying in bed, knitting, or crocheting to keep my mind off the fact that my life could be over in an instant.

Islamic radicals blew up my home in a small Christian town in southern Lebanon in 1975, forcing my parents and me below ground as our only chance to survive. My life story is detailed in my first *New York Times* best seller, *Because They Hate*.

Raised Catholic, my day started with a prayer thanking Jesus and Mary for watching over me another night and keeping me safe. Every night I prayed very hard to live just one more day while bombs rained from above.

Faith is all you have when your shadow, the shadow of death, becomes your only playmate. As a young teenager in a bomb shelter with nowhere to go and no one my age to talk to, I needed an escape.

My only window to the world was through a black-and-white television operated on a car battery. My father turned it on only at night so we could watch the evening news and hear the latest status of the war. We had three stations to choose from: Israeli TV, Jordanian TV, and Middle East Television—not a large variety of choices compared to nowadays.

Still, that television took me to places I could only dream of at the time. It was my source of therapy, along with my faith and my family. Shows like *CHiPs*, *Dallas*, *Love Boat*, *Little House on the Prairie*, and *The Waltons* took me halfway around the world to the greatest nation in the history of mankind, the United States of America.

In addition to helping me learn English, those shows enchanted me. The world they depicted was such a profound contrast to the hell I was living in at the time. I would dream and fantasize about the television magically sucking my parents and me through it and transporting us to America—this land of freedom, safety, and prosperity.

I loved the tightly knit, God-loving family units depicted on *The Waltons* and *Little House on the Prairie*. These families forged their own paths, using their ingenuity and bare hands to make a living, never forgetting what matters most is not *what* you have in your life, but *who* you have.

I learned this lesson personally when my home was bombed and nearly every material possession was taken from me. I went from having maids to eating dandelions that I would dig out around our bomb shelter when the bullets and explosions would subside for a while.

I went from having a chauffeur drive me to school to being driven to and from school in a military tank, which could fit myself and fifteen other children inside. Some days I had to run home from school as fast as I could, and I routinely dove into ditches as bombshells exploded and bullets scattered the ground near my feet. In an act of desperation, I remember using my books to cover my head, hoping they would offer me the protection I needed to spare my life.

My school began to function as a place to learn as well as a bomb shelter. A bomb shelter needed at least two roofs, so when the explosion penetrated, the second roof would dramatically decrease the number of casualties.

Still, in spite of having almost nothing, I had everything. The things that truly mattered were right next to me in that shelter—the unshakable bond and faith in God that we shared as a family, the values we lived by and were willing to die for, and even learning to reject hatred and forgive our enemies for the evil that they did to us.

I loved how shows like *CHiPs* and *Hawaii Five-0* combined adventure with humor and portrayed the American police officer as a figure to be respected and admired. Shows like *Happy Days* depicted the small-town American utopia in which I could only dream of living, and there was always an important life lesson in every episode.

That was the America to which I dreamed of coming. Those are the Judeo-Christian values that came to fruition to form the greatest nation the world has ever seen.

America became a larger-than-life word that represented a larger-than-life country where nothing is impossible with perseverance and hard work. America had no boundaries—it was just a wide-open world where the sky is the limit. America represented all the values I grew up with but captured them in a way no other country on earth ever had before.

AMERICA, WHERE HAVE YOU GONE?

They don't make many shows like the ones I watched growing up anymore. Instead, we have the chaos of *Real Housewives*, the self-absorbed materialism of the Kardashians, the racial politics of *Black-ish*, the vulgarity mixed with political propaganda on *The Late Show With Stephen Colbert*, and the list goes on and on.

Judeo-Christian values are the fundamental building blocks of Western civilization. Freedom, family, faith, and fortitude all helped provide the infrastructure for the benefits we reap today. But these principles that helped shape our nation have been slowly eroding, leaving us vulnerable to catastrophic internal collapse.

Abraham Lincoln said it best when he noted:

> At what point shall we expect the approach of danger? By what means shall we fortify against it?—Shall we expect some transatlantic military giant, to step the Ocean, and crush us at a blow? Never!— All the armies of Europe, Asia and Africa combined...could not by force, take a drink from the Ohio, or make a track on the Blue Ridge, in a trial of a thousand years. At what point then is the approach of danger to be expected? I answer, if it ever reach us, it must spring up amongst us. It cannot come from abroad. If destruction be our lot, we must ourselves be its author and finisher. As a nation of freemen, we must live through all time, or die by suicide.[1]

Just like the Roman Empire before it, America, mighty as it is, can self-destruct. But this process will likely not happen overnight. Even if our destruction were to occur in the blink of an eye, countless warning signs have preceded it.

The Catos and Ciceros of Rome predicted the empire's collapse nearly half a millennium before its actual fall. They knew that as they shifted from republic to empire, the consequences would be fatal. Freedoms were taken away, corruption was legitimized, and government entitlements bled the empire dry.[2]

So we've evidently learned nothing over the past 2,073 years!

Today even our most fundamental freedoms, such as freedom of speech, are under attack by the tyranny of "tolerance." Free speech is the new "hate speech," and the right to exercise one's opinion seems to end where the radical Left's feelings begin.

Corruption at the highest levels of our government often appears to go either unnoticed or unpunished. When the secretary of state can destroy evidence in an ongoing federal corruption investigation only to have her pals at the FBI cover for her, we do not have rule of law; we have anarchy. When an outgoing presidential administration can weaponize the justice department and intelligence agencies to attack a candidate from an opposition party even after he has left office, we do not have rule of law; we have anarchy.

Those who choose to put their lives on the line to defend this nation and enforce its laws as their patriotic and civic duty are rewarded with mockery, disrespect, and slander from its citizens. Among the audacious are professional athletes who view kneeling for the national anthem as some sort of warped heroism.

The media spreads falsehoods about the American police officer, seeking to inflame racial tensions between black and white at almost every turn. Of course, this only takes place when they're not spreading fake news stories about Russia colluding with President Trump to rig the election.

Elected officials seem particularly generous spending your tax dollars on welfare programs for unvetted Islamic refugees and newly arrived immigrants, many of whom do not respect our nation or the values it embodies.

Worst of all, our enemies seem to be as united as we are divided. While many radical Islamists from all around the globe have been flocking to join the Islamic caliphate known as ISIS, others, inspired by their progress, have chosen to wage war from right outside their Western backyards.

Foolishly, many tasked with protecting us have refused to take the threats we face seriously. In doing so, they have endangered their citizens in the name of political correctness and social justice.

Parents remain too distracted by their careers, material possessions, or modern technological devices to notice that their children are being taught in their daily classes to hate this nation, those who founded it, and even the very principles upon which it was founded. While they think their children are learning about the Judeo-Christian virtues of minds such as Jefferson, Madison, Washington, and Lincoln, in reality, they're learning the virtues of Che, Castro, Marx, Lenin, and even Muhammad.

Instead of the tight-knit, God-loving families I watched on my black-and-white television, American families have become fragmented, distracted, and self-absorbed units. That's what happens when all of a sudden, you can get any piece of information you want in the blink of an eye. Instant gratification has become a way of life, and with it, the failure to recognize the virtues of perseverance, self-reliance, and sacrifice.

These were the virtues that inspired a generation of Americans to rise and defeat the Axis powers during World War II. When the Japanese bombed Pearl Harbor, Americans came together, made sacrifices, and persevered to save the world from tyranny and genocide.

We get a clearer picture of this when we compare our response to 9/11 to that of Pearl Harbor. In the immediate aftermath of 9/11 Americans did come together with remarkable patriotism as we did in 1945. We mourned together, prayed together, and vowed to defeat this enemy as one United States of America. But as time progressed after the tragedy of 2001, our memory of the attacks faded. We forgot what we promised we never would.

We allowed ourselves to become distracted from the fundamental fight for Western civilization that was and still is at stake. The Judeo-Christian values that were so unshakable during and after World War II were not nearly as strong.

Looking back on it now, 9/11 showed us how ill our culture was. We lacked any Judeo-Christian backbone, and when it came down to it, our leaders simply weren't willing to do what was necessary to defend our land and way of life.

We are still heading down a dangerous road, with fewer and fewer exit signs left before we reach the point of no return. But if we're going to restore America to prominence, we can only do so by also recognizing and resurrecting the principles that made America the shining city on a hill we all remember it to be.

We must not be ashamed of our heritage, our nationality, or our way of life. If we as Americans cannot champion the virtues of freedom, we cannot possibly expect others to do so.

These are the sentiments that inspired me to write this book. It will highlight the most critical problems facing our nation today. It will explain how we got here and what we can do as people who love this country to see that it's saved.

Regardless of color, gender, or background, as Americans we are all united under the same flag of freedom. I believe each one of us can be used as an instrument of change in this life. This book is a rallying cry for every citizen who bleeds red, white, and blue and does not apologize for their patriotism.

Fragmented we are fragile, but united we possess the potential to save this nation from doom and restore it to its rightful place as the greatest in the history of mankind. But we cannot accomplish this from our keyboards. We must rise and take action, matching the enthusiasm of our enemies.

My sincerest hope is that each one of you who read this will not just absorb it as information, but that you become inspired to take action on behalf of your country, community, and family. I assure you, by the time you finish reading this book, you're going to know exactly what we're up against and what you can do as an instrument of change to lead this nation back to prominence, prosperity, and safety.

Chapter 1

OUR NATION DIVIDED

Septembers 11, 2001, was a day so monumentally tragic, its memory seems more like a dream than reality. The world came to a grinding halt as thousands of innocent civilian lives were cut short by the sword of radical Islamic terrorism.

Suddenly the whole world became smaller. Nineteen jihadists, all hailing from the Middle East, an overwhelming majority from Saudi Arabia, were able to pull off the most massive terror strike in world history.[1] The attacks we suffered that day were not only against our nation but also on Judeo-Christian Western civilization and all the freedoms and prosperity it provides us.

The twin towers were not only the tallest buildings in New York City, but they were also the centerpiece of the World Trade Center complex. More than just a majestic architectural feat, they symbolized capitalism, freedom, and the American dream. They represented a pinnacle of unequivocal success only achieved in a society built on Judeo-Christian values and principles. The towers said to the rest of the world, "This is what Western civilization is capable of producing: a society of unlimited achievement, innovation, strength, and success." This unmistakable message was the real target of those who brought down the towers, not just the lives they took in the process.

Like the twin towers, America also is viewed as the epitome of Judeo-Christian exceptionalism by our enemies. Some may challenge that sentiment, but such objections are not relevant to those who seek our destruction. Jihadists don't concern themselves with Western opinions about America, and in their view America is Westernization at its most powerful.

This concept is critically important to understand. Americans were shocked and confused as the world stopped turning on September 11, 2001, because they couldn't imagine how anyone could commit such a soullessly evil act. "What did we do to deserve this?" they asked.

As I outlined in my previous book *Because They Hate*, jihadists hate us because we are infidels, and they view our way of life as a direct threat to theirs. This belief, embedded in jihadist ideology, functions as the Islamist justification for the atrocities committed on 9/11.

The deeper meaning behind the twin towers made them a primary target of Islamic terrorism, not once but twice in less than ten years. If the attacks we suffered on 9/11 were merely an attempt to take life, why not the Willis Tower in Chicago? Why not the Empire State Building? Because jihadists wanted to destroy not only life but symbols of free trade, capitalism, and the inter national exchange of these values they reject.

Unfortunately, what we cherish most about America is what our ene- mies hate most about our country. While the Western world mourned on September 11, 2001, Palestinians danced in the streets with joy. Think of it this way: in the Western world we love and celebrate life. In the Islamic world they love and celebrate death. That's a contrast with profoundly dan- gerous consequences.

Our military was and is the greatest and most powerful force in the world. But the might of our armed forces couldn't defend us that fateful September morning. With the dawn of a new millennium came the dawn of new threats never before considered in our society.

The Pentagon in Washington, DC, was another target of symbolic importance to jihadists. Serving as the headquarters for the Department of Defense, the Pentagon represented our ability to defend ourselves from those who seek to destroy us.

Aside from Pearl Harbor, there had never been an attack on American soil by a foreign enemy of comparable magnitude prior to 9/11. Americans woke up that crystal-clear September day feeling the same security they'd felt their entire lives. But by mid-morning their peace of mind had evapo- rated entirely.

- No longer was our brute military force a sufficient defense for our homeland.
- No longer were we protected by two vast oceans.
- No longer could we turn a blind eye to the threats of the new millennium.
- We were all rightfully terrified.

Flight 93, the last of the hijacked planes, was screaming toward the White House at over 500 mph when brave souls on board cried out, "Let's roll," and stormed the cockpit valiantly. The hijackers intentionally took down the plane and innocent lives along with it, but they did not hit their intended political target at 1600 Pennsylvania Avenue. Instead, they crashed in a des- olate field in Shanksville, Pennsylvania, due to the selfless and heroic bravery of civilians on board.[2]

The White House symbolizes more than just power; it symbolizes our entire political system. Jihadists who adhere to Islamic law do not believe in democratic ideals. Instead, they believe in what is known as Sharia, a form of Islamic law.

Sharia law's barbaric system serves as justification for a majority of human rights atrocities that are all too common in the Middle East.[3] While America functions as a democratic republic built on equality, freedom, and opportunity for all, Sharia law builds on submission, discrimination, and brutality.

Flight 93 hijackers would have loved nothing more than to fly that jetliner straight through the heart of our political system. Thanks to the patriots who gave their own lives while saving countless other lives in the process, those jihadist plans were foiled.

THE WAKE-UP CALL FROM HELL

Jihadists put America and the rest of the Western world on notice that they would stop at nothing to destroy our economic, military, and political systems. Our entire way of life was under assault. But how did we respond to this unthinkable attack, against this unconscionable loss of innocent life?

I remember it like it was yesterday.

In the aftermath of September 11, 2001, Americans were more unified than they'd been since World War II. Flags flew on almost every porch and street corner. It seemed like patriotic bumper stickers plastered every car. If you walked around any mall, park, or public gathering, you found yourself in a sea of T-shirts displaying either our flag or patriotic slogans such as "God Bless America" or "Never Forget" as dedications to those lost in the attacks. Businesspeople and blue-collar patriots alike went to work wearing FDNY or NYPD baseball caps.

Tears dripped down the faces of athletes and fans as they stood proudly for our national anthem. Celebrities were proud to voice their love for this country and their gratitude for the opportunities and protections it provided them. It seemed we all felt as lucky to be Americans as we did to be alive. We held our loved ones more tightly and waved our flags more proudly.

Even those who disagreed with our then commander in chief, George W. Bush, respected him enough to call him our president and passionately cheered when he threw the first pitch during the World Series at Yankee Stadium later that autumn. Recalling President Bush's pitch, author David Fisher noted, "I didn't vote for him, but at that point, my personal feelings about him as a politician [were] gone. I watched him, and he was my representative, and I had never felt that way before."[4]

The political disagreements of the past were suddenly meaningless. All that mattered in the aftermath of those attacks was our American identity. We realized that what unified us was so much stronger and more important than what divided us.

Mixed feelings of sorrow, fear, and anger were seen and understood on the faces of every fellow citizen we passed in the streets. The overwhelming majority of Americans were rightfully fearful and angry about the tumultuous blow struck against our nation. We were motivated to do whatever we could to defend the country and those we loved.

Support for our troops was never greater across all industries, including leftist Hollywood. We realized full well the dangers we all faced moving forward in this fight against Islamic terrorism, and we willingly came together to restore the feeling of security that had been taken from us. How I wish for the sake of our nation that such patriotic unity lasted.

WHERE IS THAT PATRIOTISM NOW?

Fast-forward to contemporary America and the stark contrast is unmistakable. It seems that today Americans are more divided than ever and remarkably oblivious to the grave dangers facing our nation and the Western world at large.

The rapid technological advancements that have taken place since 2001 enhance this ironic tragedy. Access to information has never been easier, faster, or more affordable. There are more avenues of information today than at any other time in world history.

Still, it seems a wave of apathy has washed over our nation with respect to national security. The vigilance and activism we saw after those towers came crashing down have disappeared. The American flags that lined our porches and street corners are now considered hate symbols by the radical Left and banned from certain college campuses.

You read that right.

University of California, Irvine student government leader Matthew Guevara wrote a bill banning the American flag from being displayed on campus. This fantastically foolish bill was put forth because "the American flag has been flown in instances of colonialism and imperialism" and could be used to "construct paradigms of conformity and sets homogenized standards," whatever that means.[5]

> Radical leftists hate the flag as much as radical Islamists do because it represents ideals that are contrary to their warped worldview.

If this sounds more like a *Saturday Night Live* episode than a factual representation of today's college campuses, I regret to inform you it is not. All of this was done in the name of tolerance and inclusion. Why is it that tolerance and inclusion always seem to encompass everything except for the Judeo-Christian values America was founded on?

The anti-flag resolution at UC Irvine went on to say that "freedom of speech, in a space that aims to be as inclusive as possible, can be interpreted as hate speech."[6] Ah, and there you have it. Not only is the American flag under attack on college campuses, but the fundamentally American ideal of freedom of speech.

You know who else doesn't believe in free speech? The terrorists who flew planes into the World Trade Center, the Pentagon, and almost the White House. Radical leftists hate the flag as much as radical Islamists do because it represents ideals that are contrary to their warped worldview.

Unfortunately, UC Irvine isn't the only leftist campus that has tried banning our flag. After a campus flag-burning incident following President Trump's electoral victory, the president of Hampshire College, Jonathan Lash, removed the flag due to the fact he thought it was a "disruptive symbol."[7]

Lash stated that the move would enable the school "to focus our efforts on addressing racist, misogynistic, Islamophobic, anti-immigrant, anti-Semitic, and anti-LGBTQ rhetoric and behaviors."[8]

Host of *Dirty Jobs* Mike Rowe summed it up perfectly when he noted,

> I found myself wondering as to why the President of Hampshire College would allow his students to pay for their tuition with federal dollars—federal dollars provided by the same government whose flag was no longer suitable to fly at his school.[9]

Who would've thought fifteen years after the most devastating terrorist attack in world history—an attack that left almost three thousand civilians dead—we would have to put up with anti-American garbage like this in our own backyard and subsidize it!

Ungratefulness and disrespect for this nation have spread like wildfire not only on college campuses but also on the football field. Enter Colin Kaepernick, third-rate NFL quarterback and first-class buffoon.

The anti-American communist sympathizer stole the hearts of mainstream media pundits across the sports and political spectrums when he began kneeling during the national anthem before game time.

Kaepernick's actions sparked a repulsive trend that took off in a big way during the start of the 2017–2018 NFL season when Kaepernick found himself out of work. Although Kaepernick's grievance against the NFL accuses them of colluding to exclude him because of his politics, many fellow leftists assign "racism" as the reason he was not signed to an NFL roster that season. Whether it was based entirely on his subpar performance or a hybrid including his appalling behavior, Kaepernick no longer graces us with his disrespectful presence on Sunday afternoons, but the anti-American trend he started lingered. For two seasons players still took a knee during our national anthem, as the National Football League stood there with its hands in its pockets, after dipping its hands in our pockets through taxpayer subsidies.

Really?

NFL Commissioner Roger Goodell, who said he was proud about the so-called "protests" he enabled,[10] should have reflected on the following facts:

1. At a team practice Kaepernick wore socks depicting police officers as pigs, and the NFL did nothing to reprimand him.[11]

2. At an NFL media interview Kaepernick wore a shirt glorifying Cuban dictator Fidel Castro, a terrorist who killed and ruthlessly tortured his own people for decades as well as aimed nuclear warheads at our nation from one hundred miles away. Kaepernick's discipline from the league? Nothing.[12]

3. The NFL prevented the Dallas Cowboys from paying tribute to five Dallas police officers who were shot dead at a Black Lives Matter protest in July 2016. The decal that the Cowboys wanted to wear on their helmets read "Arm in Arm." But apparently this was unacceptable according to NFL policy.[13]

4. When Tennessee Titans' Avery Williamson wanted to wear a pair of football cleats honoring 9/11 victims, the NFL threatened to fine him and squashed it.[14]

Are you getting the picture? The NFL seemed to have an awful lot of flexibility when it came to anti-American actions, but zero tolerance for patriotism and honoring those who protect and serve. It took almost two years for NFL owners to approve a policy requiring players to stand if they are on the field during the national anthem but giving them the option to remain in the locker room. Whether the decision to approve the policy was motivated by patriotism or by a shrinking bottom line is up for debate.

Witnessing disgraceful actions such as kneeling during the national anthem would have been unthinkable in American sports stadiums in the aftermath of 9/11. We would've condemned them immediately, and so would've the league. But, as always, whenever leftists disgrace our country, military heroes, or police, they always do so under the veil of social justice, tolerance, and equality.

Antifa violently attacks those with whom they disagree under the same deceitful sloganeering. But the NFL, owners, and players insist that these protests were to combat "police brutality."[15]

First of all, the real problem plaguing this country is lack of respect for our law enforcement who risk their lives for very little pay just to protect the same self-entitled, egotistic millionaires who turn around and disgrace them on national television every Sunday. What kind of warped logic does it take to think that kneeling for the national anthem helps solve police brutality or inequality? How does wearing socks depicting police as pigs or T-shirts glorifying dictators move us forward on that issue?

Thankfully these radicals couldn't fool the fans. Polling showed that 64 percent of the public disagreed with kneeling or boycotting the national anthem, with only 24 percent supporting it.[16]

KNEELING FOR THE NATIONAL ANTHEM

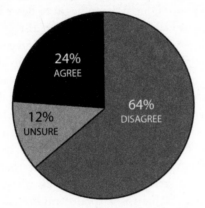

Nevertheless, we are still being lectured to by the anti-American fringe media. One of the more appalling examples of the glorification of disgracing our nation and its flag came from the sports media, which now rivals MSNBC in its radicalism.

Shannon Sharpe of Fox Sports 1 (FS1) noted he was "unimpressed" with the protest, and said he wished the players had gone even further to make a statement.[17] What else did he want them to do? Burn the flag right on the field?

Sharpe also attacked former Army Ranger Alejandro Villanueva, who did three tours overseas during his service, for standing during the anthem while his Pittsburgh Steelers teammates sat in the locker room like anti-American cowards.[18]

Sharpe's cohost on Fox Sports' *Undisputed*, Skip Bayless, joined Sharpe in attacking the veteran, who then was forced to issue an apology for his actions, in what looked like a hostage video from North Korea.[19]

I don't know about you, but in my opinion anyone who serves this nation—particularly someone who has done not one, not two, but three tours overseas—has earned the right to do whatever the heck he wants, and thankless fools like Sharpe and Bayless should just deal with it.

The American people voiced their patriotic opinions in the face of this radicalism. The day after Villanueva's brave stance, his jersey instantly became the top-selling of any NFL player on NFLShop.com and Fanatics.com.[20]

COMING TOGETHER AS A NATION

Certain concepts bring us together as a nation. One of those is standing for our national anthem. In addition to showing our patriotism and respect for our flag, standing for the anthem honors those who gave more than we can ever repay to defend the freedoms we enjoy.

The hypocrisy of the NFL, the owners, coaches, players, and sports media is more than appalling. As an immigrant who knows what it's like to grow up without the protection, freedom, and opportunities America affords its citizens, the word *ungrateful* doesn't even begin to describe this sentiment.

I'm continuously shocked to see such blatant disregard for the blessings and opportunities America affords all its citizens, regardless of color, religion, or creed. It seems as if the media wants to equate self-deprecation with patriotism and patriotism with racism or white supremacy.

Having spent my early years dodging bullets and bombs in war-torn Lebanon, I know that every American citizen is truly a lottery winner. I can assure you that those who live under Hezbollah rule in my home country of Lebanon, in famine-stricken countries in Africa, or in murderous and socialist hellholes like Venezuela would be beside themselves if they saw such ungratefulness. To scoff at the blessings of safety, freedom, opportunity, and all the human rights these spoiled millionaire athletes and their media fan base are afforded is nothing short of disgraceful.

We are now in an age when nothing is safe from the leftist anti-American propaganda movement, and we had better be prepared to fight back or continue to see the most unifying aspects of our culture destroyed.

Days after 9/11, a player taking a knee during the anthem to attack our first responders would've been rightly condemned for such behavior. But in the days after the Obama presidency, such actions are not only tolerated but even glorified. These days, if you're a minority, attacking America makes you a hero. If you're a celebrity like Snoop Dogg, you can mock an execution of our president in a music video without so much as a peep from the mainstream media condemning you.[21] If you're a wannabe political commentator disguised as a late-night comedian like Stephen Colbert of Samantha Bee, you can make outrageously vulgar and homophobic comments about our president and his family on live television, without so much as an apology from your employer.[22] If you're an actor like Robert De Niro or Peter Fonda, there's no need to hide how unhinged you've become. Feel free to make obscene comments about the president at an awards ceremony or tweet sick threats about the president's child. You'll still receive a standing ovation and have your movies release right on schedule. After all, we're living in a time when, in the wake of Sarah Huckabee Sanders and Kirstjen Nielsen being bullied out of restaurants, left-wing leaders like Rep. Maxine Waters encourage more incivility and give

> **Freedom and security are not political issues; they are American issues.**

public speeches that warn the president's cabinet members and staff to expect harassment at restaurants, gas stations, shopping places, and even their homes![23]

How classy.

It's high time we as Americans start to call out these attempts to divide us when we see them. It is a very calculated strategy by those who seek to destroy this country from within. They know that Americans, when unified, are a light for the rest of the world that cannot be extinguished. But when fragmented, we leave ourselves vulnerable to their attacks from within.

Instead of focusing on that which unites us, the radical Left has led us astray. Soros-funded anti-American organizations such as Media Matters, the Southern Poverty Law Center (SPLC), the American Civil Liberties Union (ACLU), and Antifa have launched a full-scale attack against America. They try clever tricks to divide us, such as ginning up racial and religious division, while continuing to push their false narrative that America is an inherently evil nation.

More egregious, they attempt to silence anyone who does not conform to their politically correct worldview. This divide-and-conquer strategy is their only hope to, in the words of our former failed president, "fundamentally transform" our nation.

We cannot take the bait they've laid out for us, and we surely cannot lay down when they attempt to silence us. Instead, we must rise as one cohesive, unified America—the same America that came together after the tragedies of Pearl Harbor and September 11, 2001.

After all, regardless of race or religion, all peaceful Americans are infidels in the eyes of our enemies. Jihadists don't care whether you support President Trump, Hillary Clinton, or Bernie Sanders; jihadists only care that you do not submit to their radical Islamist worldview.

> Do you believe in freedom of speech?
> They want you dead.
> Do you believe in equal opportunity for both men and women?
> They want you dead.
> Do you believe that men who beat their wives should go to jail?
> They want you dead.
> Do you believe female genital mutilation is barbaric?
> They want you dead.
> Do you subscribe to any religion other than Islam?
> They want you dead.

It's easy to find common ground when we put things into perspective. As Americans we think we are further apart from one another than we really are. Although we may voice our disagreements passionately on social media and in the media, an overwhelming majority of Americans can still achieve unity on key issues.

I'm talking about the real heart of America, not the out-of-touch DC swamp. I'm talking about people like you and me, who wake up every morning, work hard, and just want to come home safely in a country that affords them the freedom to live as they please. I'm talking about people who still believe that America is the greatest country on earth. I'm talking about those who don't want their neighborhoods transformed into Islamic no-go zones as many in Europe have been.[24] I'm talking about those who want to go to the mall without wondering whether they're in America or Saudi Arabia.

My friends, freedom and security are not political issues; they are American issues. Remember, we are all marked for death in the eyes of our enemies. So let us cast off the shackles of division holding us back and call out those pushing these destructive distractions when we see them.

America is the greatest country on earth and worthy of both our highest respect and protection. Let the anti-American haters say what they will, but as for you and me and the millions of patriots who realize how blessed we are to have been handed the lottery-winning tickets of American citizenship and residence, we know what we're thankful for and what we're fighting for.

In the next chapter we will go into detail as to how the fight for the protection of our nation has been going after spending the last two decades at war. Are we any safer?

RISE UP AND ACT

I am a firm believer that while education is important, education by itself is not sufficient. Education must be coupled with action. Therefore, at the end of each chapter I will share action tips you can take to make a difference in the protection of our freedoms.

I founded an organization called ACT for America, which has become the largest national security grassroots organization in the US. As of the writing of this book, we have helped pass ninety-seven bills nationwide at the state and federal level to protect the homeland. We empower citizens and give them the tools and the information to impact policy in their cities and states. We provide tips and send out nationwide action alerts about legislation, important town hall meetings, and other events.

The tips throughout this book are a great start and will activate anyone who wants to make a difference. However, I encourage you to go to www.actforamerica.org and sign up to receive our free emails and action alerts so you can be notified on an ongoing basis about when bills come down for a vote and so you can be empowered as a citizen to become a voice affecting your community and our nation.

Chapter 2

THE COST OF TERROR

DESPITE ALMOST TWO decades of spending massive amounts of money, dramatically expanding the size and scope of our federal government, and losing the priceless lives, limbs, and minds of our military heroes, America is no safer today than it was prior to the largest terror attack in world history on September 11, 2001.

In fact, the actions and inactions of the Obama administration made America a more vulnerable target than ever before. Let's assess how the so-called "war on terror" has been going.

Islamic terror groups are rapidly mushrooming around the globe. There are many factions with different names, but all with a unified goal of a worldwide Islamic empire. It doesn't matter what language they speak, what color their skin is, or what passport they hold—what bonds them together is their radical ideology.

The first terrorist group that grabbed America's attention was al Qaeda. Since then countless Islamic terror groups have sprouted up, such as Boko Haram in Nigeria, Lashkar-e-Taiba in Pakistan, al-Shabaab in Somalia, Ansar al-Sharia in Libya, Hezbollah in Lebanon, Hamas in Gaza, Islamic State of Iraq and Syria (ISIS), and that is just the tip of the iceberg.

Boko Haram put Nigeria on the terrorist map, so to speak, for the terrorist group's notorious kidnapping of more than three hundred girls. The Christians among the victims were forcefully converted to Islam. To this day we do not know what happened to all these girls. As it turns out, Michelle Obama's social media post of her holding a sign that read #BringBackOurGirls didn't magically solve the issue of the evil acts committed in the name of Islam.[1]

Remember that embarrassment? There are few instances that could better summarize the useless and even destructive nature of radical left-wing ideology in combatting terrorism than this example. Michelle Obama posted the photo on social media after the heartbreaking story had gone viral. Of course, the media fawned over how noble and brave the then–First Lady was to start this viral trending hashtag and photo. Unfortunately this did absolutely nothing to actually bring back the kidnapped victims, and in reality probably inspired Boko Haram to ramp up their kidnappings now that Michelle Obama had helped them make a name for themselves.[2] You see, Islamic terrorists don't give in to hashtag campaigns. They respect and understand one thing and one thing only: strength. America's strength is what Boko Haram didn't fear when they kidnapped and tortured hundreds of girls. Unfortunately their lack of fear was logical, given the pathetic lack of response by the Obama administration.

What Boko Haram did for Nigeria, Lashkar-e-Taiba did for Pakistan. This Pakistani terrorist network was the mastermind behind the Mumbai bombings in November of 2008. Over several days, twelve shootings and bombing attacks shook the Indian city to its core, killing 166 as a consequence.[3]

Ansar al-Sharia in Libya is another of the many terror networks spreading like wildfire around the globe. Their goal is to implement Sharia by any means necessary.[4] The logo of the Ansar al-Sharia includes two AK-47s, a clenched fist with one finger pointed up, a Quran, and a black flag. What was it that Obama was saying about Islam having absolutely nothing to do with terrorism?

Ahmed Abu Khattala, the Libyan leader of Ansar al-Sharia, played a significant role in the 2012 attack on the US diplomatic compound in Benghazi, which left four Americans dead, including our ambassador.[5] That's right, the one that Susan Rice, Hillary Clinton, and Barack Obama all said was the result of an "internet video."[6]

Iran's proxy army, known as Hezbollah, has been wreaking havoc in my home country of Lebanon for decades. Hezbollah has been consistently responsible for major terror attacks on four separate continents and is rapidly driving us closer to a military confrontation with Iran.[7] While radical Sunni groups such as al Qaeda and ISIS have drawn the most attention over the past two decades, Hezbollah has continued to push terror in the name of Shiite Islam, a competing branch within Islam itself.

Hezbollah's history of terror includes the 1983 attack on the US Marine Corps barracks in Beirut, the 1983 US embassy bombing in Beirut, and the bombing of Khobar Towers in Saudi Arabia in 1996, which together killed 323 people.[8] Even more frightening, Hezbollah possesses guided, long-range missiles that are capable of carrying chemical weapons. It reportedly has forty thousand to sixty thousand missiles in its arsenal, and all are within striking distance of Israel, a nation it seeks to exterminate.[9]

And while we're talking about threats to Israel, I'd be remiss if I didn't mention Hamas, the poisonous Palestinian terror network that has one goal on its mind: the total genocide of Jews.[10] Hamas knows that America and Israel remain the greatest of allies that share the same democratic and Judeo-Christian values, and thus, consider America and Israel to be equally worthy of death. Hamas builds terror tunnels to facilitate their deadly attacks against innocent Jews, while also using women, children, and the mentally disabled as human shields when playing defense.[11]

I'm convinced it's only a matter of time before an official spokesperson for Hamas earns a job as a CNN contributor. In fact, CNN doesn't even need an official spokesperson with anchors like leftist Ashleigh Banfield, who has routinely defended Hamas. While discussing a Hamas-inspired terrorist attack that occurred in the Har Nof synagogue in Jerusalem, Banfield defended Hamas' purely evil ideology, which attempts to justify the killing of every Jew in Israel, including babies.[12]

"Soldiers come in all forms....And when you have mandatory conscription and service in Israel, effectively the Palestinians will say it's war against everyone because everyone's a soldier," said Banfield.

When Alan Dershowitz responded in astonishment, "Well, that's just racism and bigotry to say that everyone is a soldier," Banfield wouldn't let it go.

"But everybody is."

Dershowitz responded again, "No, not everybody is...The law...is very clear, you can't kill a two-year-old child claiming he's going to be a soldier."[13]

Imagine watching this exchange between Banfield and Dershowitz as a member of Hamas. You'd probably be thinking to yourself, "Are we paying her? If not, we should, and if we are, let's give that gal a raise!"

How Safe Are We?

These terrorist groups are united in their hatred for us and everything we stand for as a Western, democratic republic. They will stop at nothing until they have achieved what they are seeking, a worldwide Islamic caliphate.

ISIS has already established a caliphate and is using the internet to spread its message and recruit an army of followers worldwide, including here in the United States.[14] Don't let reports that their caliphate has been destroyed fool you. Though their territory has been dramatically decreased by the firepower unleashed by the Trump administration, ISIS's digital caliphate on the internet is strong and thriving. ISIS remains a threat both abroad and here at home. In fact, with the destruction of territory ISIS had gained during the Obama administration, these terrorists will be attempting to make their way back to Western countries and blending in with the rest of society before making their next move.

Are we really safer from jihad now than we were prior to 9/11? It doesn't take a rocket scientist to know we aren't. As a matter of fact, despite the trillions of dollars we have spent for nearly two decades fighting the war on terror, Islamic terrorists screaming "Allahu Akbar" have been able to carry out a seemingly endless string of successful attacks worldwide, including right here on American soil, at an alarming rate.

Let me get something straight here right from the start. We are fighting Islamic terrorism. The Left refuses to identify the problem by name, let alone combat it. They can't stomach the fact that all religions do not possess equally radical factions, just as all cultures are not equally virtuous in their treatment of minorities, women, homosexuals, or others. Islamic terrorism conflicts with the Left's multicultural utopian fantasy, so rather than accurately attack the problem, they pretend it doesn't exist. The whole world is fighting Islamic terrorism, regardless of what watered-down name they call it, such as the "war on terror," "overseas contingency," or "man-made disasters." Although acts of terrorism have been carried out in the name of virtually every religion, it is not Buddhist terrorism, Jewish terrorism, Christian terrorism, or Hindu terrorism that is threatening peaceful civilization, but Islamic terrorism.

We need not worry about Buddhist monks ramming cars into pedestrians and mowing down innocent civilians on a shooting spree to achieve inner peace. The Jewish suicide bomber threat also seems to be contained at this point. Christians are not beheading those who draw pictures of Jesus, and atheists who drive around with COEXIST bumper stickers on their cars are probably not making pipe bombs in their garages to use in crowded public areas.

Religious conflicts take place through debates and discussions, but for the most part everyone gets along just fine, except for one particular group of maniacs screaming "Allahu Akbar" as they mow down innocent civilians in their cars, explode themselves in malls, and slice people's necks like broccoli while reciting from the Quran.

The United States has spent $2 trillion fighting Islamic terrorism since September 11, 2001.[15] Astounding! The wars in Iraq, Syria, and Afghanistan; other counter-terrorism efforts abroad; and the increased spending on homeland security and Departments of Defense and Veteran Affairs since the 9/11 attacks have cost more than $4.3 trillion in current dollars through the fiscal year 2017.[16]

US FEDERAL WAR-RELATED SPENDING IN BILLIONS OF CURRENT DOLLARS (ROUNDED TO THE NEAREST BILLION), FY 2001–2017[17]

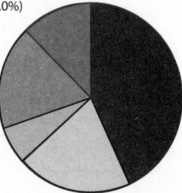

Overseas Operations by Departments of Defense and State: 1,878 (43.1%)

Other: 534 (12.3%)

Homeland Security: 783 (18.0%)

Veterans Affairs: 277 (6.4%)

Additional Department of Defense: 879 (20.2%)

(FIGURES SHOWN IN BILLIONS OF DOLLARS)

We hear these numbers thrown around, and most Americans cannot begin to fathom the real amount of dollars we are talking about. Unless you have an advanced degree in accounting, these numbers might as well be in Chinese. So here, in simple English, is what the numbers really mean: one trillion (1,000,000,000,000) is one thousand times one billion. Another way to think of it is one million times one million.

If that's not enough, the costs of post-9/11 wars are predicted to total more than a mind-boggling $5.6 trillion by the end of 2018. How much of this money came out of your pocket? The average amount every single American taxpayer has already spent fighting Islamic terrorism since 2001 is $23,386![18]

That's money out of your pocket and the pockets of your children and grandchildren—all which has left us fighting the exact same enemy and arguably more vulnerable than ever before. Think about that for a moment. That's almost $100,000 out of the bank account of a family of four! Add to that grandparents, aunts, uncles, cousins, and other extended family members and the number becomes astronomical.

Consider this: a $100,000 investment account, using, let's say, the S&P 500 Index, would net a conservative 8 percent annual return, and with the power of compounded interest over a twenty-year time frame, your family would have $466,095.71. Nearly half a million dollars! So those who think this war on terror doesn't directly affect them or their pocketbook may want to reconsider.

The Pentagon does a very inadequate job of accounting for war costs, and thus we have no assurance of where their funds are actually spent. Do you feel safer now? How has the return on your investment been?

> **Our failed leaders care more about getting reelected and catering to the PC police than serving their country and ensuring the safety of American citizens.**

A paramount cost we must consider when reviewing the true cost of war is the necessity of taking care of our brave servicemen and women when they return home. Deceptively, Pentagon reports do not acknowledge the cost of medical care and disability payments to veterans. This is because a separate body, the Department of Veterans Affairs, reports such numbers.

A report titled "Estimated Cost to Each Taxpayer for the Wars in Afghanistan, Iraq and Syria" only totals the cost of war in those regions as $1.52 trillion, and the average taxpayer's individual burden as $7,740. This is because it only counts Department of Defense spending, rather than the spending of all additional departments related to national defense, as well as the cost of taking care of those who sacrificed so much for our nation.[19] But if we're going to grasp how much these wars have cost the American people, in both blood and treasure, all these numbers need to be included.

We the American public deserve to hear the cold hard truth about the burdens of our national security strategy since we are the ones picking up the tab. We have been fighting a war that many politicians are too cowardly to name, with a military ready and able to win, but confined by the shackles of political correctness. Our failed leaders care more about getting reelected and catering to the PC police than serving their country and ensuring the safety of American citizens.

The American public doesn't mind paying for safety. But we do mind being taken for a ride by our government, which spends money we do not have on wars we do not understand and aren't making progress on, all while giving away foreign aid to countries that hate us.

Since September 11, America has used Pakistan as a useful military route to deliver supplies to our bases in Afghanistan. From 2002 to 2014 the United States paid about $35 billion to Pakistan. About $13 billion of that went for economic and humanitarian aid that has absolutely nothing to do with joint security efforts.[20]

Of course, maybe this wouldn't be such a big issue if Pakistan were a loyal ally like Israel. But this isn't Israel. This is Pakistan—the same Pakistan we didn't even trust enough to tell we were coming to kill Osama bin Laden out of fear they'd warn him. With this in mind, it's safe to say we did not give this money to worthy friends.[21] Most frightening, Pakistan has over one hundred nuclear bombs, and although the Pakistani government presumably has control over these weapons, there is concern over their security in the face of political instability in the country.[22]

We have wasted trillions of dollars on the wrong approach to this war. Despite this, we have been told our strategy was winning hearts and minds in the Islamic world. We were advised by radical Islamic lobby organizations in America when the Obama White House welcomed individuals associated with groups such as the Council on American-Islamic Relations (CAIR) and the Islamic Society of North America (ISNA).[23] Thankfully, as I'm writing this, we no longer have a terrorist-enabler at 1600 Pennsylvania Avenue, but instead a straight-talking commander-in-chief who, at the very least, is willing to call Islamic terrorism by name and do whatever it takes to win the war against it.

Wars and taking care of those who fight them are paid for with death and debt. For some reason, our government likes to hide from taxpayers like you and me the interest rate on the money we borrow to fight these wars. Future interest on money we borrowed to fight the wars in Afghanistan, Iraq, and elsewhere is predicted to add more than $7.9 trillion to the national debt over the next few decades. In fact, interest on overseas contingency operations is predicted to add more than $1 trillion to the national debt by 2023.[24]

Who is funding these enterprises now? China already owns more than

$1.17 trillion in American debt, and as you can see, that number shows no sign of slowing down if this outrageous and useless spending continues.[25] We are enslaving future generations, the generations we should be protecting, by running up outrageous debts to a Communist Asian superpower with nearly half the world's population. How do our leaders sleep at night? How can we sleep without putting a stop to this before it's too late?

> We were advised by radical Islamic lobby organizations in America with the Obama White House welcoming individuals associated with groups such as the Council on American-Islamic Relations (CAIR) and the Islamic Society of North America (ISNA).

Our military presence in two separate countries in the Middle East—Afghanistan and Iraq—tops the charts for the longest American wars, surpassed only by the time we spent in Vietnam.[26] And here at home we continue to try to spend our way to safety. In response to 9/11 we created a variety of different agencies to provide additional national security infrastructure.

One of those was the Department of Homeland Security (DHS). The DHS is a massive bureaucracy, encompassing seven separate federal agencies. These include the United States Citizenship and Immigration Services, Federal Emergency Management Agency, US Customs and Border Protection, Immigration and Customs Enforcement (ICE), Transportation Security Administration (TSA), US Coast Guard, and US Secret Service.

Some of these agencies existed before 9/11, but with the inception of the DHS, everything merged into what is now an inefficient goliath, sucking up billions of dollars from the US taxpayers. Meanwhile, the right hand has no idea what the left is doing, putting American lives at risk.

Astoundingly, despite the continued lack of safety, DHS has spent more than $650 billion since its creation in 2002. The DHS has 229,000 employees as of 2017, and a $40 billion annual budget. With that type of funding, you'd think we'd be a lot safer than we are today.

Protecting New York City's metro area alone from terrorism costs about $1 billion a year. Despite this, New York City suffered two separate terror attacks in the last three months of 2017, with one thankfully resulting in the malfunction of a homemade bomb.

In both cases, terrorists used ordinary and readily available tools to carry out their attacks. Whether it was a car, gun, or cheap and easy-to-find materials to assemble a low-tech explosive device, terrorists had no problem getting their hands on what they needed. Our enemies are constantly evolving in their methods, while we're stuck in the same tired and useless practices of the past to protect our nation.

So Why Aren't We Safer?

Spending has certainly not been the issue. As I mentioned, the Department of Homeland Security has spent over $650 billion since its inception in 2002.[27] Yet despite all that money, we have low-tech terrorists such as the Boston bombers putting together an explosive device for peanuts, while still killing and maiming many innocent civilians and costing the city millions of dollars in damage.

Omar Mateen, the Islamic terrorist who gunned down forty-nine innocent civilians at an Orlando nightclub, was responsible for the deadliest Islamic terrorist attack on American soil since 9/11, and it cost him less than twenty-five hundred dollars to carry out his evil rampage.[28] The FBI investigated Mateen twice before his attack but did not take any substantive action against him. Mateen was self-radicalized but pledged allegiance to ISIS leader Abu Bakr al-Baghdadi before his death.[29]

During the Obama administration, none other than FBI Director Robert Mueller, in an effort to please his radical leftist boss, oversaw the removal of all references to jihad, Islamic terrorism, Islamic radicalism, and jihadism from FBI training manuals.[30] This is no joke. Organizations such as the Council for American Islamic Relations (CAIR), which has been designated as a terrorist organization by even a Sharia governed country such as the United Arab Emirates (UAE), might as well have written the FBI training manuals themselves.

Terror-groups like CAIR also enjoyed meetings and visits to the White House under Obama, adding to their efforts to legitimize themselves, despite their explicit connections to terror. There have been deadly consequences for Obama's PC enabling of Islamic radicalism.

The Russians also notified the FBI about the radicalism of one of the Boston bombers, Tamerlan Tsarnaev.[31] Although FBI agents interviewed Tsarnaev, they misspelled his name in the CBP TECS database, not appearing to take the matter very seriously. Perhaps they were brainwashed during their Obama-required sensitivity classes that jihad is like yoga for the soul. Consequently, their willful ignorance ended up costing innocent civilians—including children—their lives and limbs.

The Fort Hood shooter was also able to carry out his violent jihad, despite having been on the radar of the FBI prior to the attacks. To jog your memory, the Fort Hood Shooter, Nidal Hasan, waged jihad by shooting and killing thirteen people at Fort Hood military base in Texas back in 2009. Hasan was able to carry out his slaughter, despite having been on FBI radar for at least six months before the attack, after making online posts glorifying suicide bombers and attempting to contact al Qaeda. Yet somehow Hasan was able to continue working on base as, get this, a psychiatrist. As if those facts don't make your blood boil enough, the Department of Defense later classified Hasan's jihad as "workplace violence." Generally speaking, when someone has explicit jihadist connections and yells "Allahu Akbar" during a shooting rampage, it's probably a pretty good hint we're dealing with Islamic terrorism, not workplace violence.[32]

This is the same problem we see now in Europe, whether it's Paris, Brussels, or London—the terrorists were on the radar of the intelligence community prior to the attack.

Whether the terrorism is inspired by radical Islam or not, the threat to unprotected Americans is the same. Most recently we saw how dangerously inept the FBI was at responding to potential threats when they continuously failed to adequately address explicit reports about a deranged teenager whose name we won't mention and who subsequently shot up a local high school in Parkland, Florida, killing seventeen innocent students and teachers.[33]

But the FBI is not alone in their failure to protect Americans. Of all the agencies that make up the Department of Homeland Security, TSA is the one that stands out the most. While most Americans may never have to deal with any other organization in a meaningful way, the TSA is the one agency that almost all Americans have to deal with.

The TSA hasn't exactly instilled feelings of safety within the minds of those they supposedly protect. Despite a $7.5 billion annual budget, the TSA has a whopping 95 percent failure rate in detecting weapons and fake explosives during airport screening. Yes, you read that number correctly: 95 percent failure! This figure isn't just shocking; if you've ever gone through an airport, it is downright terrifying.[34]

In 2015 a man named Blake Alford took a loaded gun through security at Atlanta's Hartsfield-Jackson International Airport, also known as "the world's busiest airport," and boarded his flight without anyone noticing. His handgun was fully loaded with seven hollow-point bullets.[35] Mr. Alford didn't even know the gun was in his bag until he arrived at his destination, but he said once he noticed, he had to come forward.

"I just want to do the right thing. I didn't want to get into trouble. I didn't want to get anybody in trouble. I guess I wanted everybody to realize we need to tighten up," he said.[36]

But Mr. Alford wasn't alone. A man named James Petrovic pulled out his bag mid-flight to do some work when he noticed his .38 Smith & Wesson revolver, which was loaded and had one bullet in the chamber. Once again, had he not turned himself in, the entire matter would've gone undetected.[37]

Imagine if these civilians were Islamic terrorists trying to smuggle firearms onto their flights intentionally! To say that the scanners used in many US airports to help detect explosives, firearms, or other threatening items aren't getting the job done is the understatement of the century.

We spent over $2.1 billion from 2008 through 2017 on scanners that the TSA said would provide "the most effective and least intrusive" way to check travelers for weapons.[38] The TSA is now using 793 useless full-body scanners, funded by you, at 157 airports as a part of their continued "we've got you covered" theatre.

In an interview with *Politico*, one TSA trainer said that he wouldn't be able to distinguish plastic explosives from body fat and that guns were practically invisible if they were turned sideways in a pocket.[39] Jason Edward Harrington, who spent several years working for the TSA, wrote in a piece for *Politico* that TSA officials knew about the flaws in the scanners with respect to detecting potentially dangerous weapons and materials, but chose to ignore it.

"Officers discovered that the machines were good at detecting just about everything besides cleverly hidden explosives and guns. The only thing more absurd than how poorly the full-body scanners performed was the incredible amount of time the machines wasted for everyone." Harrington said.[40]

A YouTube blogger, Jonathan Corbett, posted a video to YouTube in which he walked through one of the scanners while he had a gun placed sideways on one leg. This method proved to be effective, as Corbett passed through the scanner completely undetected. Most alarming, after millions had seen the video posted by Corbett, causing tremendous concern, Harrington said that supervisors instructed him and his colleagues to pat down every fifth passenger, as a means of reassuring the general public that scanners were not the only effective technique.[41]

Isn't political correctness great? Not only do we get to be harassed and herded through radiation-emitting machinery like cattle, but our government also has a one-in-five chance of catching a jihadist hiding a gun on his leg.

Let me tell you, trying to find an explosive device planted by terrorists is like trying to find a needle in a haystack. Terrorists make up a tiny portion of passengers at airports compared to the peaceful civilian population.

For this reason, the best way to locate explosives and prevent them from passing undetected through security involves significantly shrinking the pool of those receiving enhanced screening. The only way to do this is by profiling based on behavior and mannerisms.

We must also factor in the generic profile of a terrorist based on all the terrorist attacks and jihadists since 2001. But clueless leftists in Washington and their cheer squad in the media believe it would be "discriminatory" to target those of Middle Eastern or North African descent.

Listen, I don't know about you, but the idea of patting down a seventy-year-old nun while Muhammad, a twenty-five-year-old Yemeni national, walks through unscathed seems as dangerous as it is idiotic.

We're at war with radical Islamic terrorism. Logically one would expect those in charge of protecting this nation to seek out those who fit the profile of someone most likely to sympathize with radical Islamic ideology.

Maybe we should be giving the TSA and PC politicians in Washington a little history lesson concerning the nationalities of those who participated in the deadliest terror attack in world history. All nineteen were young Muslim men of Middle Eastern origin. Was this just a coincidence?

Instead of targeted screening with a purpose, like Israel, we get a sweeping, randomized selection process, delaying travel and doing almost nothing to prevent danger.

According to the most recent reporting from the TSA itself, there were more weapons confiscated in 2017 than any other year in history. Here is some startling information from the TSA's 2017 report on items found during the airport screening process in the United States.[42]

NUMBER OF FIREARMS DISCOVERED IN CARRY-ON BAGS IN U.S. AIRPORTS

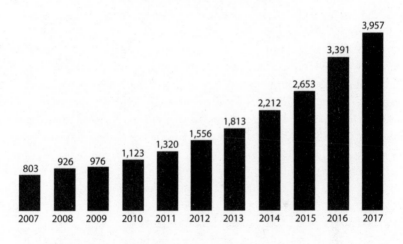

- 771.5 million (771,556,886) passengers
- 3,957, firearms discovered in carry-on bags totaling 76.1 firearms per week, and 10.8 per day. A new record!
- 3,324 (84 percent) of those firearms discovered were loaded.
- 1,378 (34.8 percent) of those firearms found had a round chambered.
- The most firearms discovered in one month, which was thirty-one, were found in August 2017 in Atlanta.
- Firearms were discovered in 239 different airports!

- There was a 16.7 percent jump from 2016's total firearms discovered.

Remember earlier when we were discussing the TSA's 95 percent failure rate? Imagine how many weapons passed through security scanners undetected and made it onboard planes that perhaps even you have traveled on!

Since 9/11 there have been two terrorist attacks on American flights, both al Qaeda related—Richard Reid, the shoe bomber, and Umar Farouk Abdulmutallab, the underpants bomber. In both cases the flights began abroad (Paris and Amsterdam), and the men made it through airport screening but were thankfully stopped by fellow passengers and had their plots foiled.

> We have a worldwide epidemic of Islamic terror spreading around the globe like the plague, but leftist loons are more concerned about protecting feelings than protecting lives.

If this keeps up, another 9/11 could be just around the corner.

But don't worry, PC politicians and their media cheer squad are prioritizing more critical issues like "Islamophobia." Federal prosecutors have already charged 121 men and women around the country in connection with the Islamic State, with seventy-two convicted so far. The FBI says that it has disrupted plots in a handful of cases targeting US military or law enforcement personnel.[43]

The FBI reported that roughly one thousand active Islamic State probes inside the United States are ongoing and that at least forty-eight of those are considered such a high risk that the bureau has deployed elite surveillance teams to track their whereabouts.[44]

These mobile surveillance teams are following suspects who are believed to be radicalized on a 24/7 basis. We have a worldwide epidemic of Islamic terror spreading around the globe like the plague, but leftist loons are more concerned about protecting feelings than protecting lives.

At this stage of the game, we are fighting for our very survival as a Judeo-Christian civilization, and we better start demanding that those who are in charge of protecting us prefer protection over PC endangerment.

- No more money given to countries that burn our flag!
- No more enslaving our future generations to debt with China in order to pay for wars we are not committed to winning.
- No more money spent on useless security techniques that do little to stop terrorism and much to harass the peaceful public.

It's time we, as a Western, Judeo-Christian society, begin to fight this war the proper way, the way our allies the Israelis do, with feelings taking a back-seat to safety every time. Not vice versa! I'll put the security of my family and myself ahead of worrying about offending the Muslim community, and I'm not alone.

In fact, plenty of Muslims also fear Islamic terror attacks and would be glad to sacrifice their personal convenience in order to feel safe. As we'll learn in the next chapter, it is the radicals that we must excise; the peaceful majority is irrelevant.

Rise Up and ACT

The next time you hear about the cost of the war on terror, don't just chalk it up to incompetent government officials. ACT!

- Attend local town hall meetings with your elected officials and convince a couple of friends to go with you. Ask the officials direct questions about radical Islamic terrorism. We have spent billions of dollars and continue losing the war because people are afraid to identify the problem due to political correctness. Do not let them beat around the bush with empty verbiage such as the war on terror, etc.

- Program your elected officials' phone numbers into your cell phone. Call them when you hear them make a wishy-washy statement about radical Islamic terrorism, trying to avoid the issue. Also call them and thank them when they speak coura-geously and identify the problem. Tell them you took notice and you will vote for them again. Remember, what they want the most is to get reelected. Hold them accountable for spending your money and keeping you safe. That is a big part of their job

Chapter 3

THE MYTH AND IRRELEVANCE OF
THE PEACEFUL MAJORITY

I F I HAD a dollar for every time I heard the phrase *moderate Muslims* in the media after an Islamic terrorist attack, Oprah would be calling me to borrow money.

Or how about *religion of peace?* That's another beauty that the radical Left loves to cough up after a jihadist has slaughtered more innocent civilians. I don't know about you, but I've heard more than enough of these clueless clichés about the nature of our enemy since 9/11.

When I speak publicly, I usually engage in a Q&A after the presentation with the audience. One question I can always count on like clockwork is: "What about the peaceful Muslims? We cannot forget about them. They're our only hope." Let me share a story with you to show you what I mean.

I'm proud to have been a part of the Benghazi Accountability Coalition, a group of leaders who came together to demand justice and truth for the attack on our consulate in Libya. As a result, a couple of years back, I was invited to speak on a panel in Washington, DC, about the attack on our consulate in Benghazi, which left four Americans dead, including our ambassador to Libya.

During a Q&A session, I noticed a Muslim woman wearing a hijab stand up and seemingly chase after the woman holding the microphone. I could tell she was going out of her way to make sure she was able to ask her question.

In my mind I said to myself, "Why do I get the feeling this is going to be about the peaceful majority?" Sure enough, this woman got the opportunity she was seeking. Below is a transcript of our exchange:

> Assalam o alaikum, peace to you all. My name is Saba Ahmed; I'm a law student in American university. I am here to ask you a simple question. I know that we portray Islam and all Muslims as bad, but there is 1.8 billion Muslim followers of Islam. We have eight million-plus Muslim Americans in this country, and I don't see them represented here, but my question is how can we fight an ideological war with weapons? How can we ever end this war? The jihadist ideology that you talk about, it's an ideology. How can you ever win this thing if you don't address it ideologically?

"Oh baby, bring it on…" I thought. I waited for another panelist to share his thoughts, and then I responded:

Great question. I am so glad you're here, and I am so glad you brought that up because it gives us an opportunity to answer. What I find so amazing is, since the beginning of this panel—which we are here about the Benghazi attack against our people—not one person mentioned Muslims [or said that] we are here against Islam or we're launching war against Muslims. We are here to discuss how four Americans died and what our government is doing. We were not here to bash Muslims; *you* were the one who brought up the issue about most Muslims, not us. And since you brought it up, allow me to elaborate with my answer.

There are 1.2 billion Muslims in the world today. Of course, not all of them are radicals. The majority of them are peaceful people. The radicals are estimated to be between 15 to 25 percent according to all intelligence services around the world. That leaves 75 percent of them as peaceful people, but when you look at 15 to 25 percent of the world's Muslim population, you're looking at a 180 million to 300 million people dedicated to the destruction of Western civilization. That is as big as the United States. So why should we worry about the radical 15 to 25 percent? Because it is the radicals that kill; because it is the radicals that behead and massacre.

When you look throughout history, when you look at all the lessons of history:

- Most Germans were peaceful, yet the Nazis drove the agenda. And as a result, sixty million people died, almost fourteen million in concentration camps, six million were Jews. The peaceful majority were irrelevant.

- When you look at Russia, most Russians were peaceful as well, yet the Russians were able to kill twenty million people. The peaceful majority were irrelevant.

- When you look at China, for example, most Chinese were peaceful as well, yet the Chinese were able to kill seventy million people. The peaceful majority were irrelevant.

- When you look at Japan prior to World War II, most Japanese were peaceful as well, yet Japan was able to butcher its way across Southeast Asia, killing twelve million people, mostly killed with bayonets and shovels. The peaceful majority were irrelevant.

- On September 11th in the United States, we had 2.3 million Arab Muslims living in the United States. It took nineteen hijackers—nineteen radicals—to bring America down to its knees, destroy the World Trade Center, attack the Pentagon, and kill almost three thousand Americans that day. The peaceful majority were irrelevant.

So, for all our powers of reason and us talking about moderate and peaceful Muslims, I'm glad you're here, but where are the others speaking out?...

And since you are the only Muslim representative in here, you took the limelight instead of speaking about why our government— and I assume are you an American? You're an American citizen. So as an American citizen you sat in this room and instead of standing up and saying a question or asking something about the four Americans that died and what our government is doing to correct the problem, you stood there to make a point about peaceful, moderate Muslims. I wish you brought ten with you to question about what or how we can hold our government responsible. It is time we take political correctness and throw it in the garbage can where it belongs and start calling a spade a spade.[1]

If you're active online, chances are you recognize this exchange. Almost thirty million people around the world have viewed a clip of this exchange on YouTube. It struck a nerve with so many because when it comes down to it, the peaceful majority have always been, throughout history, irrelevant.

I want to take a moment to clarify that I am not saying peaceful Muslims are irrelevant as people. Everyone is created by God and has value and worth as a human being. I'm saying that the argument that there is a peaceful majority is an irrelevant argument.

There are a lot of self-identified Muslims who realize full well the scope of the problem within their own religion. They are the ones most hurt by Islamic radicals and by leftists who resort to ad hominem attacks, calling everyone speaking the truth about their religion "Islamophobic." Indeed, there are plenty of peaceful Muslims in the world who do not practice or endorse the type of barbarism that threatens our way of life, but my point is that these peaceful Muslims do not magically cancel out the threats posed by violent ones.

Add to this the fact that there is also a significant amount of misinformation peddled by media propagandists and PC politicians about just how many Muslims in the world are, in fact, radicalized. When they aren't twisting the facts, they are trying to make those who dare to speak the truth about radical Islam look bad.

During the 2016 Republican presidential debates, CNN's Jake Tapper and *Washington Times'* Stephen Dinan questioned then-candidate Trump on his comments about Muslims.

TAPPER: Mr. Trump, let me start with you. Last night, you told CNN quote, "Islam hates us." Did you mean all 1.6 billion Muslims?

TRUMP: I mean a lot of them. I mean a lot of them.

DINAN: Do you want to clarify the comment at all?

TRUMP: Well, you know, I've been watching the debate today. And they're talking about radical Islamic terrorism or radical Islam. But I will tell you this. There's something going on that maybe you don't know about, maybe a lot of other people don't know about, but there's tremendous hatred. And I will stick with exactly what I said to Anderson Cooper.[2]

Tapper's questioning is par for the course when it comes to a mainstream media pundit attempting to make himself feel or appear morally superior while demeaning those who speak frankly about the threats we face. Despite the attempts of many pundits like Tapper to claim the moral and intellectual high ground, there is verifiable data that concludes there are, in fact, "a lot" of Muslims who want to kill us, and we should never fear to speak the truth when it comes to matters of national security.

> **Peaceful Muslims do not magically cancel out the threats posed by violent ones.**

Most politicians would have tried to soften their stance and play defense against Tapper's line of questioning, but not Donald Trump. The reality is, President Trump was elected in large part because he spoke candidly and unwaveringly about radical Islam, in spite of attacks from the mainstream media.

Our former jihad-apologist-in-chief, Barack Hussein Obama, was another master at spreading falsehoods about radical Islam and just how widespread the issue is. In an interview with CNN pundit and Islamist apologist Fareed Zakaria, President Obama stated the following:

> You know, I think that the way to understand this is there is an element growing out of Muslim communities in certain parts of the world that have perverted the religion, have embraced a nihilistic, violent, almost medieval interpretation of Islam. And they're doing damage in a lot of countries around the world. But it is absolutely true that I reject a notion that somehow that creates a religious war because the overwhelming majority of Muslims reject that interpretation of Islam. They don't even recognize it as being Islam. And I think that for us to be successful in fighting this scourge, it's very important for us to align ourselves with the 99.9 percent of Muslims who are looking for the same thing we're looking for—order, peace, prosperity.[3]

Reading that quote again almost triggers post-traumatic stress flashbacks from Obama's days in the White House. We can all be thankful we don't have to listen to any more of his lectures about how peaceful Islam is after innocent Westerners have been killed or maimed.

The 99.9 percent? Really?

Where did he get that brilliant number?

News flash: just because someone doesn't actively participate in a particular activity doesn't mean they don't support it or enjoy it. In the same way, just because certain Muslims may not consider blowing themselves up doesn't mean they don't support the idea of someone else doing it.

Muslims who support barbaric anti-Western practices such as suicide bombings, violence against women and gay men, female genital mutilation (FGM), or Sharia law are all radicalized Muslims. So let's take a look at just how many Muslims in the world are radicalized, according to poll data, and compare it to Obama's 99.9 percent claim.

Pew Research Data and other polls have revealed some startling statistics. Let's take a look at some real numbers of why the so-called "peaceful majority" is irrelevant and why accusations of "Islamophobia" are so absurd.

There are approximately 1.8 billion Muslims in the world. In Indonesia, which is currently the most populous Muslim majority country with 227 million Muslims, approximately 70 percent of Indonesian Muslims blame the United States, Israel, or another country for 9/11, or they say they don't know who to blame.[4] That's 159 million Muslims blaming anyone and everyone except al Qaeda for 9/11!

Even more sobering, 11 percent specifically blame the United States. This means in a country the Left loves to tout as the poster child of peaceful Islamic countries, nearly 25 million Muslims blame us for the deadliest terror attack in world history.

The percentage might sound small, but the number of individuals is alarming, especially when compared with Nazi Germany. In the early 1930s the population of Germany was 67 million, and in November of 1932, a third of them (33 percent) voted for the Nazi party.[5] That's 22 million Germans in 1932 who were radical enough to vote for Nazism compared with 25 million Indonesian Muslims today who are radical enough to blame America for an attack on our own people. In Germany 22 million Nazi-sympathizers enabled the extermination of up to 6 million Jews in the Holocaust and the death of an estimated 10 million non-Jewish civilians and prisoners of war. What could 25 million Indonesian terrorist sympathizers enable today's radical Islamists to accomplish?

Something to think about for any of you thinking of vacationing in Bali anytime soon.

A shocking 72 percent of Indonesians also believe Sharia should be the law of the land—a terrifying yet still lower number than nearby Malaysia, where 86 percent believe Sharia should be the law of the land.[6] In fact, 36 percent of Malaysian Muslims were also either favorable or unsure about ISIS.[7]

One poll exposed a shocking statistic about Muslims in Egypt, where nearly 70 percent said they had positive or mixed feelings about Osama bin Laden.[8] Also, 74 percent of Egyptian Muslims said that they favored Sharia as the law of the land and that it should extend to both Muslims and non-Muslims.[9] That's over 64 million Egyptian Muslims![10]

With such an enormous population endorsing barbarism, it's no wonder Coptic Christians in Egypt are still being slaughtered and terrorized simply for following Christ rather than Muhammad.[11] Coptic Christians make up approximately 10 percent of the Egyptian population and live in constant fear for reasons outlined in this poll data from Pew Research.[12]

Pakistan's population is about 207 million. Approximately 40 percent of Pakistani Muslims said that they supported honor killings for women who committed adultery.[13] That's over 80 million Muslims who believe it's OK to kill a woman for an extramarital affair.

Additionally, 71 percent of Pakistani Muslims were either favorable or unsure about ISIS,[14] while 84 percent believe Sharia should be the law of the land. Of those who believe Sharia should be the law of the land, 76 percent believe those who leave Islam should receive the death penalty, and a whopping 89 percent believe adulterers should be stoned to death.[15] It might be why Pakistan was so irritated that we launched a mission to capture and kill Osama bin Laden inside their country without even telling them.

A shocking 89 percent of Palestinians living in the Gaza Strip support firing rockets at Israel.[16] Approximately one-third of Palestinians surveyed in the West Bank, Gaza Strip, and Jerusalem said that a specific attack that killed five members of a family, including three children, could be justified.[17] Additionally, 52 percent of Palestinians support suicide bombings against Israelis. Perhaps we shouldn't be giving the Palestine Liberation Organization millions of dollars after all.

Pew Research Data found that 89 percent of Palestinians favor Sharia as the law of the land, and of those 89 percent, two-thirds believe that those who leave Islam should be killed. But don't worry, just 84 percent believe that those who commit adultery should be stoned to death.[18]

The Israelis are supposed to negotiate peace with this type of society? I've said it before, and I'll say it again, the difference between Israel and the Palestinians is the difference between civilization and barbarism.

Countries in sub-Saharan Africa are also home to some startlingly radical views. The poll revealed that 34 percent of Nigerians were either favorable or undecided about ISIS, as well as 40 percent from Senegal.[19]

Jordan is a country we often hear about as an ally of the United States. It's one the Left occasionally likes to mention as a "moderate" Muslim country in the Middle East. But when surveyed about their views on suicide bombings, 15 percent of Jordanian Muslims said that suicide bombings could be justified. Additionally, 71 percent of Jordanian Muslims believe Sharia should be the law of the land, and of those, 67 percent believe stoning is the proper punishment for adultery.[20]

That means that 48 percent of the total Jordanian population believes a woman accused of adultery should have her skull crushed by rocks. How's that for "moderate"?

Let's not forget about Turkey, perhaps the most moderate of all Muslim majority countries in the world. Nearly one-third of the population that is arguably the most moderate of all Muslim countries said that honor killings could be justified.[21] That's about 23 million Turkish Muslims.

I don't know about you, but I wouldn't exactly be bragging about a country's "moderate" beliefs if 23 million of them believed fathers or husbands should be able to kill their daughters or wives for "dishonoring" them. How about you?

To summarize, here are the percentages of Muslims in each country who believe that Sharia should be the law of the land:[22]

Russia	42 percent
Turkey	12 percent
Pakistan	84 percent
Palestine	89 percent
Jordan	71 percent
Lebanon	29 percent
Malaysia	86 percent
Afghanistan	99 percent
Bangladesh	82 percent
Egypt	74 percent
Iraq	91 percent
Thailand	77 percent
Indonesia	72 percent
Niger	71 percent
Senegal	55 percent

The next time a leftist tries to tell you that there is no connection between Sharia and radicalism, be sure to remember this shocking summarized data. In every Middle Eastern and North African country surveyed except Morocco and Iraq, 40 percent or more of the Sharia-supporting Muslims believe that Sharia should apply not only to Muslims but non-Muslims. This means that they believe you too should submit to Allah or be put to death.[23]

Here are the percentages of Muslims who believe in the death penalty for leaving Islam:[24]

Russia	15 percent
Turkey	17 percent
Pakistan	76 percent
Palestine	66 percent
Jordan	82 percent
Lebanon	46 percent
Malaysia	62 percent
Afghanistan	79 percent
Bangladesh	44 percent
Egypt	86 percent
Iraq	42 percent
Thailand	27 percent
Indonesia	18 percent

Now take a look at the percent of Muslims in each country who believe in stoning as punishment for adultery:[25]

Russia	26 percent
Turkey	29 percent
Pakistan	89 percent
Palestine	84 percent
Jordan	67 percent
Lebanon	46 percent
Malaysia	60 percent
Afghanistan	85 percent
Bangladesh	55 percent
Egypt	81 percent
Iraq	58 percent
Thailand	51 percent
Indonesia	48 percent

How do Muslims around the world view the United States? A World Public Opinion Poll concluded the following percentages of Muslims approved of attacks on American troops in Iraq:[26]

Turkey	40 percent
Pakistan	26 percent
Palestine	90 percent

Jordan	72 percent
Egypt	83 percent
Indonesia	26 percent
Morocco	68 percent

Only a minority of Muslims disagreed with terror attacks on American troops, and about half of those opposed to attacking Americans were sympathetic with al Qaeda's attitude toward the United States.[27] Do you still think there's a "peaceful majority"?

WESTERNIZED MUSLIMS

Let's turn our attention to Muslim views from the Western world since the radical Left will inevitably argue that Western Muslims are more civilized in their approach to such barbaric practices. When surveyed about their views, 16 percent of French Muslims said that suicide bombings could be justified.[28] In a separate study the same percentage answered that they viewed ISIS favorably.[29] That's around one million Muslims in France! In nearby Belgium about 16 percent of young Muslims were found to support terrorism.[30]

In the UK 78 percent of British Muslims said they wanted to see those who drew Muhammad as a cartoon legally prosecuted.[31] Approximately one third of British Muslims refuse to completely condemn the practice of stoning women to death for adultery, with their survey answers ranging from condemning it to some extent, to being neutral about it, to "I don't know."[32] After the July 7 London bombings in 2005, a terrorist attack often referred to as 7/7 that killed 52 civilians, approximately one in five British Muslims expressed sympathy for the suicide bombers who carried out the attack.[33]

How about in the United States?

When surveyed, 12 percent of Muslim Americans had favorable views about violence toward civilians,[34] and 19 percent said they either supported (5 percent) or were undecided (14 percent) about al Qaeda.[35] That's half a million Muslim Americans! *Half a million!*

A 2015 survey by the Center for Security Policy shows that 51 percent of Muslims living in the United States said they preferred having "the choice of being governed according to shariah" or Islamic law.[36] Contrary to media narratives, an overwhelming 60 percent of Muslim-Americans under age thirty told Pew Research they're more loyal to Islam than America.[37]

As one can see, these terrifying statistics show a stark contrast to the deceptive 99.9 percent peaceful fantasy that Barack Obama perpetuated. The problem is far more widespread than many Americans realize. In fact, approximately 680 million Muslims worldwide have endorsed radical Islamic views.[38] That's about twice the entire US population, without even surveying all Muslim majority countries in Africa and the Middle East.

It's figures like these that make the Left's greatest boogeyman "Islamophobia" seem all the more ridiculous, and their "peaceful majority" cliché seem all the more inconsequential.

The typical leftist response in the media to Islamic terror attacks always includes an "Islamophobia" or "peaceful majority" reference because this is straight out of the radical Islamic lobby's PR playbook. It's the radical Islamic lobby's way of framing themselves as the victims, and the media buys it hook, line, and sinker. Now that you've got the facts, you won't.

The great irony, of course, is that the Left also holds itself up to be the great defender of human rights, particularly minority rights.

There is a deliberate misinformation campaign being waged by leftists in the media as well as Washington in an effort to keep the American public in the dark about our nation's most dangerous enemy. There is a go-to playbook that leftists and the radical Islamic lobby utilize every time an Islamic radical commits a terrorist attack against the West.

First, they set up a straw-man argument in an attempt to distract from the real issue at hand. For example, instead of having a serious discussion about the root causes of Islamic terror, the Left puts out irrelevant statements such as "not all Muslims are terrorists," as if anyone with anyone with any political power or influence has ever stated that all Muslims are terrorists, which would be an absurdity.

Next, they try to conflate radical Islam with other religions such as Christianity, Judaism, Hinduism, etc. in an attempt to argue that all religions have their violent zealots, and none is more dangerous than another. Take, for example, an exchange I had with radical leftist and professional jihad apologist Peter Beinart, who attacked me on Twitter in 2017 over my dedication to exposing the truth about radical Islam. (By the way, if you aren't familiar with Peter Beinart, the best description of him I ever heard came from Ben Shapiro when he said that Beinart is the type of leftist that gives Hamas a reason to celebrate when he's on television.)[39]

Beinart tweeted, "hey @ACTBrigitte, I know u think Koran is uniquely murderous + Jews dislike violent texts. But we just celebrated a holiday called Purim…"[40] He was implying that Purim commemorates a twenty-five-hundred-year-old example of Arab-Israeli violence.

My response: "We seem to have the Jewish suicide bomber threat under control."[41]

By that, I meant that his attack illustrates perfectly just how delusional the Left is about Islam and how desperate they are to cover up the truth. We don't hear a whole lot about Jews, Catholics, Mormons, or Lutherans detonating suicide bombs, hijacking airlines, or beheading others in the name of their religion for a reason. All religions are not created or exercised equally.

For us to defeat radical Islamic terrorism, we must be able to have a rational discussion about the topic and not resort to such insane and irrelevant comparisons.

This desperate attempt to paint over the connection between Islam and terror is not only wrong, but it's also dangerous. Islam is the fastest-growing religion in the world according to the latest Pew Report in 2017. Muslims are expected to exceed the number of Christians in the world by the end of the twenty-first century.[42]

Unless we can speak truthfully about the nature of radical Islamic terrorism, the ideology driving it, and why we must rise in defense of our great nation's culture and values, its tentacles will continue to stretch further into the Western world, resulting in more lives lost and the destruction of Judeo-Christian civilization as we know it.

Poll data has shown that our way of life is simply incompatible with the barbaric practices endorsed by hundreds of millions of Muslims worldwide. This radical ideology can only be defeated if we can identify the scope, magnitude, and implications of its opposition to all the values we cherish as a Western, Judeo-Christian society.

RISE UP AND ACT

When you hear people talk about the peaceful majority of Muslims, don't just hope someone else will set the record straight. ACT!

- The next time a leftist tries to conflate Islamic terrorism with extremism in other religions, revert back to these facts and poll data. The evidence is resoundingly clear that Islam has a far more prevalent case of extremism than any other religion, and the statistics mentioned in this chapter reveal that.

- Do not fight fire with fire. When hostile leftists resort to ad hominem attacks, labeling you bigoted, Islamophobic, racist, or worse when facts you've outlined conflict with their feelings, stick to a fact-based response as best you can. The leftists know they have no verifiable way of backing up their worldview, so personal attacks are all they have. We, on the other hand, have truth on our side, and truth is a powerful weapon when properly utilized.

- Share this poll data, which can be retrieved online at our website www.actforamerica.org, with friends and family who may have fallen for the fallacies perpetuated by the media or politically correct politicians with respect to the roots of terrorism. More to it, if your senator or congressional representative is one of those misrepresenting the truth about radical Islam, send them an email with the link and share this data with them.

Chapter 4

WEAPONIZING THE INTERNET

JUST AS IT has become easier for civilians to communicate with one another, so too it has become easier for Islamic terrorists to recruit and inspire fellow radicals to commit deadly attacks against the West. Radicals are now able to mobilize and connect with one another in ways not possible even just a decade ago. Though on different continents, from different cultures, and speaking different languages, all are able to march in unison for the same radical cause, thanks to technological advances, most notably the internet.

No longer is it necessary to grow up in a radicalized community in the Middle East to absorb the same radical values. Instead, the internet has created a borderless cultural exchange, where radical values from abroad can inspire deadly attacks from any location around the globe.

To put it another way, prior to modern advancements such as the internet, smartphones, and social media, jihadists were mainly limited to inspiring those they met in person. Now Islamic radicals can connect with people half a world away from them and spread poison to all those who will listen.

On September 11, 2001, the technological revolution was still in its infancy. Internet speeds moved like tortoises compared to modern Wi-Fi. Half the US population didn't have cell phones yet, and texting wasn't nearly as common as it is now.

Logging on to the internet was a somewhat laborious process filled with never-ending wait times, clogged up phone lines, and a painfully irritating dial-up sound as you waited to gain access. Social media outlets such as Facebook and Twitter were nonexistent and would remain so for several years. Still, even with all the technological advancements of today unavailable to them at the time, al Qaeda was able to organize the deadliest terror attack in world history. Nineteen jihadists were able to hijack four major airliners, destroy two of the world's tallest buildings along with the Department of Defense headquarters at the Pentagon, and kill thousands of innocent civilians all in about two hours.[1]

That level of deadly destruction requires precise execution and organization. For the terrorists to achieve such coordination in a time when almost none of the tools we use today to connect with one another or obtain information existed is beyond startling. The events of September 11 are all the more terrifying when considering all the additional tools that Islamic terrorists have at their disposal today for recruitment, incitement, organization, and execution.

Fast-forward to contemporary technological advancements, and jihad-ists can literally hold access to the entire world in the palms of their hands. Social media gives us the ability to connect with whomever we choose when-ever we choose. Unfortunately, an object of blessing for peaceful civilians remains a weapon for those who seek to do evil.

ISIS has truly capitalized on modern communications to destroy the Western world. The Paris Massacre in 2015 involved absolute precision between three teams of jihadists who set off consecutive bombs and coor-dinated shootings, using contemporary internet communication to their advantage.[2] Additionally, the 2013 Boston Marathon bombing, the 2015 San Bernardino attack, the 2016 Pulse nightclub shooting in Orlando, Florida, and many others were all carried out by individuals radicalized online.[3]

Anwar al-Awlaki was one of the most overt in utilizing the internet to spread his radical philosophies.[4] Al-Awlaki frequently uploaded sermons in which he promoted jihadism and encouraged violent attacks against Westerners whom he deemed oppressors.

He tried to convince impressionable Muslims around the globe that the only true course of action for a real Muslim was violent jihad. While he helped terrorists carry out their deadly plans, al-Awlaki's most notorious impact was his viral videos, which instantaneously spread his radical-Islamic message around the globe.

At the height of his power in Yemen, where he'd been forced to take refuge, al-Awlaki was the English-speaking mouthpiece for al Qaeda, as well as the cocreator of its official *Inspire* magazine, which would publish mate-rial about how to make homemade bombs and other tips for terrorists. This content by al-Awlaki was even picked up by the Boston Marathon bombers, Tamerlan and Dzhokhar Tsarnaev.[5]

Al-Awlaki's impact is a critically important concept for the Western world to understand. Our Judeo-Christian culture has always been allowed to prosper because it has existed as a mutually exclusive civilization to that of the Islamic world.

Muslim Americans who were born in America and grew up absorbing only the Western values that it embodies would have a much better chance of assimilating into our Judeo-Christian culture. But now the internet has made it impossible to contain the spread of jihadism and has thus eliminated the geographic advantage that Western countries traditionally had, having existed apart from the Islamic culture of the Middle East.

In the past the only way young Muslims in the West could become radical-ized was if they traveled to the Middle East or had close communication with someone who had. But the internet has transcended borders, language, and culture, and opened a can of worms with potentially deadly consequences.

Although al-Awlaki perfected the art of utilizing the internet to spread radical Islamic propaganda, Junaid Hussain took it to a whole different stratosphere. Hussain was the internet mastermind for ISIS, utilizing and weaponizing technology to become the massive worldwide threat it is today.

While you'd probably expect the top internet guru for ISIS to hail from Syria or Iraq, Hussain was raised in Birmingham, England. He became an internet hacking expert as a teenager, and at age fifteen he founded a group of hacking terrorists known as "TeaMp0isoN." The group claims to have hacked Mark Zuckerberg's Facebook page, NATO, and the British Ministry of Defense.

After serving six months in prison for leaking the address book of former prime minister Tony Blair, in 2013 Hussain made his way to Syria and became the main hacker for ISIS, helping them pull off a number of hacks worldwide, including the social media accounts of US Central Command—the military unit responsible for fighting ISIS. He tweeted "AMERICAN SOLDIERS, WE ARE COMING, WATCH YOUR BACK" to the 109,000 followers of the CentCom Twitter account and posted two ISIS propaganda videos on their YouTube page.[6]

Hussain continued to absorb jihadist propaganda online and became a master ISIS propagandist himself. He became known as one of the four "Beatles," a nickname for a group of four British jihadists who became notorious supporters in the ISIS cause. This group of four jihadists included Mohammed "Jihadi John" Emwazi, who gained international attention after his horrific execution of American journalists James Foley and Steven Sotloff and British aid workers David Haines and Alan Henning.[7]

This nickname ISIS gave their British supporters illustrates how clever they are with propaganda and inspiration. They gave these four a sense of purpose and prestige akin to that of rock stars. They appealed to them not through Islamic means alone, but through a sly mix of Islamic values with Western methods.

Hussain led what is known as the "Cyber Caliphate" of ISIS and was compensated accordingly. He took charge of hacking and social media outreach, including on YouTube, Facebook, Twitter, and other outlets. In June 2015 Hussain was able to gain access to the personal addresses of US military personnel and released the information in August 2015 on Twitter, encouraging ISIS followers to execute them.[8]

Al Qaeda, as well as other well-networked Islamic terror groups, used the same method in the past to target me personally. The toll this has taken on me cannot be overstated.

One Sunday morning in 2011 my name was published in an American newspaper by a leftist reporter, including the city where I lived, my husband's name, and other personal information. On Monday morning the Council on American-Islamic Relations (CAIR) put out a press release that was picked up by Al Jazeera network, sharing my name and location.

By Tuesday I received a call from the FBI informing me that my name, as well as the names of my children, was posted thirty-five thousand times on various radical Islamic websites, along with my address.

Consequently, the FBI advised me to move. By Wednesday morning I received an urgent warning from the FBI saying that our names and address were posted 165,000 times on different Islamic websites around the world.

I had to leave my home in a matter of hours with only two suitcases. I had to live in hiding for eight months before moving to a more permanent and secure location. Keeping myself and my family away from danger ended up costing us close to $100,000; not to mention the drastic and irreversible emotional toll this took on us.

The terrorization of any individual in any location at any time is now possible thanks to jihadist internet masterminds like Hussain, whose techniques continue to threaten the lives of both military personnel as well as civilians. Hussain was also in online contact with one of the gunmen behind the Draw Muhammad terrorist attack in Garland, Texas. Before the massacre, an attacker posted online statements on Twitter, calling for others to follow Hussain's account.

After the shooting Hussain tweeted: "Allahu Akbar!!!! 2 of our brothers just opened fire."[9]

The fact that the Pentagon once listed Hussain as the third-highest ISIS target on the their "kill list" (behind ISIS leader Abu Bakr al-Baghdadi and Mohammed Emwazi) simply for his internet expertise shows how weaponized our internet has become for jihadists.[10]

Thankfully Hussain was killed in a drone strike in Raqqa on August 24, 2015. His death marked the emergence of his wife, Sally Jones, who later became known as the "White Widow." Jones was a British-born, quintessential Westerner until she became entranced by ISIS propaganda. Following the death of her husband, Jones took up the cause of recruiting young Western girls for ISIS.[11]

LIONESSES OF ALLAH

The most shocking revelation in the online propaganda campaign by ISIS is their ability to recruit young, impressionable, Western-born-and-raised women. These women have been dubbed "Lionesses of Allah" and are deceptively deadly.

The primary purpose of an ISIS "lioness" is to bear the next generation of soldiers, known as "cubs." These children of lionesses will be raised to do one thing: kill the nonbeliever.[12]

One particular sixteen-minute video circulated far and wide across the Islamic State's media outlet, Telegram, as well as on Twitter. It showed young Indonesian and Malaysian men, dressed in combat gear, pointing

AK-47 assault rifles in the air with a crowd of children beside them chanting, "Allahu Akbar," an Arabic phrase meaning "Allah is great," and the seemingly go-to phrase for terrorists, frequently shouted before any terrorist attack.[13]

The narrator in the video will send chills down your spine when he states, "While the cubs of the Caliphate prepare themselves to be the conquering heroes in the near future, their fathers never stop waging jihad in the battle-fields and being garrisoned on the front lines to expand the territory of the Caliphate and protect every inch of its lands."[14]

One of the boys holding a rifle declares in response, "We in the nations of Nusantara—Indonesia, the Philippines, and Malaysia—by the grace of Allah, we have immigrated to the land of the Caliphate, and we left from the land of ignorance, the land of humiliation, the land of the lie, to the land that Allah had dignified."[15]

In Iraq, ISIS militants were also found to have trained young children to behead their victims, practicing on homemade mannequins constructed from a rubber girl's head taped to a plastic torso.

"This figure was for teaching children how to slaughter people. They showed them how to use a knife to sever the head on this figure, so they would know how to do it on a real person," an Iraqi special forces soldier stated. After decapitating the mannequin, they reattached the head so the children could continue to practice their killing.[16]

In sickening irony the same ISIS militants who used the mannequins to train children to kill also banned all mannequins in clothing shops across its territory because they felt mannequins were idolatrous.[17]

It is the "Lionesses of Allah" who are being recruited from all across the Western world and given the specific task of giving birth to as many future killers as possible.

While Western military wives and mothers spend sleepless nights tossing and turning, trying to take their mind off the dangers their husbands and sons are facing abroad, for an Islamic State lioness, a dead husband or son brings joy and honor.

The joy that Western wives feel when they can finally hug and kiss their husbands after a long and dangerous tour abroad, a lioness can only feel from learning of her husband's or son's death. A dead husband or son brings with it a sense of honor that she was the wife or mother of a brave and heroic martyr for Allah.

Western mothers do all they can to protect their children from harm; an Islamic "lioness" dreams of a day when her boy will die a martyr's death. While Western mothers dream of their boys growing up to be doctors, law-yers, athletes, etc., lionesses dream of their boys being brave enough to blow themselves to pieces for Allah. In the West we celebrate life. In the Islamic world they celebrate death.

For every ISIS soldier killed in battle, there are many more lying in wait, trained by their mothers to replace their fathers. ISIS rewards its widows for their loyalty, paying them a monthly stipend for each "cub" they deliver as well as a maternity and marriage bonus.[18]

These are the values that the internet is bringing to the homes of unsuspecting Westerners.

> In the West we celebrate life. In the Islamic world they celebrate death.

So where does ISIS find these deranged women? Thanks to the weaponization of the internet, right in your own backyard. No longer is this barbaric mentality reserved exclusively for those who grow up in a radicalized, Sharia-abiding community.

While their territory is shrinking, ISIS remains a particularly powerful online force. They continue to have an extremely strong presence on the web, having established over thirty thousand websites or "virtual caliphates." These so-called "virtual caliphates" are likely to live on long after we eliminate ISIS territory in Iraq and Syria. The thousands of websites circulating radical messages from the group continue to draft and inspire new recruits and homegrown jihadists on a regular basis.[19]

The internet is currently transitioning from the means of fighting the war on terror to becoming the actual battleground of the war on terror.

This new type of warfare no longer requires jihadists to travel thousands of miles to become radicalized at extremist training camps; instead they can gain all the radical training they need in the click of a button.[20] However, after having been radicalized online, virtual caliphates also allow others around the world to travel directly to the Islamic world for hands-on training in weaponry and explosives, if they so choose.

In addition to their seemingly countless websites, ISIS also frequently publishes online magazines. These magazines print jihadist propaganda and serve as a source of inspiration for potential supporters to attack the West.[21] ISIS online sources produce high-quality publications that cater to their supporters while attacking their enemy, the nonbelievers. They were the mother ship that inspired ISIS supporters to conduct coordinated attacks in places such as Iraq, Afghanistan, France, and other Western nations during Ramadan.[22]

In the new age of online warfare there is no invasion necessary. The soldiers have already crossed into enemy territory and are waiting for their orders from headquarters. This is why having a strong military, while necessary, is not sufficient to win the war on terror.[23]

TERRORISM IN 280 CHARACTERS OR LESS

ISIS's external outreach is complex, sophisticated, and dangerous. It is the threat that keeps growing at an alarming rate, especially as they continue to lose physical ground.

Social media has been a fundamental aspect of ISIS's internet strategy. Perhaps the most popular online outlet has been Twitter, which has played a tremendous role in homegrown jihadist attacks against the West.

ISIS militants used Twitter and the communication application called Telegram to post links of gruesome videos, detailing how to make home-made improvised explosive devices (IEDs) as well as instruction manuals on how to attack the United States using chemical weapons.[24]

In its biannual transparency report Twitter publishes data on requests it has received from the government and other legal entities to regulate content. In the last half of 2016 Twitter suspended 376,890 accounts for promoting terrorism-related content. That is no small number!

More startling, of the 376,890 suspended accounts, only 2 percent were the result of government requests to remove data![25] Twitter noted that automated spam tools, not human methods, actually found 74 percent of extremist accounts.

It makes one wonder how many terrorists are operating in our midst without any law enforcement tracking them! In February 2016, Twitter announced several initiatives, including partnering with outside organizations, training its policy team, and attending government-sponsored summits,[26] but in my opinion, those efforts are failing.

In the grand scheme of things extremism via social media comprises a significant aspect of radicalization, thus, until social media networks begin to properly assist law enforcement in the identification and removal of extremist propaganda, this is a deadly threat here to stay.

Failure to get serious about this threat from social media giants will result in more radicalization and more death. Estimates indicate that over forty thousand individuals have left their home countries for Iraq and Syria to join the fight for an Islamic caliphate.[27] Imagine how many have not left their homes!

YouTube has also been instrumental to ISIS in their relentless quest to recruit Westerners. ISIS creates propaganda films to attract young, disenfranchised Muslims, and even non-Muslims from the West, and have been very successful in doing so.

These videos are not what you'd expect from a barbaric jihadist group. They portray ISIS fighters as the strong, intimidating force they view themselves as, while at the same time also showing a "gentler" side of jihad, cracking jokes with one another or even playing with kittens.[28] This is their way of making Jihad look fun and exciting to a Western viewer, and tragically it works.[29]

The breakdown of the Western family creates a perfect opportunity for ISIS to brainwash and recruit more members. Parents are often aloof on their own tech devices and are not paying close enough attention to the poison their children are soaking up in the room right next to them. While the Western world seems to place an increasing amount of attention on material possessions, ISIS sees an opportunity to fill a spiritual void that exists within many young Western children as well as adults.

It might seem crazy from an outside perspective, but Islam gives many recruits structure. Men can play the hero, and women can have someone to support and take care of them, regardless of their outward appearance.

Now men can fill the leadership role and receive affection they have been craving, not because of how much money they make, but simply because they are a man. Women can be desired—even if they feel unattractive—because draped in a black burqa there is no feeling of inferiority compared to other women.

If you find this hypothesis hard to swallow, consider the tragically explosive opiate overdose epidemic sweeping across the United States. In 2016 more than sixty thousand Americans died of drug overdoses—that's more than all the soldiers killed throughout the entire Vietnam War.[30] In a three-year time period, deaths caused by Fentanyl, a particularly powerful opiate, increased by 540 percent.[31] We still do not know the total number of those killed from opiates in 2017 as the CDC is still calculating, but numbers are expected to rise even further.

> **The breakdown of the Western family creates a perfect opportunity for ISIS to brainwash and recruit more members.**

US Vietnam War Fatalities vs. Fatal Drug Overdoses

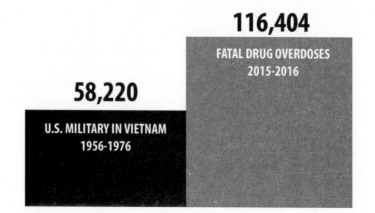

116,404

FATAL DRUG OVERDOSES
2015-2016

58,220

U.S. MILITARY IN VIETNAM
1956-1976

An epidemic like that doesn't come about without a spiritual vacancy. The breakdown of the Western family and the distancing of God as the central spiritual unifier at home has left a generation of young people hungry for unconditional love and acceptance from the highest person they were taught to love and revere. It used to be God in the Western family. Technology has made things easier, faster, and more available, yet many in the West have become more withdrawn from authentic human interaction, feeling lonely, and longing to have a purpose, while pleasing a father-type figure like God.

We've become distracted, impatient, and unfulfilled by the same devices we can't seem to live without. While some have found comfort in a bottle or needle, others have found comfort and even meaning in jihad—particularly young, impressionable Westerners, who have never known a world without high-speed Wi-Fi, social media, and instant access to a borderless virtual culture.

One of the most fundamental bedrocks of Western civilization has always been the family unit. In America it was not only the family unit, but also local places of worship that provided care, comfort, and meaning to the community. Whether it was the local parish, synagogue, or another place of worship, there was a unified spiritual connection between citizens.

Parents would take their children to the local pastor, priest, or rabbi for guidance and repentance for misdeeds they had committed, and there was a cohesive effort amongst the community to help one another. But regardless of religious background, they all recognized the existence of "God" or a higher being who guided their lives and played a role in how they conducted themselves because "God was always watching."

Over the past several decades religious attendance has dropped precipitously, and we've replaced the human relationships of the past with the virtual connections of today. Gone are the days when everyone knew their neighbors and would recognize and interact with others while out in their local community. Nowadays, you can have thousands of followers on Twitter, most of whom you've never actually met, and use this virtual reality as a substitute for authentic personal connections.

Children aren't outside playing with their friends, scraping their knees, and interacting with their peers. Instead, they sit in the same room with one another, while each is separately glued to his or her own tech device. They're in a constant state of competition with one another, to see who can project the best virtual lifestyle. Posting pictures of where they are and who they're with is more important than where they actually are and who they're actually with. It's all a big front for the emptiness and longing for true human connections that every man, woman, or child needs.

HEADS IN THE SAND

Despite the fact that social media and other evolving forms of technology have been exploited by the most dangerous terrorists on the planet in order to grow their following, spread propaganda, and launch cyber warfare, big tech companies such as Google, Facebook, and Twitter seem more antagonistic toward conservatives than they do jihadists.

Google has gone to great lengths recently to silence and smear conservative websites by installing a partisan fact-checking feature when viewers come across content from conservative publications. This feature, of course, was not made available for Far Left websites and has since been removed for what Google attributed to "systemic challenges." Google used FactCheck.org, Politifact, and Climate Feedback, all partisan, left-wing outfits to "fact check" conservative news. They were caught red-handed and had to walk back their partisanship.[32] Such bias is unsurprising given that Eric Schmidt, chairman of Google's parent company, Alphabet, is a vehement supporter and contributor to the Democratic Party.[33] If only Google went to such lengths to remove jihadist propaganda from its search engines.

Google, Facebook, and Twitter all caught well-deserved flack in late 2017, when British Prime Minister Theresa May told them to take down terrorist websites within two hours or face heavy fines.[34] Considering how much money these tech giants are making, the fact that they have failed to get their arms around this epidemic of jihadist propaganda is beyond absurd. The first two hours are the most critical time to remove such propaganda because jihadists can install notifications whenever an update is posted, leaving future efforts to remove extremist posts rather meaningless. Once the message is out, it's too late.

If tech giants continue to run rampant while silencing voices they disagree with politically, freedom of speech will be a thing of the past.

All of these outlets have failed to live up to their responsibility of combatting terrorism online, yet we continue to see overwhelming and explicit evidence of political partisanship on behalf of these leftist tech giants.

One of the more egregious examples of this leftist bias is Twitter's notorious "shadow banning" of conservatives and really anyone who doesn't fall in line with the ideological worldview of the Far Left. Shadow banning is a clever little trick undercover reporter James O'Keefe uncovered, in which tweets from a shadow-banned user still appear to their followers but will not show up in search results. Essentially the content is not reaching new audiences, and the users who have been shadow banned are none the wiser. This practice was exposed by O'Keefe when he spoke to Twitter employees about the practice itself. Former Twitter engineer Conrado

Miranda clarified to O'Keefe that shadow banning of Trump supporters was in fact taking place and that it was far more common than most realize.[35]

Twitter employs content reviewers who often use shadow banning as a means of silencing the political opposition at their own discretion. Mo Noral, a former Twitter content review agent, explained the practice to O'Keefe, "Let's say if it was a pro-Trump thing and I am anti-Trump, I was like, I banned his whole account. It goes to you, and then it's at your discretion."[36]

He continued, "If this is pro-Trump I don't want it because it offends me. And I say, 'I banned this whole thing…'" Noral also pointed out that employees at Twitter are at least 90 percent, and most likely, 99 percent anti-Trump.[37]

Gosh, you'd think with the constant onslaught of jihadist propaganda flooding Twitter, the company would spend a little more time on combatting Islamic terrorism than on American conservatism.

Facebook also has a reputation for blacklisting and shadow banning users with political bias. When a German Facebook page started listing and mapping all migrant-committed crimes reported by police, the page's followers suddenly reported not seeing the posts anymore. The page's owner told Breitbart investigative reporters that he noticed a sudden and drastic decline in their reach, after having a lengthy history of continuous growth in audience.[38] Such bias would not be surprising at Facebook, considering founder Mark Zuckerberg's ardent loyalty to and support for refugees. One thing remains certain: if these tech giants, who control modern communication on a monopolistic scale, continue to run rampant while silencing voices they disagree with politically, freedom of speech will be a thing of the past. Still, even with the reputation Silicon Valley has garnered for silencing conservatives, the voices of violent jihad continue to permeate these outlets on a dangerously high scale.

PROFILE OF THE NEW ISLAMIC TERRORIST

If I asked you where you were raised, you'd probably give me the name of your home city and be able to tell me all about the cultural impact of growing up in that particular place. Nowadays a child can reside in Brooklyn, New York, but be raised as if on a completely separate continent. It all depends on the material they absorb and the values of people with whom they interact. Consequently, those they socialize with—who can be anyone, anytime, from anywhere—become their community substitute.

Shannon Maureen Conley was sentenced to four years in prison for attempting to join ISIS in Syria. Conley, a Denver woman, was nineteen years old when she was sentenced and looked barely fifteen.[39] Not exactly the typical profile of an Islamic terrorist, is it? Welcome to the new world.

Conley joined the US Army Explorers to be trained in US military tactics and in firearms, intending to train jihadists in US military tactics. She intended to travel to Syria, where she planned to marry a Tunisian jihadist whom she met online.[40] Impressionable and brainwashed, Conley quickly converted to Islam and jumped headfirst into the radical abyss.

The Colorado teen was arrested when trying to board a plane to Turkey at Denver International Airport and was charged with conspiracy to provide material support to ISIS. She "repeatedly referred to US military bases as 'targets,'" in an interview with the FBI.[41]

Conley said she wanted to "wage jihad" and viewed women and children as targets if they were visiting a military base at the time. In her interview with the FBI, Conley coldheartedly noted that it is OK to harm innocents if they are part of a target.[42]

Conley practiced shooting at a local shooting range and had access to several firearms. She noted that she needed to go overseas to be "trained in jihad," but did not need to be overseas to "wage jihad."[43]

Welcome to the age of internet weaponization. Without the use of the internet, Conley never would have been able to connect with a smooth-talking jihadist halfway around the world, nor would she have been radicalized at such an alarming speed.

Thankfully a diligent local pastor reported Conley to law enforcement. The pastor suspected she might have been casing his church building for a terrorist attack. Church members and staff saw Conley walking the church grounds several times, wearing a hijab and a backpack, and taking notes and sketching diligently.[44]

When confronted about why she was casing the church in her FBI interview, Conley simply replied, "I hate those people."[45] If not for the courage and sense of this pastor, Conley could possibly have slaughtered hundreds in her planned rampage.

The case of Shannon Conley demonstrates just how easy it is with contemporary technology for an Islamic radical on the other side of the world to influence the mind of a typical teenage girl. It also displays how creating a profile of potential jihadists within our communities is not exclusive to those whom you'd typically suspect on paper.

Conley grew up a typical teenage girl in a quintessential American town, only to then turn on the community that raised her. As the Islamic State shrinks, hundreds if not thousands of other Conleys recruited online and trained in the Middle East are going to be roaming our streets as ISIS soldiers.

Roughly forty thousand people from over one hundred countries made their way to Iraq and Syria to join ISIS both before and after it became a self-declared caliphate in 2014. Thousands of the Islamic State's foreign fighters are already returning to Western countries, including the United States, as their territory fades away in Iraq and Syria.

While eliminating ISIS territory is a tremendous accomplishment for our military, we must now face the reality of bitter, militant Islamists returning home with a vengeance. A recent report from the Soufan Center indicates at least two thousand former ISIS members have gone back to Western countries.[46]

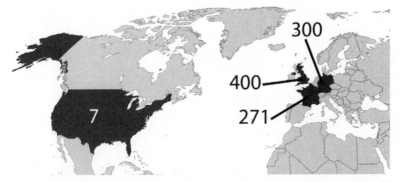

Approximately 1,500 fighters have returned to Europe, with about 400 going back to the United Kingdom, 271 to France, and about 300 in Germany. Meanwhile, 7 have returned to the United States out of the 129 Americans we know have joined ISIS. Overall, 5,600 citizens or residents from thirty-three countries have returned to their home countries.[47]

The online sphere of influence is ever expanding, and no parent, spouse, or child should turn a blind eye to suspicious behavior by those they love. Westerners must take hold of this emerging threat before it is too late. The internet has opened the floodgates to threats never before posed to Western society and the Judeo-Christian values it embodies.

Welcome to the twenty-first century, where the world is smaller, and everything is faster, easier, and more dangerous than ever before.

RISE UP AND ACT

When you notice something or someone suspicious online, don't just look the other way. ACT!

- Get involved and learn how to use social media because social media is the future of communication. The world is changing more rapidly every day. Today the new theater of war is not a geographical location. It is on your computer on the internet. Anyone can be a soldier in this fight for the good against the bad. We need as many patriots active online as possible to help spread our message to the masses. Join us as an activist at www.actforamerica.org, and we will train you on how to use the internet to put out information and influence opinion on your social network.

- If you see radical postings online from jihadist accounts, report the accounts to the FBI immediately, and make sure to take a screenshot of the account, as well as the radical posting. We must stay vigilant against this enemy both in the real world as well as the cyber world.

- We cannot win this fight on our keyboards alone. Countries cannot be saved by tweets and hashtags alone. Social media and utilizing technology, while necessary, is not sufficient to win this fight. We must also become engaged and active in our local communities to ensure that we remain connected as individuals and restore interpersonal connections with our neighbors, a concept that has seemingly eroded due to changing technology. Take walks in your neighborhood and pay attention to who lives there and their habits. Not only will you get to meet your neighbors and make a few new friends, but you will also develop a network of people keeping an eye on the neighborhood. This also will make you aware of someone changing their ways and possibly becoming radicalized.

- If someone you know experiences a sudden change in personality, becomes more withdrawn, or begins posting strange or radical material online, please take notice and contact authorities. Radicalization can strike any person, in any town, at any time.

- My organization, ACT for America, the nation's largest and most powerful grassroots national security organization, has a campaign dubbed Open Eyes Save Lives, specifically dedicated to identifying and stopping this very type of potential attack. Please go to www.actforamerica.org to learn how you can help protect your community.

Chapter 5

REPLACEMENT CIVILIZATION

THE FUNDAMENTAL TRANSFORMATION of society doesn't happen overnight. The larger the population and the more embedded the values within that population, the longer it will take to change the foundation. But the fundamental transformation of the United States has been underway for half a century, and we can already see the disastrous consequences.

You've probably heard it said, "We're a nation of immigrants." This is not true. America is a nation of citizens who welcome immigrants that come in legally and assimilate to benefit those already living here.

To put it another way, America is a nation of citizens, not immigrants. Citizenship is what every immigrant should aspire to, and only something that should be obtained through genuine assimilation into the fabric of a Western, democratic society built on Judeo-Christian principles.

This is not a knock on immigrants. I myself am an immigrant. I legally immigrated to the United States and became a United States citizen through marriage. From the moment I arrived, I wanted to be as American as apple pie.

I didn't even teach my children my native Arabic when they were growing up, though it was the easiest language for me to speak. I wanted them to be 100 percent American and bleed nothing but red, white, and blue.

My love affair with America began in my bomb shelter, while watching American television programming. A tiny black and white box operated by a car battery became my only window to the outside world, but it was more than enough to captivate my attention. Watching my favorite series like *The Love Boat*, *The Waltons*, *Little House on the Prairie*, and *Dallas* took me out of the hellhole bomb shelter I was trapped in and transported me to the safe and beautiful streets of the United States. To me, English was synonymous with a better way of life. I knew that if I ever had a chance to make it to America, which was my newfound dream, learning English would be a necessity. Learning a new language was a small price to pay for the comfort it brought me and the opportunity to one day live in the paradise I dreamed of as a little girl.

These American television shows were more than just entertainment. They became my English classroom. I would hang on every word and read the Arabic subtitles meticulously. I started writing words on my arm so I could memorize them. Since we barely had enough water to drink, let alone shower, we could only afford to bathe once a week. This being the case, I practically accumulated the entire English dictionary on my body. I never studied English in school, but because I was determined enough, I was able to learn better than any formalized method would have allowed. When the heart is as passionate as the mind, you can learn and do just about anything in this world.

Learning English meant more to me than just memorizing words—it meant salvation. It meant a new lease on life. I may have been living in an underground bomb shelter, but by helping me learn English, my television became a secret escape route, leading me out of Lebanon and right to the dream called America. Despite all the bullets and bombs, the terrorists could never touch my imagination, and therefore, they could never fully break my spirit. Today America the dream has become my address.

America is a nation of citizens, not immigrants. Citizenship is what every immigrant should aspire to.

Speaking English was important to me, but it was the Judeo-Christian values that America was founded upon that I wanted to impress upon my children the most. It was these values that formed the greatest nation the world has ever seen and inspired a democratic revolution that would change the world forever.

Don't get me wrong, I still love to converse in Arabic with old friends from Lebanon now and then, and when my children pushed my buttons while they were growing up, I sometimes had to let the native tongue fly. I still cook traditional Lebanese meals for company, and belly dancing is still as natural as riding a bike. These things will never leave me, and I wouldn't want them to. But these are not the things that make one a true Westerner.

What separates the Western world from other civilizations are things such as freedom of thought, freedom of speech, democracy, the pursuit of happiness, the right to self-determination, and endless limits to human achievement.

We take these things for granted as Westerners. We think that most human beings share these treasures we call human rights because they are such a natural part of our everyday lives.

The writing of the Magna Carta, the Enlightenment, the Declaration of Independence, the abolition of slavery, and the Industrial Revolution—none of these things took place outside Western civilization for a reason. They require a society built on Judeo-Christian values.

America is the greatest testament to that. From electricity to cars, chemotherapy, polio vaccines, a man on the moon, cell phones, the internet, the iPhone, and the list goes on and on, America was always a beacon of hope and progress for the rest of the world. It has been the "shining city upon a hill" that President Reagan famously noted and proof of what a society built on individual ingenuity and human rights could achieve.

But in recent years we've seen a concerted effort by America's enemies, both abroad and within, to put a stop to that progress and extinguish that flame of hope in exchange for political correctness and a borderless world. If you've ever had the unfortunate experience of being stuck in the waiting room at a doctor's office while CNN or MSNBC is on, you've probably come across the propaganda they spread about our nation's past concerning immigration.

REWRITING HISTORY

Contrary to what you may have heard, from the late 1800s our immigration system had limits, and starting in 1921 it had quotas. Today this quota system is but a relic from the past, thanks to a disastrously destructive piece of legislation that was passed in order to fundamentally change the demographic makeup of America, with seemingly no regard for assimilation whatsoever.

The 1965 Immigration Act removed the national origin quota system and opened floodgates that we still haven't closed. It provided preference to refugees and immigrants who were family members of US citizens. This was the beginning of the effort to "diversify" America and marked the initiation of "tolerance" over common sense. Never again would the American immigration system serve to benefit Americans first. Instead, immigration became a charity for the rest of the world to take advantage of, courtesy of the hardworking American taxpayer.

Post-1965 arrivals consisted of a wider mix of people seeking family unification and a much higher share from the Islamic world. It was no longer about who was most likely to assimilate and benefit America, but racial and religious diversity instead. In other words, it became the very antithesis of what Martin Luther King Jr. preached about—judging one based on their character rather than the color of their skin. The 1965 Immigration Act flipped Dr. King's dream on its head and betrayed everything that America was supposed to represent.

Suddenly the United States began to function like a government-run charity dedicated to serving anyone who walked through its doors. Still today it seems to have no regard for policies that will benefit those already living here, particularly concerning safety and culture.

WHERE AM I?

Too many Westerners look around their hometown communities today and barely recognize them. They turn on the news and hear horrific stories of crimes committed in their own backyards, leaving them wondering what changed.

They go to their local shopping malls and wonder whether this is the same shopping center they have been coming to for decades, or whether they were somehow teleported to Saudi Arabia. Women draped in full *niqabs* (coverings for the face with only a small eye slit) shop alongside them. It startles most people to see a woman draped in black garb from head to toe because for her to reveal more than her eyes would bring shame to her husband. By the way, forcing women to dress this way does not reflect a *moderate* ideology—not to mention it is demeaning to women and would never be tolerated by the Left if Christian men were subjugating women this way.

Churches and synagogues are disappearing, while mosques are spreading like wildfire. In fact, more than nine hundred new Islamic centers have been established since 2000.[1] Maybe that fact doesn't concern you in and of itself, but what about the realization that inside these mosques radical imams preach hateful sermons in Arabic about the West to their congregations with citizens of the surrounding community completely unaware.

> The 1965 Immigration Act flipped Dr. King's dream on its head and betrayed everything that America was supposed to represent.

When we hear about terrorist attacks committed by "lone wolves," the community itself is shocked and terrified. They ask themselves, "How could this happen here?" But if Americans were aware of just how many immigrants from the Islamic world were entering their communities over the past few decades and the hateful rhetoric that was being preached at the local mosque down the street, their only surprise would be that it hadn't happened sooner.

When I travel the country to speak and educate communities about the threats facing this nation, I'm often approached by ordinary citizens who have no real interest in politics. These are not right-wing ideologues who watch Fox News religiously or attend every Republican meeting they can; these are average, nonpartisan, hardworking citizens.

When I ask what motivates them to come and listen to me speak or get involved with our organization ACT for America, one of the most common reasons they give is that they no longer recognize the communities they live in. These small-town American communities that their families have resided in for generations have—to borrow a phrase from Barack Hussein Obama—"fundamentally transformed."

I recently had a conversation with a middle-aged man from Lackawanna, New York, a blue-collar, former steel town just outside Buffalo. He told me that he and his wife were now terrified of the community where they grew up and raised their children. Prior to 9/11, in the spring of 2001, six men from Lackawanna traveled to a bin Laden–run terrorist training camp in Afghanistan.[2]

In June 2001 a concerned citizen sent a letter to the FBI warning, "I am very concern[sic]. I am an Arab American...and I cannot give you my name because I fear for my life. Two terrorist [sic] came to Lackawanna...for recruiting the Yemenite youth...the terrorist group...left to Afghanistan to meet...bin Laden and...stay in his camp for training."[3]

The bin Laden–trained jihadists returned to Lackawanna later that year.[4] All of the "Lackawanna Six" eventually pleaded guilty to providing material support to a terrorist organization and were sent to federal prison. Imagine if these were your neighbors.

The Lackawanna man I spoke to said that the arrest of the Lackawanna Six should have been a wake-up call for the community, but sadly he was no less fearful today than he was a decade ago. Now he and his wife are awakened by Islamic calls to prayer every morning as local Islamists blast the chants, conceivably waking up the entire street. Although he's complained, the police do nothing.

He told me the value of their house has depreciated due to massive Islamic immigration, leaving him and his wife in a terrible bind. But this man said he would still sell, even taking a loss on the house, if not for having to leave his mother-in-law who lives just one street over and is too attached to her home and community to leave it.

Lackawanna's story touched me because it's a story not exclusive to one city, but a rapidly growing number of American communities that have been radically transformed due to an influx of unvetted Islamic refugees and immigrants. To ask hardworking Americans to pack up and leave the communities their families have called home for generations due to irresponsible and dangerous immigration policy is unacceptable. People grow attached to their communities for a reason. This is where they grew up, bought their first house, got married, and raised their children and grandchildren.

Now these citizens are forced to leave all those memories behind because the community they have called home for so long has been transformed. This is the reality for many American towns that are witnessing a replacement civilization before their very eyes.

WELCOME TO SOMALIA

Take, for example, the tragic transformation of Minnesota, which currently has the nation's largest Somali population. Law enforcement in Minnesota has struggled for years to combat the recruitment of young Somali men by ISIS and the East Africa–based militant group al-Shabaab, and for good reason. Census numbers put the state's Somali population at about forty thousand, but community activists have said it's probably significantly higher.[5]

The largest share of that group has settled into one neighborhood in the Minneapolis area, which is now dubbed "Little Mogadishu." But significant numbers have also settled in St. Cloud, Willmar, and other smaller cities in the state.[6]

Wouldn't you love to live in a community known as Little Mogadishu? No? When you consider that the US State Department and most Western nations have posted an advisory, warning people to avoid all travel to the real

Mogadishu because of terrorist activity, I can understand why you might not want to see your community named after it. However, the mainstream media and community activists might just call you a racist for feeling that way.

Mogadishu is the capital of Somalia, which, by the way, is a country where residents will pay hundreds of dollars to sit in a room with a live hyena. I'm not joking. Many Somalis believe that the hyena will cure them of drug addiction by scaring away the demons inside.[7] Hearing this, the leftist politicians in Minnesota must have thought to themselves, "We need that type of culture over here!"

In the 1990s the head of the Minneapolis Foundation, Emmett Carson, lobbied vehemently for Somali Islamists in order to compensate for Minnesota's previous "lack of diversity." Sure, Minnesota was more culturally unified before its Somali invasion, but wasn't that boring? Now Minnesota can proudly call itself "multicultural!"

Leftists like Carson must have figured since so many Minnesotans didn't have the money to spend on a luxurious vacation to Mogadishu—as is every American family's dream—he ought to bring all the same dangers and cultural plagues that exist in Somalia right here.[8] Forgive me for being sarcastic, but it's hard not to be when the situation is this unbelievable.

The Minneapolis Foundation ran a PR campaign that displayed a photo of three Somali women draped in their native garb with a caption that read: "Maybe you're just not sure what to make of all these new Minnesotans bringing in all these strange new cultures and customs..."[9] This was, of course, to imply that if you didn't think it was such a good idea to import massive waves of Somalis, you're probably just uninformed or a racist.

This has nothing to do with race. This has everything to do with character, as Dr. Martin Luther King famously emphasized in his speech. This has to do with values.

A Somali gang ring was indicted in 2010 on charges related to hundreds of thousands of dollars in credit card fraud and child prostitution.[10] "They were trying to find identity," said Hassan Mohamud, the imam at Islamic Da'wah Center, a youth-oriented mosque and cultural center in St. Paul.[11]

Community centers and mosques have come together to create basketball and soccer programs to try to keep kids busy. They've also held forums to discuss issues including sex trafficking. Perhaps the unfortunate reality in Mogadishu makes it necessary for local religious centers to commonly hold discussions discouraging sex trafficking, but here in the Western world, it's a bit unusual.

Since the unemployment rate of Somalis is about three times the rate for the general population, it's unsurprising that credit card fraud is so high on the list of crimes committed by Somali immigrants. The median household income of Minnesotans from Somalia in 2016 was $25,500 a year, compared to $65,600 for average Minnesotans.[12] Half of Minnesota's Somalis are unemployed and the other half make significantly less than that of the average Minnesotan. Does this sound sustainable to you?

A startling 42 percent of Somalis in Minnesota live at or below the poverty line.[13] Nearly 40 percent of Somali adults over twenty-five have not graduated from high school, compared with only around 8 percent of non-Somali Minnesotans.[14] This problem is not exclusive to Minnesota or even America. In Sweden only 21 percent of Somali immigrants have jobs.[15]

ECONOMIC STATUS OF MINNESOTA'S SOMALI REFUGEES[16]

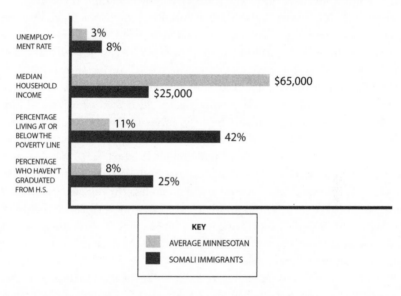

These problems, of course, could have been foreseen, given the fact that the World Health Organization estimates that one-third of Somalia's population is mentally ill.[17] With this in mind, perhaps we should press pause on the massive importation of Somalis to Minnesota, at least until after they've had a thorough mental evaluation.

Surely the biggest concern out of these revelations is not the effect it's having on American citizens who are footing the bill for almost-doubled public welfare consumption,[18] but whether or not the Somali community feels culturally welcomed or not. Don't worry, the Catholic University of St. Thomas installed Islamic prayer rooms in 2013 in order to show tolerance.

In a political television commercial aired across Minneapolis, Mayor Betsy Hodges—wearing a hijab, mind you—began by addressing viewers with "Assalamu alaikum," an Islamic Arabic greeting. The submissive mayor then proceeded to tell local residents how she would be sure to hire a very "inclusive" group of individuals from "the community" so that they could have their eyes and ears on public policy decisions.[19] When I heard this, I thought, "How wonderful. I'm sure this will bode well for counterterrorism efforts." Sadly, my point was proven when, in July 2017, a Somali police officer (whose position on the police force was celebrated by the mayor in a Facebook post) shot and killed a woman and was charged with murder and manslaughter.[20]

SANITARY CONDITIONS OPTIONAL

Should a Muslim surgeon be allowed to wear a headscarf into surgery if it poses an unsanitary risk that could lead to a deadly infection? If you answered no, then according to the Royal Hallamshire Hospital in Sheffield, England, you're an intolerant bigot. The UK hospital suspended a consultant anesthesiologist for allegedly exposing a Muslim surgeon's unsanitary and dangerous behavior when she refused to take off her headscarf during surgery.[21]

Dr. Vladislav Rogozov, a Czech-born doctor, raised serious concern for his patient's well-being and was promptly suspended by the hospital. "I came into the operating room, where I met the surgeon, a woman shrouded in a Muslim headscarf," Dr. Rogozov wrote. "I immediately stopped the operation of the hall and asked her to put down her scarf and replace it with the prescribed headgear. After a long discussion held with respect, decency, and factual arguments, the surgeon refused and left the operating room. We managed to subsequently find another surgeon who performed the operation. After the end of the operating day, other members of the surgical team came to me (in a low voice and with the door closed) to share their concerns about the threat to patient safety."[22]

Did the Muslim surgeon apologize for her dangerous defiance of medical etiquette? Of course not. In her mind the anesthesiologist's concerns were obviously a result of racism.

That's right—the Muslim surgeon accused Dr. Rogozov of racial discrimination. Of course, Islam is a religion, not a race, but why let facts and common sense get in the way of politically correct victimhood? Surely any attempt by a fellow physician to ensure proper hygiene standards before performing surgery could only be the result of bigotry.

According to hospital regulations, religious coverings are "excluded in areas such as theatre, where they could present a health and cross-infection hazard."[23] But of course, this Muslim surgeon's right to wear an unsanitary headscarf should clearly trump patient safety. Because, surely, it's better to be dead than intolerant.

But this particular surgeon wasn't the only Muslim endangering the lives of patients during surgery. Dr. Rogozov reported other Muslim staff members taking breaks in the middle of operations for Islamic prayers as well as distractingly reciting verses from the Quran during surgery.

I wonder what the response of the hospital would have been had it been a Christian doctor abandoning her obligations to pray or wearing a veil during surgery. Can you imagine this happening while a doctor operated on you or one of your loved ones?

NEXT STOP: EURABIA

Welcome to what I call Eurabia, where millions of Muslim migrants and so-called refugees from the Middle East and North Africa have flooded into Western countries. There has been something of a culture clash, to say the least.

But the economic effects have also been dire. Home values drop as much as 2 percent in areas where Middle Eastern refugees settle, according to experts. Working-class towns in the northern UK, where a typical home can lose more than £3,000 (more than $4,000) of its value, seem to be the worst affected.[24] So much for all the hard work these residents put into paying off their homes.

Former prime minister David Cameron's commitment for Britain to take in twenty thousand additional Syrian refugees before his long overdue exit from office didn't help matters either.

Academics calculate that "a 1 percent rise in the number of migrants in a community causes a 1.7 percent fall in property prices."[25] Researchers attribute this to a fall in demand for housing because of a pattern of wealthy Brits leaving their neighborhoods as soon as immigrants move in. They've also concluded that immigrants are usually less able to afford a high-end house and are more likely to rent, explaining why prices in these neighborhoods do not rise as quickly and demand drops.

A report by Nils Braakmann of the University of Newcastle backs up this claim and has also indicated that massive influxes of migrants have a negative impact on house prices.[26] These effects are even more drastic when the immigrants have lower educational backgrounds. Research shows that the current population tends to prefer living closer to those with similar education levels.[27] Of course, mainstream media pundits who live in Manhattan or London high-rises or gated communities would likely call this a racist move.

When Iran's Hassan Rouhani recently visited Rome to meet with Italian Prime Minister Matteo Renzi, statues among the historical collections at the world famous Capitoline Museums were hidden.[28] The museum said the Italian prime minister's office requested the cover-up so as to not offend Rouhani. Additionally, no wine was served amongst any of the attendees at an official dinner for Rouhani.

"The level of cultural subordination of Renzi and the left has exceeded all limits of decency," was said quite correctly by Italian politician Giorgia Meloni, who also posted on social media about whether they should cover St. Peter's Basilica "with a huge box" when the emir of Qatar visited.[29] When

Rouhani, the leader of the foremost state sponsor of terrorism,[30] receives a submissive welcome from a country with a cultural history as rich as Italy's, it shows just how far Western civilization has fallen.

The West continues to choke itself to death by refusing to stand up for the values that made it so free and prosperous in the first place. You might say that we're so beholden to the tyranny of tolerance, we now seem to tolerate only the intolerant!

Meanwhile, London's Islamist mayor, Sadiq Khan, who once stated that preparations for terrorist attacks in his city were simply a normal part of urban life, continues to try to ban President Trump from setting foot on UK soil.

Islamic culture is the only one for which nude statues in Rome would be covered up, and it is the only culture that requires female diplomats to cover their hair in the presence of male world leaders.[31] The Dalai Lama doesn't require such outrageous gestures. Neither do Pope Francis nor high-ranking Orthodox Jews. Only in the Islamic world is it expected that the differing culture should submit to them, even when they travel to other countries.

In tragic irony the very same values that created Western countries—tolerance, inclusivity, freedom, and individual thought—are now being used to destroy them. These Western, Judeo-Christian values have been perverted to suddenly mean giving up such principles in order to not "offend" or be "intolerant" of those who do not share such values.

CLASH OF CULTURES

Cultures are clashing in Europe and across the Western world at an alarming rate. Many in the West have been stunned by the difference that exists between them and the Islamic world.

Things as simple as how to properly use the bathroom have now become an issue. Believe it or not, many recent Muslim migrants have no idea how to use toilets in the Western world. One German bathroom manufacturer is trying to solve this startling dilemma by designing a special "multicultural toilet" that the migrants can use.[32] Yes, really.

Many Muslim migrants say they're baffled by Western toilets and have resorted to defecating outdoors, on the floors, in showers, and even on top of toilets themselves. They basically just go everywhere except for actually in the proper location.

The problem has gotten so out of control that the government is now passing out instructional leaflets, including pictures for educational purposes, pleading with migrants to learn the proper way of relieving themselves. The leaflets—not the actions of the migrants—have predictably come under criticism by social justice leftists, who say such efforts are "racist" and "insensitive" toward Muslims. But I'm sure the creation of a special "multicultural toilet" by the German manufacturer Global Fliegenschmidt will solve the problem entirely.[33]

What do you expect from a society that, up until 2015, did not permit the use of toilet paper? However, progress has certainly been made in the Islamic world concerning this issue. In 2015 Turkey issued a fatwa allowing Muslims to use toilet paper. I'm not kidding, a fatwa. Talk about progression. My gosh, could this be a sign of a coming Islamic reformation?

Call me crazy, but I believe knowing how to use a toilet properly as an adult, or anyone over the age of three, should probably be one of the prerequisites to earning legalized status in any Western country.

Thanks to open borders, leftists, and politically correct politicians, the problem has also made its way to the United States. The city of Denver passed an ordinance in May 2017 to reduce the penalty for public defecation. You read that right. Mark Silverstein, legal director for the American Civil Liberties Union of Colorado, cheered this "progressive" policy, noting, "Many times it becomes a deportable offense if you've been convicted of even a minor ordinance violation that's punishable by a year in jail."[34]

The law basically protects illegals and refugees who come from countries described in colorful language by President Trump from being arrested and deported. After all, we want to make it as easy as possible for these poor, culturally diverse people to come and live here and prove to them our unshakable tolerance.

Perhaps public defecation is a minor offense to lawless leftists like Silverstein and his army of ACLU apologists, but to civilized twenty-first-century Americans it defies all common decency and is a direct threat to public health. Here's some free advice for Denver politicians who refuse to hold adults accountable for their infantile actions: reducing the consequences for reprehensible behavior only enables such behavior to continue.

How are these illegals ever supposed to assimilate the way the Far Left says they already have if they relax the disciplines for not abiding by our laws and codes of common decency? It's no surprise that Denver is having issues, given that they have a larger illegal migrant population than Philadelphia and San Francisco.[35]

DOUBLE STANDARDS

Whether it's sexual assault, stoning, honor killings, death to gay men, or suppression of free speech, Westerners should be just as outraged if it comes from an Islamist as they would if it came from a Christian, Hindu, Buddhist, or Jew.

Leftists love to talk about the genocide of Native Americans hundreds of years ago but are silent about the current genocide taking place in the Middle East against Christians.

The world made major progress in the past century with respect to democracy, individual freedoms, and basic human decency, but one culture remains more than a millennium behind. Now the radical Left, which ironically markets itself as "progressive," wants to take us backward more than one thousand years by importing millions of unvetted Islamic immigrants from Middle Eastern countries, many of whom possess anciently barbaric values.

The radical Left sees Western civilization as the enemy, not the solution. They view massive immigration as an obligation to pay for the sins of our colonial past, and believe that we are no better than the Islamic world from a moral standpoint. This is cultural relativism at its finest. That's the type of poisonous false equivalency that is going to get many more people killed.

> We are fighting two battles at the same time: one against radical Islamists who want to kill us and one against the radical Left.

While unsuspecting Westerners continue to run into issues of terrorism, sexual assault, threatening behavior, unsanitary conditions, and other cultural clashes with the Islamic world, the goal of the radical Left marches onward. Anything that gets in the way of their efforts to replace Western civilization must be destroyed.

Unless the West wakes up to the fact that their culture and way of life is eroding through immigration from the Islamic world, the values of the Islamic world will soon overtake us. We are fighting two battles at the same time: one against radical Islamists who want to kill us and one against the radical Left.

The answer is to celebrate our values and the historic accomplishments they've led to. Contrary to what you might hear from the mainstream media propaganda machine, all cultures are not equal. There's a reason why Afghanistan and Saudi Arabia weren't the first to put a man on the moon and still haven't done so. There's a reason why they didn't invent photography, antibiotics, or discover DNA—their value system simply doesn't allow for such progress to take root.

We cannot separate the tremendous human progress that has taken place over the past few centuries across the Western world from the values that allowed it to blossom. But that is exactly what the radical Left seeks to do through unlimited, unvetted immigration. If we don't stop this unchecked influx and civilization transformation soon, our culture and all the progress it has made will soon be eradicated.

RISE UP AND ACT

The next time you hear a news report about immigration and refugees, don't shrug your shoulders helplessly. ACT!

- Teach your children, grandchildren, and any young person you know about the values of Western civilization that make us superior to cultures that do not embrace them. Teach them that it is not only OK but proper to celebrate how virtuous this nation is compared to others with respect to freedom, prosperity, and human rights. Teach them about countries that reject the very ideals we uphold and the problems they have as a result. Give them examples such as Castro in Cuba or Chavez in Venezuela. If you are able, take your children on an educational vacation to a part of the world where they can see poverty and how different America is. If you cannot afford an educational trip such as this, go on YouTube and show them videos of slums in India, pollution in China, or crime-ridden favelas in Brazil. Teach them to be grateful for the chance to live in a country as great as America. This will solidify why we must protect our culture from those who seek to import the destructive values from abroad.

- Share stories on your social media accounts about experiences you may have had abroad that made you understand how lucky you are to be an American or a Westerner. Those of us who understand the values that made us such a free and prosperous wonderland must do more to educate others, especially those who were taught to reject the Constitution, capitalism, and Judeo-Christian principles by leftist educators.

Chapter 6
TRANSFORMATION THROUGH IMMIGRATION

WHEN DID OUR immigration system start functioning like a charity to benefit third-world countries rather than America? When did it become the case that the interests of foreigners should take precedent over those of American citizens?

It's a peculiar thing. A massive wave of third-world immigration has been engulfing America for half a century,[1] yet all American citizens hear about from the "lamestream media" is what a racist, intolerant country we live in. If we don't openly accept millions of individuals who have no desire to embrace the language, culture, and values that made America the greatest country in the history of the world, we must be racists.

Of course, it's easy to make that argument from the Manhattan high-rises that leftist pundits reside in or from the gated DC communities of our politicians. It's not the elites who have to suffer the consequences of hundreds of thousands of unvetted foreigners flocking to the United States. It's not the elites who have had their communities transformed, endangered, and eroded by ten million illegal aliens. Like always, it's the average American citizen who bears that burden.

You might be wondering why I use the word *unvetted* when technically there is a vetting process in place. I say *unvetted* because I haven't fallen for the mainstream media lie that we have a legitimate vetting process in this country, which I'll expose in detail in this chapter. The truth is, this so-called "vetting process" is merely a smokescreen used by leftist politicians to keep the public from knowing the dangerous reality involved in refugee resettlement. More on this momentarily.

Still, even after decades of putting up with an immigration system that seeks to benefit those outside the United States rather than its citizens, we still get lectured by PC pundits and the frauds who pretend to represent us in Washington about how we need to be a more "tolerant" and "diverse" country.

As a legal immigrant from war-torn Lebanon, I understand firsthand the plight of those seeking shelter from violence and oppression from their native countries. I also understand the very legitimate fears that common Americans have about their country and local communities being transformed before their very eyes. America is great for the very reason that it does not allow lawlessness and embodies a set of Western principles that the countries many are fleeing fail to uphold. The problem arises when those fleeing lawless, violent, and corrupt countries seek to benefit from the safety, prosperity, and generosity of the United States while not realizing that the reason America is a country they want to flee to is because we do not allow anarchy. We do not allow anyone to come here simply because it's convenient for them. We do not look the other way when someone violates federal immigration policy.

For the open-borders leftists who would call me a hypocrite because I do not support lawlessness and the massive cultural transformation of America, your PC demagoguery won't fly with me. Let me set the record straight: I immigrated to this country legally through marriage. I paid thousands of dollars and waited for years even after I was married before I was eligible for citizenship. Had I never married an American man, I would not have gotten on a plane, flown halfway around the world, and set up shop in a Lebanese community, demanding that America take me in.

John F. Kennedy said it best when he declared, "Ask not what your country can do for you, but what you can do for your country." What a profoundly inspiring message that is, and to think it was one of the most quintessential lines of any American president, let alone a Democrat. Not ironically, that line was delivered just a few years prior to the 1965 Immigration Act, which I mentioned in the previous chapter as a dramatic turning point. Can you imagine a Democrat saying that in a campaign speech today? They'd be booed off the stage, and radicals like Antifa or Black Lives Matter would probably start a riot. The mainstream media would immediately frame the comments as racist, and every PC celebrity would release a cliché television advertisement condemning the candidate. That's how far America has fallen in the last half-century.

Nowadays it's all about what America can do for me. Of course, many who did not grow up learning to embrace the culture and ideals of America have no idea that America is great because it allows the individual to pave his own path, rather than rely on the government, a.k.a. you and me the taxpayers, to take care of them. We have experienced a tidal wave of unfettered immigration from non-Western countries and have not only failed to assimilate those arriving but even encouraged them not to assimilate.

The mainstream media has spread falsehoods about how America is America because we accept anyone from anywhere at any time and do not expect anything in return for our generosity. Wrong! America is America because it serves as a beacon of light that the rest of the world can embody for themselves by recognizing certain unalienable rights, such as freedom, self-reliance, and rule of law. Should we as Americans help those struggling in dangerous and impoverished countries? Yes, I certainly believe that there is a role America needs to play to help those in need, regardless of nationality. But the way we do that is not by transforming who we are and what we stand for simply to appease the rest of the world. We should help others through leading by example and helping other countries understand how to fix their own house.

For example, if we truly want to help refugees, we could work with our European allies to set up a safe zone for them in the Middle East, rather than spending hundreds of millions of dollars that we don't have to bring unvetted, ISIS-infiltrated refugee camps to the Western world.

While I share President Trump's compassion for immigrant children that led him to sign an executive order on June 20, 2018, to keep illegally entering families together at our southern border, if we really want to help families fleeing crime-ridden Latin America, we should do more to secure our borders so that the drug cartels that have harnessed control of those countries are not able to continue profiting from selling dangerous narcotics on American streets. We should also do more to as a nation to condemn the oppressive and poisonous policies of socialism that have doomed so many Latin Americans to poverty and starvation, most recently in Venezuela. Socialism is as anti-American as it is anti-humane, and we ought to stop pretending like it's merely a peaceful and democratic alternative to capitalism.

Notice how none of these solutions would involve granting amnesty to millions of illegal immigrants, nor allowing anyone who wants to come to the United States the ability to do so without any consideration for the cultural, economic, and national security consequences of doing so. If America becomes a country that fails to stand for what made it great in the first place, how long will it be before America is not even a country worth wanting to come to? How long before we're just another Banana Republic, plagued by massive corruption, poverty, and crime?

The radical Left wants to misrepresent the history and founding principles of this nation so they can continue to import as many future Democratic voters as possible. That's why they preach entitlement rather than gratitude to the immigrants who come here. They patronize them, telling them they don't need to learn English, they don't need to work hard, and that if they don't feel successful enough, it's probably because of how racist America is. This is pure garbage, and I as an immigrant take it particularly personally, as should all Americans.

NUMBERS DON'T LIE

If Americans knew just how many immigrants, both legal and illegal, our nation has taken in over the past half-century, they'd be marching on Washington every day, demanding immediate action.

As I mentioned in chapter 5, before 1965, immigration generally worked to benefit Americans. But that all changed when Democratic politicians came up with a scheme to change the demographics of the United States to electorally favor the Democratic party. The Immigration and Nationality

Act of 1965 (H.R. 2580; Pub. L. 89–236, 79 Stat. 911, enacted June 30, 1968), also known as the Hart-Celler Act, eliminated the concept of quotas that had been in place for several decades.

Representative Emanuel Celler of New York sponsored the bill in the House of Representatives, Senator Philip Hart of Michigan sponsored it in the Senate, and Senator Ted Kennedy of Massachusetts bent over backward to help promote it. By removing the concept of national quotas, this bill significantly, and in my opinion intentionally, transformed the demographic makeup of the United States forever.

The new law changed the order of preference for visa categories to one that focused on family relationships with citizens or US residents, rather than the skills that had previously taken precedent in visa decisions. This is what opened the floodgates to the concept of "chain migration." If this was a scheme by the Democrats, as I believe it was, then it was a brilliant one. Now they could brand those who oppose their efforts to diversify America as racist or xenophobic while also importing generations of future voters. From then on, immediate relatives of US citizens and "special immigrants" had no restrictions or quotas, regardless of skill or country of origin. Let the chain migration begin!

America's Foreign Born Population

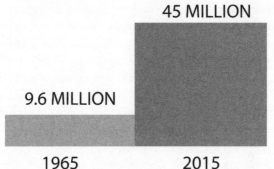

45 MILLION

9.6 MILLION

1965   2015

The nation's foreign-born population has more than quadrupled from 9.6 million in 1965 to 45 million in 2015! According to Pew Research, immigrants and their descendants accounted for 72 million in population growth between 1965 and 2015. If this trend continues, immigrants and their descendants are projected to account for 88 percent of the US population growth by 2065![2]

America is actively being transformed before our very eyes. A nation that defeated the mighty British Empire to gain its independence, helped defeat Hitler, beat the menacing Soviet Union, put a man on the moon, pioneered countless scientific and medical breakthroughs, and changed the world forever, is now strangling itself with its own suicidal blindness.

Many Americans know that immigrants to the United States are not assimilating to our culture. When polled by Pew Research, two-thirds of adults said that immigrants in the United States today "generally want to hold onto their home country customs and way of life," and 59 percent of Americans also said "most recent immigrants do not learn English within a reasonable amount of time."[3] Having to press a button for English every time they need to speak to a customer service representative, regardless of whether they live in Arizona or Maine, was probably a pretty good indication.

Despite lectures about our racist intolerance from PC elitists, the United States has the world's largest immigrant population, and it's not even close. One in five of the world's immigrants live in the United States of America! Our foreign-born population since 1965 has gone from 5 percent to 14 percent today and will push to a projected record of 18 percent in 2065.[4]

Don't be fooled by leftist lies on CNN about how this immigration explosion has always been the norm for our nation either. The number of US immigrants between 1965 and 2015 is 59 million, surpassing the European-dominated immigration waves during the nineteenth and early twentieth centuries. Between 1840 and 1889, 14.3 million immigrants arrived in the United States, compared to 18.2 million between 1890 and 1919.[5] More importantly, the immigrants America was taking in prior to 1965 were overwhelmingly from countries far more likely to share our values and Western culture.

After the replacement of the nation's European-focused quota system, immigration from non-Western countries exploded. By comparison, both of the US immigration waves in the mid-nineteenth century and early twentieth century consisted almost entirely of European immigrants. While the Left likes to brand this a racist historical policy, it would make sense for us to take in mostly Western hailing immigrants considering, you know, we're a Western nation!

Between 1890 and 1919, a time period the radical Left loves to cite as justification for our currently suicidal immigration system, 88 percent of immigrants to the United States came from Europe. A mere 2 percent of immigrants during that time period came from the Middle East,[6] and those that did were mostly Christians fleeing persecution who shared our values. Immigrants from Africa during this time period were mostly students. Now, only 12 percent of our immigrants originate from Europe, the percentage of immigrants we take from Africa and the Middle East has quadrupled since the early twentieth century, and those from the Middle East are predominantly Muslims as opposed to Christians.[7]

In 1993 Islamic terrorists, most of them immigrants, made their first attempt at bringing down the World Trade Center when a truck filled with a 1,200-pound nitrate-hydrogen gas bomb exploded inside the parking garage beneath the buildings.[8] The hope of the jihadists who orchestrated the attack was to send the North Tower crashing into the South Tower, bringing both towers down simultaneously and killing tens of thousands in the process.[9]

At the time of the first World Trade Center bombing, the US Muslim population was approximately 1 million. Since then, that number has more than tripled to approximately 3.45 million.[10]

What kind of a response is this to a potentially catastrophic terrorist attack? To not only continue to allow massive immigration from the Islamic world, but to triple the Islamic population in America in two decades while we're at war with radical Islamic terrorism?

REFUGEE RESETTLEMENT

Refugees have had a dramatic effect on Islamic immigration into the United States over the past several decades. The United States has resettled far more refugees than any other country—about 3 million since 1980, despite ongoing lectures about our intolerance from CNN. Between 1982 and 2016, 69 percent of the world's refugees resettled in the United States. That's more than two-thirds of the refugees in the entire world. Canada was next with 14 percent, and Australia was third with 11 percent.[11] No report yet on how many CNN pundits have offered up their Manhattan lofts to sponsor Islamic refugees from Syria.

REFUGEE RESETTLEMENT

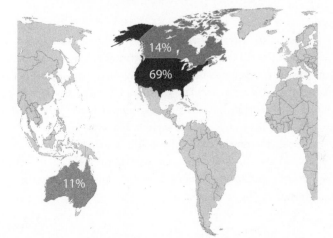

After holding fairly steady between 2012 and 2015, the number of refugees jumped to 97,000 in 2016. This was the Obama administration's response to the rise of ISIS in Iraq and Syria.[12] Leave it to an administration who tried to intimidate ISIS with an acoustic performance by James Taylor to increase the number of potential soldiers of the Islamic State entering the United States.[13]

Today a rapidly increasing number from Middle Eastern and African countries make up our refugee intake. In 2002 only 17 percent of refugees entering the United States were from Middle Eastern and African countries. By 2017 that number exploded to a mind-boggling 68 percent![14]

"Brigitte, do you mean to tell me that in response to the deadliest terror attack in world history, the United States quadrupled the number of refugees from terror-ridden nations, and we have no verifiable way of vetting them?"

Sadly, that's exactly what I'm telling you.

The fact is, while our brave men and women in the military have lost lives and limbs fighting terrorism overseas, our PC politicians back home oversaw a dramatic increase in the amount of virtually unvetted Islamic refugees from countries such as Syria, Iraq, Somalia, and others.

In 2014, the year ISIS formed their caliphate stronghold, the United States brought in twenty thousand Iraqi refugees, about 62 percent of whom were Muslim.[15] I guess Obama didn't get the memo about Christians in Iraq being slaughtered by ISIS simply for their religious identity.

About thirty-nine thousand Muslim refugees entered the United States in Obama's last year in office—the highest number on record.[16] This took place in spite of ISIS's pledge that they had infiltrated the refugee camps,[17] and Obama's own FBI admitting that it had no verifiable way to weed out terrorists.[18]

How Do They Get Here?

So how are all these so-called refugees getting here? Here's how it works.

Application

A refugee needs to show a "well-founded" fear of persecution due to a political view or membership in a racial, ethnic, religious, or social group. The definition of a refugee has been so widely stretched that it is essentially meaningless. As an example, US law declares China's one-child policy to be an example of persecution based upon a political view.[19] Not surprisingly, China now tops the list of successful asylum seekers.[20]

People can seek asylum in the United States for things such as domestic abuse, FGM, and even lack of services for the disabled.[21] In other words, almost the entire population of every Muslim-majority nation in the world is potentially eligible.

Selection

So how are they chosen? About 95 percent of the refugees coming to the United States are picked by the UN High Commissioner for Refugees (UNHCR) or are relatives of refugees selected by the United Nations.[22] Great idea, let's outsource our immigration policy to a useless globalist body like the UN, which allows countries like Saudi Arabia to serve on their Human Rights Council.

Until the late 1990s, just before 9/11, the United States picked the majority of its refugees. Timing for the outsourcing of our vetting could not have been more dangerous.

Even more alarming, the UNHCR has been infiltrated by the Organisation of Islamic Cooperation (OIC), a Muslim supremacist organization based out of Saudi Arabia. Since refugees who become US citizens are allowed to sponsor relatives thanks to the 1965 Immigration Act, I don't believe it's a stretch to say that the UN, influenced by a radical Islamic organization, has been effectively controlling both our refugees and overall immigration system for the past two decades.

Thankfully, President Trump recently unveiled a plan to dramatically reduce the number of refugees allowed to resettle in the United States, bringing the number to less than half of what Obama had previously proposed. The bottom line is, we should not be taking in anyone we cannot properly vet for extremist ties or ideology, nor anyone we cannot ensure will be able to provide for themselves without skimming off the American people.

Many refugees are not even processed in their home countries of citizenship. Instead, they're waiting for resettlement in a nearby country, where they often conveniently lack any verifiable identification.

Screening

After being picked by the UNHCR, refugees are supposedly screened by the State Department, the Department of Homeland Security's US Citizenship and Immigration Services, and other federal agencies.

Here's the real truth about this "screening" process. First of all, if the TSA has a 95 percent failure rate at spotting dangerous devices in airports, why in the world would we believe the federal government is able to properly vet thousands of third-world Islamists with no verifiable documentation?

On top of that, in April 2016, the State Department, desperate to get Obama's promised ten thousand Syrians into America before he left office, reduced the vetting process to just three months![23] The Obama administration even sent a team of interviewers to Jordan, a Muslim-majority country bordering Syria that obviously has a vested interest in getting every single refugee out of their country, to push the paperwork through as quickly as possible.

The Trump administration tried several times to institute a pause in refugee resettlement to revamp the vetting process, but time and time again such efforts were struck down by radical leftist judges, who seem to think it's within their constitutional

> **Refugee resettlement has become a massively lucrative global enterprise for those who know how to play the game.**

authority to determine US immigration policy. (Thankfully, the Supreme Court upheld the president's executive action on June 26, 2018.[24])

Even Obama-appointed former FBI Director James Comey repeatedly stated that refugees from Syria cannot be thoroughly screened because there are no records on them.[25] The same applies to many of the other countries from which mass numbers of refugees are fleeing. These are third-world countries, and we expect them to have verifiable documentation?

Settlement

Once they've gotten past a useless screening process, a network of private, so-called "nonprofit" agencies choose where refugees will settle. Here's where the corruption comes in.

Funding for these so called "nonprofits" is based on the number of refugees serviced. Logically these affiliates have an incentive to maintain or increase the number of refugees they resettle each year in order to keep the cash cow fed. Consequently, refugee resettlement has become a massively lucrative global enterprise for those who know how to play the game.

According to a fact sheet published by Refugee Resettlement Watch, here are some of the federal contractors getting paid to drop thousands of unvetted Islamic refugees into your community:

> Church World Service (CWS)
> Ethiopian Community Development Council (ECDC)
> Episcopal Migration Ministries (EMM)
> Hebrew Immigrant Aid Society (HIAS)
> International Rescue Committee (IRC)
> US Committee for Refugees and Immigrants (USCRI)
> Lutheran Immigration and Refugee Services (LIRS)
> United States Conference of Catholic Bishops (USCCB)
> World Relief Corporation (WR)[26]

Notice that six out of these nine contractors are "religious organizations." They are doing more than passing the collection plates on Sunday morning to collect more than $1 billion annually to resettle these refugees. They're getting some of it from the US Treasury Department, meaning you, the American taxpayer.

These contractors work with 350 subcontractors to resettle unvetted refugees anywhere within a hundred-mile radius of the contractor's location. If you have a contractor within a hundred-mile radius of you, then your community is at risk of being overtaken by refugees, courtesy of your own money.

The refugee gets a one-time payment of $2,125 per person, of which the contractor gets $1,000 to keep for themselves.[27] After the refugee has been housed with their one-time allocated amount, the contractor is supposed to keep occasional tabs on them for three months, after which they are no longer responsible for them whatsoever.[28]

These so-called "volunteer agencies" collect money from federal grant programs such as Marriage Initiative, Faith-based, Ownership Society, etc., as well as other state and local grants. The program is so lucrative that some churches have reduced their focus on traditional charities and increased their efforts on refugee resettlement.[29]

Be mindful of this the next time your pastor, priest, or rabbi tries to guilt you into supporting refugee resettlement in your church or synagogue. You don't need greedy lectures cloaked in compassion! It's easy to claim moral superiority when you're the one getting rich off an enterprise that is not paid for by you, but by taxpaying citizens.

These contractors do have a vested interest in their refugees being able to claim "self-sufficiency," as this leads to more refugees being sent their way. However, while hardworking Americans usually define *self-sufficiency* as, you know, being self-sufficient, the government has broadened that definition to mean not receiving cash welfare, meaning "self-sufficient" refugees can be using programs such as food stamps, public housing, or Medicaid.[30] In other words, not self-sufficient.

Refugees and asylum-seekers are eligible for all federal, state, and local welfare.[31] Refugees can be deemed "self-sufficient" by our government while still using all of the following welfare programs:

- Medicaid
- Supplemental Nutrition Assistance Program (formerly known as the Food Stamp Program)
- Public Housing
- Administration on Developmental Disabilities
- Child Care and Development Fund
- Independent Living Program
- Job Opportunities for Low-Income Individuals
- Low-Income Home Energy Assistance Program

When welfare use is included in the cost of the refugee resettlement program, it totals about $1.8 billion a year.[32] We could set up a safe zone in the Middle East for these individuals for a fraction of this cost, but such efforts wouldn't result in lining the pockets of any of these contractors who lobby Congress.

A 2013 report to Congress showed that 21.1 percent of refugees are on Supplemental Security Income, which gives a monthly check, as well as Medicaid, to elderly or disabled individuals.[33] This shockingly high rate is more than eight times that of the US population as a whole!

REFUGEES ON WELFARE PROGRAMS

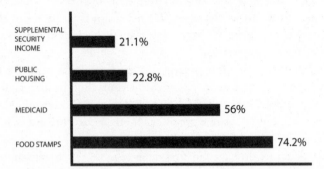

The report also stated that 22.8 percent of refugees who arrived in the previous five years were in public housing, 56.0 percent were on Medicaid, and 74.2 percent were receiving food stamps.[34] Let's keep in mind that these are individuals our government is actually choosing to bring to the United States of America.

What could possibly be the upside to this for the average American? Why do we, as the greatest nation on earth have to take in populations that make us poorer, less culturally united, and more dangerous?

Do professional sports teams recruit players they know cannot play at the professional level out of tolerance, equality, and fairness? If the NFL used our government's refugee resettlement logic, I could play quarterback for the Dallas Cowboys.

CHEAP LABOR

Many of the refugees who do find work find it with a company that receives taxpayer subsidies to hire people who receive Temporary Assistance for Needy Families or Supplemental Nutrition Assistance Program from the government. So even for those refugees who do find work, you'll be paying their paycheck through federal tax credits. How generous of you.

We're constantly being told by the mainstream media that refugees will do jobs that American citizens just won't do. In reality American citizens are being driven out of the labor force because companies such as Chobani Yogurt, a major refugee hirer, would rather hire the cheap labor subsidized by you than hire an American citizen.

As usual, if you want to get to the truth, all you need to do is follow the money. The meatpacking industry is particularly money hungry for refugees since the low-skill labor involved allows refugees to complete the tasks required, despite having limited language, education, or cultural assimilation.

Refugee contractor Lutheran Immigration and Refugee Service and meatpacking conglomerate JBS Swift have teamed up to capitalize on their mutual interest in flooding the nation with even more refugees and lecturing those who disapprove of "tolerance." JBS Swift agreed to pay Lutheran Immigration and Refugee Services $155,000 to help send them additional refugee workers in Iowa, Michigan, Georgia, and Texas.[35]

Notice these are all states that voted for Donald Trump. This creates a significant interest among Democratic politicians who want to import more welfare-dependent voters in areas of the country that will prove advantageous for them. Why else would religious agencies get paid such a staggering amount of money by massive foreign corporations to transform the demographics of the United States of America?

This is a direct assault on the American heartland. The alliance between JBS and the Lutheran agency was dubbed "Rebuilding Dreams." Yes, rebuilding dreams for refugees while causing nightmares for Americans.

In the UN's 2030 Agenda for Sustainable Development, approved by President Obama and 193 UN member states in September 2015, citizens of underdeveloped countries "are seen as human capital to be shifted around the world like pieces on a chess board. As migrants, they are granted UN 'rights' to access everything from jobs to affordable healthcare, affordable transportation, and housing."[36] This is a direct financial link between a resettlement agency, which is supposed to be a religious charity, and corporations who seek cheap foreign labor to replace Americans.

Tiny towns like Noel, Missouri, have been completely transformed in less than ten years. An estimated five hundred Somali and Sudanese refugees have significantly increased the population of this southwestern Missouri town, which had only slightly more than 1,800 residents at the time of the 2010 US Census.[37]

Noel is home to a Tyson Foods chicken plant, which started hiring African refugees to fill jobs in the 2000s, and their influence has become evident over the last one and half decades. In October 2011 more than one hundred Somalis temporarily walked out over a dispute with management at Tyson Foods about prayer times for workers.[38] Apparently they felt management had made an unacceptable demand that they refrain from stopping work to pray five times a day in the middle of their shift. In 2017 Mayor John Lafley said that refugees were determined to practice Sharia law within the community, and a man who is a frequent visitor to Noel and has relatives in the area indicated that many local residents are too afraid to drive through town unless it is absolutely necessary.[39]

We've seen the same tragic formula repeat itself over and over again in small towns all across America that have seen their communities destroyed by refugee resettlement. When you mix third-world Islamists with Western, Judeo-Christian communities, the results are never promising. The reality is, what holds true for meatpacking holds true for any industry in which

Americans are being shoved aside for cheaper labor paid with the tax dollars of those being shoved aside.

Starbucks openly criticized President Trump when he issued an executive action putting a temporary hold on immigration from a list of seven terror-ridden nations, all which were flagged by the Obama administration. In response, Starbucks pledged to hire ten thousand refugees over the next five years.[40]

The result? Starbucks' brand reputation fell by a startling two-thirds.[41] Americans are fed up with lectures from PC corporatists getting rich off of endangering the nation.

HEALTH RISKS

It's not just the jobs they are taking; it's also the diseases they are bringing. Refugees are not required to meet the same immunization requirements as other immigrants before entry into the United States. What could go wrong?

In a study published by *The New England Journal of Medicine* in 2004, refugees from four states—New York, Minnesota, Washington, and Virginia, which combined to account for 23 percent of all refugees taken in that year—were studied to determine the disease rate amongst the refugee population. The study found that the rate of tuberculosis among refugees was about eighty times the US national rate![42] I repeat, eighty times!

Americans have been warned about refugees carrying dangerous diseases that are rarely seen in the West. However, physicians who speak out about such threats have been ostracized, silenced, and attacked as racist or xenophobic by the mainstream media.

This is what makes globalist Angela Merkel's decision in 2015 to allow more than 2 million African, Asian, and Middle Eastern migrants into Germany all the more frightening![43] To put that number in context, if those migrants alone were to form an American city, they would make up the fifth largest city in America. These migrants are unscreened for infectious diseases and are entering a country that is a small fraction of the size of the United States. That, my friends, is truly terrifying.

According to the July 2017 Infectious Disease Epidemiology Annual Report by the Robert Koch Institute, Germany has already seen a surge in dangerous diseases such as dengue fever, leprosy, malaria, HIV/AIDS, tuberculosis, rubella, syphilis, typhus, whooping cough, and many others. The report showed that measles was up more than 450 percent between 2014 and 2015, hepatitis B was up 300 percent over three years, and tuberculosis (TB) was up 30 percent (and 40 percent of all tuberculosis pathogens are multi-drug-resistant).[44] The list goes on and on.

SURGE OF DISEASES IN GERMANY

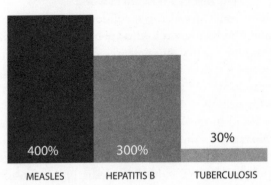

400%	300%	30%
MEASLES	HEPATITIS B	TUBERCULOSIS

We've seen a similarly dangerous pattern emerging all across the Western world. Those most at risk are babies who are not yet old enough to safely receive vaccinations and the elderly who have weakened immune systems.

A Centers for Disease Control and Prevention (CDC) study from 2016 revealed that the state with the lowest incident of TB is Wyoming. Wyoming was also the state that took in the lowest number of refugees.[45] Coincidence?

The four most populous states in America—California, Florida, New York, and Texas—accounted for more than half of the TB cases for the entire country with more than five hundred cases each. Of all TB cases reported in 2016, 67.9 percent came from foreign-born individuals, which was twice the rate of US-born cases.[46]

In 2015 twenty-seven students tested positive for tuberculosis at one high school in Kansas City, Kansas, alone. That's how contagious TB is, particularly for children without fully developed immunities.[47] Still, politicians are placing you and your loved ones in danger with politically correct recklessness.

In times past, immigrants at Ellis Island were all thoroughly medically examined and were either quarantined or sent back to their home country if they posed a health risk to Americans. But suddenly, common-sense measures have taken a backseat to "tolerance."

To protect the health and safety of American citizens, we must reinstate our prior customary medical screening as outlined on our own CDC website.[48] In reality, disease and public health are not political issues—they are human issues. Disease doesn't discriminate based on nationality, race, or political ideology.

Failure to recognize the severe dangers that open borders pose to the health of you and your loved ones will have deadly consequences. Diseases can mutate over time, and those who have no immunity to such mutations will be sitting ducks.

At the rate we're going, we're practically begging for a pandemic. The health and safety of Americans is being put in direct jeopardy in order to fulfill the political endgame of a borderless world.

For the sake of yourself and those you love, we must shut off the massive influx of unvetted immigrants, who are bringing never-seen-before dangers to our communities, the consequences of which can never be undone. The Western world has done so much to eradicate the spread of dangerous and deadly diseases over the past few centuries, only to have radical leftists voiding such efforts through reckless unfettered immigration.

We can't be afraid to speak the truth when our values, culture, and very lives are being threatened. The worst part is, we're doing it to ourselves! We've come too far as a society to have radical leftists destroy us from within. It's time for a return to borders, culture, and the protection of citizens over politically correct endangerment.

RISE UP AND ACT:

The next time you hear about this culture invasion, don't just marvel at the shortsightedness of politicians. ACT!

- Write a Letter to the Editor (LTE) of your local newspaper about the costs of refugee resettlement. Be sure to include three main facts, such as:

  - On an annual average, it costs $15,900 to resettle each refugee in America.[49]

  - Fifty percent of refugees remain on Medicaid for five years.

  - There are some eighteen federal and state programs refugees can tap for financial assistance.

- Consistently call in to local radio stations to talk about the costs of refugee resettlement. Be sure to include facts similar to the ones in your LTE.

- Attend your local city council meetings and sign up to speak on issues relating to the budget. Your city council members need to hear about the costs of refugee resettlement as well as your opposition to this costly program. Your efforts will be more effective if you 1) consistently show up at city council meetings to speak about the budget and 2) recruit your family and friends to join you in opposing the high costs of refugee resettlement.

Chapter 7

TERROR AT THE GATES

DESPERATE TO CONTINUE their fundamental transformation of Western civilization, radical leftists are hell-bent on keeping citizens in the dark about the explicit link between refugees and terrorism. Globalist politicians, who envision a world without borders, know that once the average citizen realizes the dangers associated with those they're importing, their vision for a borderless utopia is finished.

There is explicit evidence, admitted by our own federal government, of a direct link between refugees and terrorism. DHS records have shown that refugees account for nearly one third of all FBI terrorism cases.[1] This is an admission by our own government, which nevertheless has continued to allow refugees to enter the country during a time of war.

This is why President Trump's executive order, which temporarily banned travel to those without valid visas from terror-ridden nations, was so critical to our national security. Art del Cueto, president of the Local 2544 in Tucson, the Border Patrol's largest regional division, summed it up well when he voiced his ardent support for President Trump's hard-line belief in a border wall with Mexico. "I'm not anti-immigrant, but my job is to catch the people who think it's OK to break the law to come into this country," he said. "I lock my front door not because I hate the people outside, but because I love the people inside."[2]

I'll bet my bottom dollar that the left-wing politicians opposing President Trump's immigration policies are also fond of locking their doors at night, as well as living in gated communities. Wouldn't it be great to see just one mainstream media pundit exercise some real journalism and ask a wall-opposing politician if they themselves live in a gated community, and if so, why? Imagine the complete shock and utter embarrassment that would befall them. First, the shock of having been tossed a question that was not softer than a baby blanket, and then, the sheer panic that would overwhelm them as they struggled to justify their blatant hypocrisy. But I digress.

Thankfully, on June 26, 2018, the Supreme Court upheld the president's executive action, citing the fact he is well within his constitutional authority to do what he feels is necessary to protect the homeland.[3] This was a huge victory, considering the rogue radicals round the country prefer to jeopardize your safety in order to continue their political endgame of a borderless world.

Even former FBI Director James Comey admitted that nine hundred terror investigations were being conducted across every state in America during his time serving under the Obama administration.[4] You know the problem is bad when even Obama officials have to admit it.

As critical as it is to stop the Islamic radicals sneaking their way into our country, we mustn't lose sight of the unending flow of human traffickers and drug smugglers who continue to pour across our southern border illegally. The problem has gotten so out of hand that in early 2018, President Trump sent National Guard troops to the Mexican border in an effort to stem the tide of illegal crossings and criminal activity.[5]

Though this particular focus on illegal immigration was sparked by a caravan of more than a thousand migrants from Central America who were headed for the US border, the decision to militarize our southern border defense was the long overdue result of millions who had entered illegally. The result of this has been a surge in violent drug gangs, such as the notorious MS-13 from El Salvador, one of the most brutal gangs in the world, now popping up in virtually every major American city.

When you leave your front door open, you don't merely leave yourself vulnerable to one threat, but unlimited threats. That's exactly what we've done as a nation with our porous southern border, and now we must face the reality of Islamic terrorists and violent gangs setting up shop in our own backyard. Decades of carelessness have not proven favorable for the safety of our American family.

The problem isn't unique to America; it touches all of the Western world. What you are about to read in this chapter is irrefutable evidence that we are importing those who wish for our demise and the destruction of our entire way of life. We'll first look at Europe, or more accurately Eurabia, and then we'll examine the United States. The facts presented in each case are clear warning signs the West is choosing to ignore to our own detriment. The following is just a small example of cases where refugees have been directly involved in perpetrating terror attacks all across the Western world.

ISIS has made it very clear through their video messaging that they have infiltrated the refugee population with sympathizing operatives in order to carry out terrorist attacks in the West. ISIS claimed that they have embedded almost four thousand ISIS members into refugee populations entering Europe in the last three years alone.[6]

Knowing that the refugees who enter Europe do not all stay in Europe but get divided around the world through the United Nations, ISIS knew that infiltrating refugee camps would prove as effective as it was evil.

EURABIA

The Islamic transformation of Europe over the past several decades should serve as a warning of the highest magnitude to the United States. Europe is not what it once was, and taking a stroll around London today can cause one to wonder whether they're in England or Egypt.

A startling four million "refugees" have invaded Europe since the creation of ISIS, and at least one of those was a terrorist who helped carry out the notorious Paris Massacre, which left more than 120 dead. The so-called Syrian refugee gained entry through an emergency passport found near what was left of his body after he blew himself up for jihad.[7]

The terrorist defrauded Greek authorities upon entry to the European Union by falsely portraying himself as a Syrian man named Ahmad al Muhammad. He then made his way to a refugee camp in Croatia where he was able to register as a refugee.[8]

After the last leg of his journey, the trip to France from Croatia, he decided to blow himself up at the Stade de France in Paris, along with two other jihadists who were carrying fraudulent Turkish passports.[9] This is the thank you that "Ahmad al Muhammad" and his jihadist buddies decided to pay the EU for their red-carpet welcome.

The case of Ahmad al Muhammad is not one that should be taken in isolation. It should be looked at as a microcosm of the deadly cost of political correctness as well as the penalty of thinking you can soften the hearts of radical Islamists by catering to their desires.

It's as if we've learned nothing as Westerners since 9/11 with respect to this enemy. Islamists didn't come to Paris to take pictures of the Eiffel Tower; they came to blow themselves up in front of it. They viewed the gesture of Europeans kindly welcoming them into their society not as something to be grateful to them for, but as something to kill them for.

Jihadists, many of whom have cleverly infiltrated refugee populations, don't value the same things we value in the West. They don't care that you're willing to give them welfare, language classes, cultural training seminars, or any of the other things leftists believe will lead to the jihadists' eventual "assimilation"—at least to the point that they won't kill us. Jihadists view these things as a sign of submission and weakness. It only feeds their preconceived notion that the West is weak and that, sooner or later, Islam will reconquer Europe along with the rest of the Western world.

Many other refugees, or people posing as refugees, have engaged in terrorist acts against the West or have at least plotted them. Here are a few quick examples from a very long list:

- Fake refugees were involved in the terrorist attack on Brussels in March of 2016, which killed thirty-two people.[10] Ironically, Brussels is the site of EU headquarters, the institutional mother ship for open-border leftists. After taking advantage of the EU's open-border policies that allowed them entry with ease, jihadists chose to thank them with a stream of suicide bombings.[11] It's as if leftist EU politicians are screaming to jihadists, "Come on in! Islam is peace! Diversity is a strength!" leaving jihadists wondering, "Is this a trick? It can't really be this easy, can it?"

- Ayoub el-Khazzani, who shot up a train from Amsterdam to Paris in August of 2015, passed through Hungary as a fake Syrian refugee.[12]

- In 2016, Tunisian asylum seeker Anis Amri mowed down a crowd of innocent civilians at a Christmas market in Berlin, killing twelve and injuring forty-eight others. Amri was a soldier of ISIS, who gave him instructions about how to use vehicles as weapons. ISIS also released a video of Amri pledging allegiance to Abu Bakr al-Baghdadi before being killed several days later in Italy by police.[13]

- That same year, a teenage Afghan refugee used an ax to hack passengers on a train in Wuerzburg, Germany, leaving four severely wounded before he was shot to death by authorities.[14]

- Days later a twenty-one-year-old Syrian refugee used a machete to kill a pregnant woman and wound two others in Reutlingen, Germany.[15]

- ISIS also claimed responsibility when a Syrian asylee blew himself up and injured fifteen people outside a music festival in Ansbach, Germany.[16]

- On May 22, 2017, twenty-two-year-old Salman Ramadan Abedi, who had proven links to ISIS, blew himself up using a homemade bomb at an Ariana Grande concert in Manchester, England. Twenty-two people were killed, many of them children, and around 120 were injured.[17]

  Although he was born in Manchester, Abedi's parents were Libyan refugees,[18] illustrating a crucial point regarding refugees. Often the media will cover up the refugee status of a terrorist when it exists, but quickly point out non-refugee status. However, as was shown in this case, the issue at hand is not refugees, but refugee resettlement. In other words, even if those who immigrate do not commit terrorist acts, if their children or grandchildren do as a result of extremist views, is the damage any less painful for a nation to endure? One cannot deny that if Abedi's parents were not granted refugee status in the UK, it is highly unlikely he would have committed this unspeakable atrocity. Refugee terror transcends generational barriers. This was also the case with the Pulse nightclub shooter in Orlando, Florida, which we'll discuss later.

TERROR IN THE USA

Think the links between refugees and terrorism are exclusive to Europe? Think again! Here is a small sampling of the many terrorist attacks linked to refugee resettlement that have been committed in the United States in just the last decade.

Mohamed Osman Mohamud

Mohamed Osman Mohamud was a Somali refugee arrested and convicted of terrorism charges after plotting to blow up a local Christmas tree gathering in a small town in Oregon.[19] He also wrote articles on physical fitness for the English-language publication *Jihad Recollections* as part of his attempts to be involved with violent jihadist ideology.[20]

Mohamud planned to detonate a bomb in a van close to the site of the gathering. FBI agents posed as terrorists and led Mohamud to believe that the explosives inside the van were so massive that thousands of gatherers would be killed.

Mohamud told the undercover agent, "I want whoever is attending that event...to leave either dead or injured."[21] Had Mohamud's bomb been as real as he thought when he pushed the fake detonator, we could be talking about more casualties than 9/11.

Mohanad Shareef Hammadi and Waad Ramadan Alwan

These two jihadists were actually arrested by Iraqi security forces prior to being allowed to come to the United States and settle in Kentucky as Iraqi refugees. (Talk about not being properly vetted!) Waad Ramadan Alwan admitted to using improvised explosive devices (IEDs) against US soldiers in Iraq, and he also attempted to send weapons and money to al Qaeda. Alwan recruited Mohanad Shareef Hammadi to help load weapons and money that they believed would be shipped to al Qaeda operatives in Iraq. While honorable American charities like Wounded Warrior Project have been set up to care for our injured vets, these scumbags were trying to supply the weapons that led to their injuries. Alwan said of his efforts to kill US soldiers, "Lunch and dinner would be an American."[22]

Abdullatif Ali Aldosary

Abdullatif Ali Aldosary came to the United States as a refugee from Iraq in 1997. This jihadist set off a homemade bomb at an Arizona Social Security office on November 30, 2012. Authorities who searched his home found ammunition and instructions on how to make a bomb.[23]

Due to a 2008 felony conviction for aggravated harassment, Aldosary was not legally allowed to have a gun or ammunition.[24] It didn't seem to matter to Aldosary though. I know, shocking.

Here's a question for our federal government: Once he committed a felony, why was Aldosary still in the country? Because apparently the court didn't find that he was enough of a threat to deport him. I say we pass a law that if you commit a felony as a refugee, you're out of here within twenty-four hours. Better yet, how about until we can properly vet refugees for terrorist sympathies, we hit the pause button on refugee resettlement?

Tsarnaev brothers

The Tsarnaev brothers came to the United States as asylum seekers from Kyrgyzstan and were responsible for the Boston Marathon bombing that left three dead, sixteen without limbs, and over two hundred severely injured on April 15, 2013.[25] The two brothers carried out their jihad by setting off pressure cooker bombs in the middle of a crowd of marathon runners and onlookers.

Fazliddin Kurbanov

Fazliddin Kurbanov came to the United States with his family as a refugee in 2009 and plotted to bomb a military base near Boise, Idaho.[26] US District Judge Edward J. Lodge said, "He intended to explode a bomb in the U.S. to send a message, much like that delivered in the 9/11 attacks." His plans were thwarted when he attracted attention from the FBI by uploading more than one hundred terrorist videos to his YouTube account. Kurbanov was ordered to serve twenty-five years, after which he will be deported back to Uzbekistan. Thank God!

Kurbanov's defense attorney, Chuck Peterson, said he was disappointed because the sentence "was harsher than those given to others convicted of creating a bomb or setting one off." The slimy attorney didn't think it was anything worth getting so worked up about. "The judge felt it was a very serious offense. We disagree," Peterson said.[27]

Kurbanov also later pleaded guilty to charges of attempted murder of a federal officer after attempting to kill the warden at the prison where he is being held.[28] It's safe to say the United States can survive without the diversity Kurbanov adds to our nation.

Omar Faraj Saeed Al Hardan

This Iraqi refugee plotted to set off bombs at two Houston malls and provided aid to ISIS.[29] Omar Faraj Saeed Al Hardan pledged allegiance to ISIS in November 2014 and immediately received tactical weapons training with an AK-47.[30]

This "refugee" came to Houston from Iraq in 2009, and it took him all of seven years before he was arrested on terrorism charges. As the saying goes, "You really can't make this up." The guy flies halfway around the world only to immediately turn around and pledge allegiance to the Islamic caliphate he left.

Al Hardan also planned to bomb two large Houston malls using cell phones as detonators for C-4 type explosives. This could just as easily be your local mall, and if not Al Hardan, one of the many other jihadists that have infiltrated refugee populations.

Al Hardan explicitly stated, "I want to blow myself up. I want to travel with the Mujahidin. I want to travel to be with those who are against America. I am against America."[31] Before his arrest, he was coordinating his attack with Aws Mohammed Younis Al-Jayab, another Iraqi refugee living in California, and the two talked about sneaking into Syria to fight for ISIS.

Thankfully, Al-Jayab is also currently in jail. It's winners like these that really add to the diversity and multiculturalism of the American fabric. How would we ever survive without contributions like these?

Dahir Adan

Dahir Adan was a Kenyan refugee who became part of the Somali community in Minnesota. He went on a stabbing rampage at a local shopping mall in Minnesota, using steak knives to stab ten people, including a child.[32]

Adan shouted "Allahu Akbar!" and asked his victims if they were Muslim before plunging a knife into them. Adan charged at an off-duty police officer, who was forced to fatally shoot him inside a department store.[33] The FBI later said that Adan had taken "interest recently in Islam, withdrew from his friends, and encouraged his sisters to be more religious."[34] After the attack, ISIS praised Adan as a "soldier of the Islamic state."[35]

Abdul Razak Ali Artan

Abdul Razak Ali Artan is another refugee who went on a stabbing spree, this time at Ohio State University.[36] He hit several people with his car, before exiting the vehicle and attacking several students with a butcher knife. Artan was thankfully shot and killed. In total, eleven people were injured and sent to the hospital following the attack.

Prior to the attack, Artan publicly complained about Islamophobia on campus and the lack of places for Muslims to pray. He was interviewed for the Ohio State newspaper and said:

> I just transferred from Columbus State. We had prayer rooms, like actual rooms where we could go to pray because we Muslims have to pray five times a day. There's Fajr, which is early in the morning, at dawn. Then Zuhr during the daytime, then Asr in the evening, like right about now. And then Maghrib, which is like right at sunset and then Isha at night. I wanted to pray Asr. I mean, I'm new here.

This is my first day. This place is huge, and I don't even know where to pray. I wanted to pray in the open, but I was kind of scared with everything going on in the media. I'm a Muslim, it's not what the media portrays me to be. If people look at me, a Muslim praying, I don't know what they're going to think, what's going to happen. But, I don't blame them, it's the media that put that picture in their heads so they're just going to have it and it, it's going to make them feel uncomfortable. I was kind of scared right now. But I just did it. I relied on God. I went over to the corner and just prayed.[37]

Well, one way to certainly enhance feelings of mistrust and fear amongst your fellow classmates is to hit them with your car and stab them.

Seddique Mateen

Seddique Mateen, the father of Pulse nightclub shooter Omar Mateen, is an Afghan refugee.[38] Although there has been no direct linkage between Seddique Mateen and the Orlando nightclub shooting, this displays how the refugee resettlement program can endanger American citizens for future generations, especially when coming from a part of the world known to be hostile to Americans, as was true in Mateen's case.

Reflecting on case after case of refugees committing acts of terrorism, anyone with half a brain can see that the refugee resettlement program is a first-class ticket to national and cultural suicide. It's a system that gives preference to the interests of foreigners over citizens and seeks to transform the country demographically at the expense of national security.

Tolerance of intolerance is not tolerance; it's cowardice. David French of the *National Review* put it best when he noted: "When 'diversity' brings death, it's time to shed the fairytale ideologies and recognize the grim truth. The Muslim world has a problem. It's time our nation responded accordingly."[39] It's time to wake up, America!

One of the most profound takeaways from the 9/11 Commission report is that we lacked imagination.[40] In the case of refugee resettlement, almost twenty years after 9/11, there is no excuse for us to say we lack imagination. Never before have we been faced with an enemy who tells us exactly what their plan is for our destruction and how they will go about pursuing it.

Tolerance of intolerance is not tolerance; it's cowardice.

If we continue to ignore the incontrovertible evidence of their plans for our demise, we will have no excuse if their nefarious plans come to fruition. Future generations will not look back favorably on us if we continue to bury our heads in the sand.

Refugee resettlement is the silent killer of America. It took less than two hours to bring down both twin towers on 9/11, but in this case the fall will not happen so suddenly. Instead, ours will be an incremental collapse, orchestrated by those who pretend to represent us. This slow drip of destruction has plagued us for decades, and it is high time Americans rise and demand we change course before missing the last exit. For Europe, it may already be too late, and for America, the hour is drawing ever closer to midnight.

RISE UP AND ACT

When you hear about porous borders, weak immigration laws, and a lack of the ability to properly monitor visas working together to provide the perfect ingredients for terrorists to both enter our country unchecked and overstay their visas, putting all Americans at risk, don't just complain about the problem. ACT!

- Write a letter to your federal legislators (congressional representatives and senators) and send a copy to the editor of your local newspaper about the need for immigration reform. Be sure to include three main facts, such as:

    1. Sayfullo Saipov, a radical Islamic terrorist, murdered eight in New York City (Diversity Immigrant Visa program).

    2. Akayed Ullah, a radical Islamic terrorist, detonated a bomb in New York City (chain migration).

    3. Luis Bracamontes, an illegal alien, murdered two police officers and said he would kill more.

- Register your support for the RAISE Act by going to the ACT for America website (https://actioncenter.actforamerica .org/app/onestep-write-a-letter?6&engagementId=453973). The bill will eliminate the diversity immigrant visa category, end chain migration, and set a limit of fifty thousand refugee admissions per fiscal year. The bill defines: 1) *immediate relative* as "the under-twenty-one-year-old child or spouse of a US citizen" and 2) *family-sponsored immigrant* as "the under-twenty-one-year-old child or spouse of an alien lawfully admitted for permanent residence." The worldwide fiscal year level for family-sponsored immigrants is reduced. The bill establishes a nonimmigrant alien W-visa for the parent of an adult (at least twenty-one years old) US citizen. (And remember, beyond the RAISE Act, we are involved in passing legislation in many states on an ongoing basis. Please sign up to receive our alerts, and you'll always be in the know!)

- Attend the town hall meetings of your elected officials and sign up to speak. Voice your support for an immigration and refugee vetting system that will ensure public safety and the safety of our families.

- Make an appointment to speak with your elected officials when they are in their district offices.

- Your efforts will be more effective if you 1) consistently show up at various town hall meetings, and 2) recruit your family and friends to join you in voicing your concerns and requests.

Chapter 8
TARGETING THE INNOCENT

I WANT TO PREFACE this chapter by indicating that this may be very difficult for some to read. The details I will be discussing are quite heartbreaking, but I feel it is important that we do not turn a blind eye to the evils we are facing, or water down the fact that our enemy operates in a sphere of hatred. I will also be giving critically important information for how you can make a difference in the protection of others.

Those who suffer the most from the erosion of Western, Judeo-Christian values are the most vulnerable among us. Never in the history of the world have women and children ever been treated with as much dignity and respect as they are in the Western civilization.

Alvin Schmidt makes a great case for this in his book, *How Christianity Changed the World*. In the next several paragraphs I'll summarize some of the points he makes.[1]

As Christianity spread throughout the world, its teachings and influence elevated women and liberated them in many ways. Christianity declared men and women as equals in value and worth in the eyes of God.

In the New Testament, Paul told the Christians in Ephesus: "Husbands, love your wives, just as Christ also loved the church and gave Himself for her" (Eph. 5:25, NKJV). And he added, "He who loves his wife loves himself" (v. 28, NKJV). In a Christian wedding ceremony it is very common for the man to pledge to love, comfort, and honor his wife in sickness and in health, forsaking all others for as long as he lives.

These Christian principles created a stark contrast with the values of the Roman Empire. Roman families typically kept all healthy boys born to them, but only kept their oldest healthy girl. Any additional daughters were abandoned at birth and left to die. The daughter who remained alive was typically forced into an arranged marriage at age twelve and often pushed to remarry if widowed later in life.

Christians took in abandoned infants; allowed girls to marry who they wished, when they wished; and provided support for widows. This compassionate set of values caused women to convert to Christianity at a significantly higher rate than men.

Even though some Christian leaders throughout history have not truly adhered to New Testament teachings about women, this is the failure of imperfect people, not of Jesus' example and teaching. Over time Christianity's respect for women and the upholding of female dignity within the faith led to the spread of Christian values all over the world. This included the changing educational opportunities women had historically been denied in many countries, just as they still are today in many non-Western nations. Christian values helped change that in country after country. For example:

- When Christian missionaries were allowed to enter British India, the ancient practice of suttee, a barbaric practice in which Hindu widows were forced to burn to death after throwing themselves on top of the flaming corpses of their husbands, was finally abolished.

- Chinese Christian women in the late 1800s began speaking out about the extremely painful practice of forcefully binding the feet of little girls, which often left them permanently crippled. One of these Chinese Christians was a medical doctor named Shi Meiyu, who not only helped bring an end to this abusive tradition, but also served as a shining example of what women can accomplish in a Judeo-Christian society.

- In Japan a woman named Tsuda Umeko, who was educated in the United States, became the private tutor of the prime minister's children. Umeko played such an instrumental role in securing the right for women to get an education that the most prestigious private women's college in Japan, Tsuda College, was named in her honor.

In Judaism, every Friday evening, before the family sits down for the Shabbat meal, the most important meal of the week, Jews the world over sing a special poem to honor a very special Jewish woman. According to Jewish tradition, "After Moses received the Torah from God at Mount Sinai, he offered it first to the Jewish women, for he knew that if they accepted it, it would become part of the Jewish people for all time," illustrating the importance that Judaism places on women.[2]

The song is called "Eishet Chayil" (woman of valor). If no women are present at the meal, "Eishet Chayil" is still sung in praise of Jewish women everywhere.[3] The song beautifully declares the words of Proverbs 31:10–11, "A wife of noble character who can find? She is worth far more than rubies. Her husband has full confidence in her and lacks nothing of value." The song continues praising the woman for her business skills, her homemaking skills, her motherhood, and what she contributes to the family. The song ends with: "Her husband…praises her: 'Many women do noble things, but you surpass them all.' Charm is deceptive, and beauty is fleeting; but a woman who fears the LORD is to be praised. Honor her for all that her hands have done, and let her works bring her praise at the city gate" (vv. 28–31).

The rights enjoyed by women in Israel contrast in a profound way to those lacking in the Arab countries surrounding them. All women, including Muslim women, enjoy astronomically more freedom and safety in the Jewish nation of Israel than they do in any of the Sharia-abiding neighbors.[4] Sharia prevents them from getting an education, justifies domestic abuse against them, values them less than half of a man, and even legitimizes killing them should their male family members decide they have in some way dishonored them. While men who beat and rape their wives are a plague on Judeo-Christian society, in the Islamic world, they are normalized.[5]

This combination of Judeo-Christian principles came together to form the contemporary Western world we know today. Ironically the same fraudulent leftists who claim to stand for the protection of those most vulnerable, such as women, children, and minorities, are actively participating in the destruction of the only culture that ever afforded them such honor and protection.

When a radical Islamist like Linda Sarsour, who defends Saudi Arabia's treatment of women and personally advocated for the removal of my and Ayaan Hirsi Ali's genitalia, can pass as an advocate for women's rights, you wonder whether you're watching CNN or an episode of *The Twilight Zone*.[6]

THE REAL WAR ON WOMEN

We hear a lot about the so-called "war on women" happening in America from the mainstream media, which loves to portray the United States as some sort of oppressive hell-hole for women to live in. But compare that to the lack of air coverage of real women's issues such as human trafficking. Women and girls make up 96 percent of the victims of trafficking for sexual exploitation worldwide, totaling more than 11 million every year. Those numbers are unconscionable.[7]

VICTIMS OF SEX TRAFFICKING WORLDWIDE

The human trafficking epidemic is one of the most under-covered epidemics in the media, yet it's one of the most important struggles facing women and children today. Young girls from all over the world are being taken as property to be sold on the black market as objects. This heartbreaking reality, though still an issue in the United States, is an overwhelming pandemic in non-Western countries. Perhaps this fact alone is enough for the mainstream media to largely ignore it.

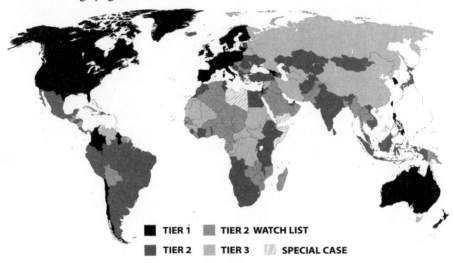

The US Department of State has a special ranking system of three tiers for countries with respect to human trafficking compliance, which is based off the Trafficking Victims Protection Act (TVPA). The TVPA was created by the US Department of State to hold other nations accountable for their actions and inactions toward human trafficking. Tier 1 countries are in compliance with the minimum standards. Tier 2 countries are those who are not in compliance with minimum standards but are making some progress toward one day fulfilling their obligations. For Tier 2 Watch List countries, in addition to the standard Tier 2 qualifications, the number of victims of severe forms of trafficking is high or is significantly increasing; no evidence has been provided of increasing efforts to combat trafficking from the previous year; or the determination the country is making progress toward minimum standards is based on commitments to take future steps. Tier 3 countries are neither in compliance with minimum standards, nor making any progress toward combatting this issue, and in many cases are enabling it. The Special Case rating is for countries that have extreme political instability or other circumstances that prevent the government from being able to address trafficking issues.

Unsurprisingly more than half of the Tier 3 countries for human trafficking are on the continent of Africa.[8] Violence, civil unrest, poverty, lack of education, and laws which allow or fail to protect women and children from modern-day slavery are all demonstrated by Tier 3 countries consitently. Traffickers in Tier 3 countries often force young girls into marriages and domestic sexual slavery, as well as international sex trafficking. As you can imagine, countries that implement Islamic Sharia law, which treats women as property, are also huge enablers of sex trafficking and slavery. In the Middle East only one country was classified as a Tier 1 nation. Can you guess which nation that was? That's right, Israel. The most demonized nation in the Middle East by the media is the only country living up to the minimum standards set forth to protect against modern-day slavery, human trafficking, and sexual exploitation.

This is an epidemic which deserves far more coverage than it gets, and Western countries living up to their responsibility of protecting the most vulnerable among us should not lose sight of the values and foundational principles that have allowed them to do so. They should also not fail to chastise and condemn other countries for not living up to their responsibility as members of the United Nations, in the name of political correctness. Isn't that what the United Nations was supposed to be for, to hold nations accountable for failure to uphold basic human rights? Or was it just to sit around and talk about the evils of colonialism and blame every problem plaguing the planet on the freest, most advanced Western nations, which have given women and children more protection and dignity than their critics ever have?

It's time we stop tolerating intolerance in the name of tolerance. It's time to hold others accountable for their lack of respect for human life, regardless of age, gender, or race. We owe it to the victims of human and sexual trafficking to speak truthfully and openly about this issue and do all we can to end it.

Across the Ocean

On New Year's Eve 2014, more than twelve hundred women were sexually assaulted across several German cities; more than six hundred assaults took place in Cologne and about four hundred in Hamburg.[9] About half the suspects were foreign nationals.[10] Half!

German officials linked the dramatic rise in sexual assaults to the influx of refugees, mostly from North Africa. One twenty-three-year-old victim stated, "They all looked foreign. They managed to separate us in the crowd and got close to us...we tried to fight off their hands...everywhere I looked I saw girls crying and being comforted."[11] Women had their underwear ripped off and some were molested by at least thirty men.[12]

In many countries in the Islamic world, according to Islamic teaching, a woman needs four male witnesses to testify in her support to prove rape. If she cannot get four male witnesses, it becomes her fault, her crime, and therefore, she must be punished for having nonmarital sex.[13] Because of that, almost all women in the Islamic world never utter a word about being raped out of fear of punishment.[14]

In Saudi Arabia a woman was sentenced to ninety lashes after she was gang-raped by seven men. Her sentence

> **In the West rape is a crime. In the Islamic world rape is a punishment.**

was later increased to two hundred lashes and six months in prison because she spoke to the media. Saudi officials justified the sentencing because she was sitting in a car with an unrelated man before she was raped.[15] Multiculturalism isn't all it's cracked up to be by the media.

If a woman has been raped in the Islamic world, she has two choices: 1) keep her mouth shut or 2) report it and potentially be shunned, demonized, or killed by her community. In the West rape is a crime. In the Islamic world rape is a punishment.

Thanks to unfettered Islamic immigration and refugee resettlement across the West, such problems do not remain confined to the Middle East but have arrived in our own communities. Two Iraqi men in their twenties raped a middle-aged woman in Colorado so brutally that she had internal bleeding, needed immediate surgery to repair her body, and required a colostomy bag for her body to function properly. Police described the rape as "one of the worst in Colorado history." Three other Iraqi men were convicted as accessories to the crime.[16]

All of the attackers received permanent residency status in the United States, due in part to helping US military members as informants and interpreters during the Iraq War.[17] Jasim Ramadon, one of the perpetrators of the rape, was the main character in a war memoir written by one of the soldiers he served with in Iraq. The book, A Soldier's Promise: The Heroic True Story of an American Soldier and an Iraqi Boy, was an instant hit and even led to Ramadon being a featured as a guest on Oprah.[18]

While living in the home of the sergeant who sponsored Ramadon for visa status, he was disrespectful to the wife of the sergeant.[19] Being that Ramadon comes from a culture where women are treated as slaves, he probably thought nothing of it. Such cultural differences should serve as a lesson to US immigration officials—assimilating men from cultures that view women as human property is not as easy as it seems.

This tragic case is an important example of what happens after decades of a pie-in-the-sky, let's-all-hold-hands-and-sing-Kumbaya immigration policy. It's a reminder that political correctness is not only illogical—it's dangerous.

KILLING HIS OWN DAUGHTER

It's not just sexual assault that Islamic values bring to the West; it's death.

"Do you know that you are going to die tonight?"

This is how Zein Isa, a Palestinian Muslim and naturalized United States citizen living in Missouri, told his sixteen-year-old daughter, Tina, she was going to die.[20] He told her she brought dishonor to the family by finding part-time work, dating a boy outside her faith, playing high school soccer, going to the prom, and becoming "Americanized."[21] Tina was brutally stabbed to death by her father with a butcher knife while her mother, Maria, held her down.

The FBI had a recording device in the home as part of an investigation into Zein Isa, but unfortunately the recording was not being monitored. It wasn't until the next morning that an FBI agent heard the horrific events and Tina's screams for mercy that had been recorded:

> Tina begins to shriek in fear.
> "Keep still, Tina!" says her father.
> "Mother, please help me!"
> "Huh? What do you mean?" the mother says.
> "Help! Help!"
> "What help?" the mother responds.
> Tina screams, and Maria says: "Are you going to listen? Are you going to listen?"
> Screaming louder, Tina gasps "Yes! Yes! Yes, I am" then coughs and adds, "No. Please!"
> Six wounds in the chest.
> The mother says, "Shut up!
> Tina continues to cry, but her voice is unintelligible.
> "Die! Die quickly! Die quickly!" her father says.
> The girl moans, seems to quiet, then screams one last time.
> "Quiet, little one! Die, my daughter, die!" the father says.[22]

Tina's father attacked and stabbed his daughter to death with his foot over her mouth to keep her quiet. She was stabbed six times in the chest.[23]

Both parents were convicted of first degree murder and sentenced to death in 1991. Tina's father died in prison in 1997 while awaiting execution; her mother's sentence was commuted to life imprisonment without parole, and she died in prison in 2014. Neither parent ever expressed an ounce of remorse for brutally murdering their own daughter.[24]

While this case may seem incomprehensible to any Westerner, it is an act that not only takes place regularly in the Islamic world, but actually is encouraged under the Islamic law of Sharia. In the West we call this murder. In the Islamic world they call it "honor killing."

In the United Kingdom eleven thousand cases of honor violence occurred in five years (from 2010 to 2014).[25] We would be wise to pay closer attention to what's happening there because it's a picture of our future if we don't act now to stop it. In fact, these acts of "honor" are already happening here in America to the tune of an estimated twenty-three to twenty-seven honor killings per year. A recent study commissioned by the US Department of Justice looked at four types of honor violence emerging in the United States: forced marriages, honor-based domestic violence, honor killing, and FGM.

The report noted that being "too Westernized" was the reason behind 91 percent of North American cases, and when victims were eighteen or younger, the father was involved 100 percent of the time. It also stated that Muslims committed 96 percent of honor killings in Europe.[26]

The experts involved said that for every honor killing, there are many more instances of abuse—both physical and emotional—all being carried out in the name of Islam. They believe the numbers are much higher than reported because families typically obstruct police investigations of these crimes and sometimes pressure the victims to commit suicide. The DOJ report states, "The National Crime Victimization Survey (NCVS) is inappropriate for collecting data on honor violence...in part because it collects data from all persons in the household. In honor violence, the household is the source of the threat."[27]

When was last time you heard about an honor-killing case on the news or even your local news? We are sacrificing our values and our standards on the altar of diversity and multiculturalism.

In the Islamic world, when two parents gruesomely murder a precious daughter like Tina, they are assigned honor. Perhaps we shouldn't be importing individuals from cultures that view murdering their own child as honorable.

Groups such as CAIR and the SPLC continue to work tirelessly to defend the values that enable murders such as Tina's. In the name of the anti-American hatred that consumes them, they smear those who dare to speak out against these violent acts.

Radical Islamist and mainstream media darling Linda Sarsour has explicitly expressed a desire to implement Sharia in the United States, a policy that would not only justify but also encourage what happened to Tina. I'll talk more about Sarsour in chapter 11.

Honor violence can take many forms, including physical violence, sexual abuse, verbal abuse, threats, stalking, harassment, false imprisonment, forced marriage, and homicide. Information about honor violence is closely concealed by families and communities who tend to communicate in Arabic amongst themselves only. Victims or potential victims may not report victimization out of fear. Further, victims may not report honor violence because in their home culture what has occurred is not viewed as a crime.[28]

Thankfully President Trump has mandated that the Secretary of Homeland Security regularly collect and make publicly available "information regarding the number and types of acts of gender-based violence against women, including so-called 'honor killings' in the United States by foreign nationals."[29] We must do more to ensure that we are not importing or fostering religious practices in the name of political correctness. The choice is clear: stand with victims of this type of barbarism or stand with the barbarians who engage in such behavior.

FEMALE GENITAL MUTILATION

Female genital mutilation (FGM) is a barbaric practice implemented regularly in the Middle East and increasingly in the Western world. FGM is the removal of a girl's external genitals. Physicians know that the female body is physically and often irreparably damaged when the healthy tissue of her genitals is cut away. Medical consensus is that there are no health benefits to FGM at all.[30]

According to the World Health Organization (WHO), more than two hundred million girls have been victims of FGM.[31] The United States is no exception. In fact, in the name of "multiculturalism," the American Academy of Pediatrics issued a policy statement in April 2010 supporting FGM—right here in the good old USA! Thankfully, after a public outcry driven by ACT for America, they rescinded the statement.[32] Still, the CDC says that about 513,000 women and girls in the United States have either been victims of FGM or are potential targets of FGM.[33] This is three times higher than an earlier CDC estimate based on 1990 data.

Many of these young girls are subjected to FGM when their parents take them back home to visit family in their home countries where the practice is sanctioned. After it's over, the family brings the girls back without a peep. (Taking a girl from the United States for the purpose of mutilating her abroad is illegal, by the way.) In other cases FGM circumcisers are actually brought to the United States to do the procedure here, even though FGM is illegal in the United States.

The purpose of FGM from the Islamist perspective is that it will eliminate pleasure from sexual intimacy, and thus, the chances of a woman having an affair when she gets older. This warped view, as twisted as it is, serves as a legitimate reason in Islamic culture to cut a young girl's genitalia.

Muslim doctors in Michigan were recently arrested for performing FGM on two girls, but it was revealed in a trial hearing that at least one hundred girls might have been mutilated in their office.[34] Dr. Jumana Nagarwala, Dr. Fakhruddin Attar, and his wife, Farida Attar, were arrested in April 2017 on three federal criminal counts, including aiding and abetting FGM, as well as conspiracy and transportation of an individual with intent to engage in criminal sexual activity.[35] This was a landmark case in that it exposes a secret, sickening practice that has existed underground in America for decades.

The Muslim doctors said they practiced FGM for "religious and cultural reasons."[36] While some in the mainstream media have disgracefully attempted to defend FGM, such as Imam Shaker Elsayed of the Dar al-Hijrah Islamic Center in Falls Church, Virginia, who said that FGM is great for controlling "hypersexuality,"[37] here in the Western world we take a more civilized point of view.

We know from court proceedings that the Islamist physicians were caught specifically for cutting two seven-year-old girls from Minnesota, but that the full scope and magnitude of how many they had mutilated during their time practicing could not be determined. However, prosecutors did say that they know the number is certainly north of one hundred victims.[38]

Dr. Attar admitted that he allowed Dr. Nagarwala to use his office at least six times a year to perform mutilations. Both are facing possible life sentences. Attar's wife tried to calm the terrified girls down during the extremely painful procedure by holding their hands. She is facing up to twenty years in prison for her aiding and abetting.[39]

The girls from Minnesota who were genitally mutilated were told by their parents that they were going to Michigan for a "special girls' trip," but instructed them not to speak about the procedure after it had taken place.[40] One has to wonder, if the parents of these poor girls really felt justified in their actions, why the need to lie to the girls about it or tell them to keep their mouths shut?

One of the victims said that she was told that the procedure was necessary to "get the germs out," while another said she could barely walk after the procedure and was in agony all the way down to her ankles.[41]

DOMESTIC DEATH

Orchard Park, New York, is an all-American suburb just outside Buffalo and the site where Bridges TV executive Muzzammil "Mo" Hassan committed a heinous crime soaked in both blood and tragic irony. Bridges TV was a television station set up by Hassan and his wife, Aasiya, founded for the specific purpose of combatting stereotypes, such as Muslims being violent.[42]

Today and hopefully for the rest of his life, Hassan is in prison—for beheading his wife. You read that right. The founder of a TV station dedicated to convincing us that Muslims aren't violent felt his wife deserved to die for dishonoring him. What had she done to bring him such dishonor? She tried to divorce him for his violent temper.[43] The upper-middle class neighborhood of Orchard Park hadn't seen a homicide since 1986, let alone a beheading! When a crime that gruesome takes place in a safe and small town like Orchard Park, it shocks the community to its core. While not unusual in the Middle East, honor killings have been virtually unheard of in towns like Orchard Park. Now, thanks to multicultural immigration policies, they no longer are.[44]

Not only did Hassan decapitate his wife, but he also went to the police station and proudly told officers about her death and where they could find her body. Talk about brazen! Police found her decapitated in the hallway of the Bridges TV studio where both Hassan and his wife had worked closely together.

Prosecutors tried to claim this was strictly a case of "domestic violence."[45]

As I explained on *Real Time With Bill Maher* shortly after this brutal killing, while in the West it's normal for those who commit murder to try to cover up their crimes, in the Islamic world it is something to be proud of.

The irony about this case is that Hassan was a darling of mainstream media outlets, appearing on various networks to talk about how moderate Islam really is, and how terrorists do not represent the true Islam. He was specifically used as the example of an Americanized, successful Muslim businessman trying to make a difference to benefit his faith and community. The media used him as a poster boy for peaceful Islam. Big mistake.

When Bridges TV was launched, it was promoted all over national mainstream media networks because it fit the PC worldview that all cultures are equal in their treatment of women. Then, the man who founded the network decapitated his wife in the very television studio that promoted this false worldview. While Hassan was giving Americanized, polished, and phony talking points to gullible, mainstream network anchors and producers, his wife was suffering in silence from his abuse.

True to his core Islamic values, Hassan blocked Bridges TV from airing a story about the first Muslim woman to win Miss England in 2005.[46] He viewed this as shameful, all while trying to keep up appearances on air.

The brutal and tragic irony of this case clearly outlines that sometimes stereotypes are not stereotypes, but legitimate depictions of the contrasting cultures of Islam and the West. Those who choose to ignore them do so at their peril.

BRINGING MOGADISHU TO YOUR DOORSTEP

I spoke of the issues with Somali "refugees" in Minnesota in an earlier chapter, but it bears another look as we discuss the need to protect women and children in this chapter. More than 136,000 Somalis were resettled in unsuspecting American cities between 1983 and 2016 by our own State Department![47] Over the last decade an average of six thousand Somali refugees have been resettled per year, of which the Minneapolis area has seen the largest share.

Consequently, massive Muslim enclaves have transformed the local population into a completely different civilization. That massive influx has created terrorizing consequences for the surrounding communities, particularly for women.

Recently a mob of about thirty young Somali men terrorized their way through an upper-middle class community, shouting intimidating comments and sexually threatening female homeowners. One female resident told local news a Somali man explicitly threatened to kidnap and rape her.

"They were screaming at the house that they were going to kidnap me, and 'we're going to rape you,'" she told local KSTP TV. "It just was a very traumatizing experience."[48]

It appears that no hate-crime charges were ever considered by either the Minnesota authorities or the Obama Justice Department. How predictable.

The Somalis randomly showed up in front of a woman's house at about 9:30 in the morning and started shouting threats and insults at her. Almost all the Minneapolis media refused to cover the story after it happened, and out of the news networks that did cover it, most never pointed out that every single aggressor was of Somali descent.

"We couldn't get them out. We didn't know what to do," the woman was quoted as saying.

The Somalis then began driving onto the sidewalk and tearing up lawns of residents while shooting off bottle rockets and yelling, "Jihad!" while waving a Somali flag. They screamed, "We're going to rape you!" toward the female homeowners. Imagine this was your mother, your sister, or your daughter being threatened by third-world Islamists when you weren't there to protect them.

The women couldn't even count on their own governor, Mark Dayton, to protect them. Months before the incident Dayton had told Minnesota residents that if they weren't comfortable living among Somali refugees, they "should find another state."[49] Maybe Dayton should find another country, like Somalia, if he seems to love the culture so much.

It doesn't seem to matter how many terror incidents occur, a leftist enabler like Minnesota's governor will never do what is necessary to protect Minnesotans because "tolerance" is the ultimate religion for leftists. Assimilation? There's assimilation alright, but not in the way you'd expect. Instead of Somalis becoming Americanized, it's Minnesotans who have been Somalianized.

WAR ON CHILDREN

It's not just women who have been endangered by importing Muslims who do not share Western values. Children, including young boys, are also vulnerable.

Take the case of Amir, a newly arrived Iraqi refugee, who settled in a peaceful Austrian town. A trip to the local public swimming pool was organized as part of public integration efforts for Amir. Unfortunately these assimilation efforts had horrifying consequences.

Amir dragged a ten-year-old boy into a cubicle in the changing room of the public pool, locked the door, and brutally raped him.[50] The traumatized child reported the attack to a lifeguard, and shockingly, when police arrived, they found Amir had returned to the pool and was playing on the diving board, seemingly carefree and making no attempt to flee.

While raping ten-year-old boys in the Islamic world may be seen as petty as jaywalking, Austrian authorities were shocked by Amir's casual, happy-go-lucky attitude about the incident. Amir admitted to the attack as soon as police questioned him, telling them openly that it was simply a "sexual emergency" because he had not had sex for four months.[51]

So what was Amir's sentence for raping and permanently scarring a young boy for life? He was initially given a pathetic seven years in prison for his attack, but that seemed too harsh for the radical leftists on the Austrian Supreme Court. They later overturned the seven-year prison sentence, ruling that the lower court had failed to establish whether or not Amir, the refugee, knew his victim did not consent.[52]

How about the fact that he was ten years old and screaming for his life? Would that be a sign?

The court did not dispute the "watertight" evidence that Amir had engaged in sexual intercourse with a ten-year-old, but they found that Amir could not be held liable because Amir, being a new refugee, was not yet capable of understanding concepts such as consensual versus nonconsensual sex or distinguishing children versus adults.

Afghan journalist Najibullah Quraishi's documentary *The Dancing Boys of Afghanistan* exposed how the UN has known and done nothing about Afghan police raping and sexually trafficking entire generations of young boys.[53]

Here in the United States, Maj. Jason Brezler was robbed of his reputation and his military career after he warned colleagues of a sexual assault on an American base in the Helmand province.[54] The Marine's request for information involved Afghan police chief and child molester Sarwar Jan.

Jan was accused of raping at least nine boys on base. Shortly after Brezler's warning, which was brazenly ignored, one of Jan's "tea boys" went on a shooting spree at Delhi military base. Marine S.Sgt. Cody Rhode was shot five times but survived. Three other heroic marines—S.Sgt. Scott Dickinson, Cpl. Richard Rivera, and Lance Cpl. Greg Buckley—died of gunshot wounds in the incident.[55] Buckley's relatives filed a lawsuit against the Department of Defense, the Marine Corps, and a top general over their deliberate attempt to suppress details of the attack.[56]

Something's wrong when a hero like Brezler gets thrown under the bus by the Obama administration for using his personal Yahoo account to try to protect fellow marines and young children while Hillary Clinton still walks a free woman.[57]

In a separate case the army denied an appeal by Green Beret Sgt. First Class Charles Martland, who was discharged in 2011 for confronting an Afghan police commander accused of kidnapping, chaining, and raping a boy, as well as beating his mother and laughing about it. Another soldier who joined Martland in the confrontation, Capt. Daniel Quinn, was also punished and subsequently resigned.[58]

During his time in office Obama wanted to spend billions combatting climate change in order to save future generations of children from pollution, but he couldn't even lift a finger to protect this generation of Afghan children from being raped. Michelle Obama put out a Twitter post with the caption "Bring Back Our Girls" after Boko Haram jihadists in Nigeria kidnapped three hundred girls but had nothing to say about forced prostitution and pedophilia rings of young boys that had been explicitly witnessed by United States military men. Not only that, the Obama administration punished and railroaded those who did speak out.

Obama continually looked the other way when the reality staring back at him contrasted his multicultural utopia. Better for him and his media minions to whitewash Islam's sins against Christians, Jews, gays, apostates, cartoonists, and genitally mutilated girls than to jeopardize his politically correct ideology.

REAL HOMOPHOBIA

In addition to women and children, gay men are another group of individuals who are routinely brutalized in the Muslim world. Homosexuals are beheaded and stoned to death in countries such as Saudi Arabia, Iran, and others where Sharia law rules the land. Many Islamic theological debates in countries such as these do not focus on whether it's OK to kill gay men, but how to kill them.

Regardless of how those in the West feel about homosexuality on a personal level, our culture allows for rigorous public debate on the subject and how public policy should approach the issue of gay marriage.

Christians will often passionately pray for those they disagree with—even their enemies. But there is no Christian or Judeo practice that sanctions the killing of another human being simply for disagreeing with their beliefs.

Islam is a different story.

One of the earliest and most respected authorities on the Quran, Ibn 'Abbas, said that "the sodomite should be thrown from the highest building in the town and then stoned."[59] This is why ISIS throws gay men off buildings and then stones them. Everything ISIS does is fundamentally Islamic and adheres to the most trusted sources and practices of Islam, which have been in place for over fourteen hundred years. Homosexuals are to be thrown off of buildings. That's just the tragic reality.

This appalling view is not only held by Muslims in the Middle East, but also right here in our own backyard. A British Islamic scholar speaking at a Florida mosque in 2016 said that killing gays should be done "out of compassion."[60]

When facts outlining the widespread abuse of women and homosexuals in Islam come to light, the only thing we hear from radical Islamic lobby groups like CAIR or their enablers like the SPLC is "Islamophobia."

Leftists love to lecture us about the joys of multiculturalism while simultaneously claiming the moral monopoly on human rights. But when real life issues smack them square in the face like this one, they're strangely silent.

Suddenly the real world contradicts everything they bought hook, line, and sinker from their Marxist professors.

They can't face the fact that the A they got in a sociology seminar taught by a middle-aged man wearing a beanie and all those hours spent watching Fareed Zakaria didn't teach them everything they needed to know about the world and life in general. The Middle East is not as it's portrayed in Marxist college textbooks, and neither is the real world. It's a dangerous place filled with evil people who do evil things. But the Western world has done better than any other civilization in the history of mankind to contain such evil, only to have it now demonized in the name of multicultural insanity.

Unless we can speak truthfully about how Islamic values directly contrast those of our Western world and rise in defense of our own values, which are without a question superior to those we are importing from radical third-world countries, the tentacles of this sick virus will continue to stretch further into our societies, resulting in the erosion and even death of them.

RISE UP AND ACT

When you read about these senseless tragedies in the news, don't just reach for the tissue box. ACT!

- If you or someone you know is a victim of sex trafficking and needs help, call 1-888-373-7888. You can also report an anonymous tip at www.humantraffickinghotline.org/report -trafficking.

- Donate to and volunteer at your local women's shelter.

- Support federal legislation to further strengthen laws against FGM. One particular federal legislation is H.R. 3317, the SAFE ACT; it easily passed the House in December 2017, but at the time of this book's publication has not been voted on in the Senate. The bill: increase the federal penalty for FGM from up to five years of imprisonment to up to fifteen years of imprisonment. The bill also calls on states to ensure that they have proper laws in place for health care providers, school officials, and adults to report suspected FGM to local law enforcement. Call and write your senator asking them to support H.R. 3317, the SAFE ACT.

- Beyond H.R. 3317, ACT for America is involved in passing legislation in many states to ban this horrible practice and penalize parents who do this to their daughters. You can sign up to receive our action alerts and to work on FGM legislation in your state.

Chapter 9

LAMESTREAM MEDIA

THE MAINSTREAM MEDIA, or what has become widely known as the "lamestream media," is an institution of pure groupthink, in which one radical leftist ideology controls the news. This institution sees itself as a great liberator of oppressed individuals. In reality, the media demonizes the very Western, Judeo-Christian values that serve as the foundation for the most liberating civilization in human history. They not only demonize these principles, they detest them. Just the sound of the words *Judeo-Christian values* to any leftist reporter is offensive, if not repulsive.

All news is now dependent upon an increasingly bizarre ladder of oppression, of which Islam has risen directly to the top, leapfrogging over all other previously victimized minorities. Any story that potentially demonizes Islam will be either ignored or deceptively covered.

Choices regarding headlines written, words spoken on television, and which stories to cover in any capacity are now completely beholden to the mainstream media's politically correct agenda. The manner of reporting a terrorist attack depends on which tribe the media place the victims. In many cases, if the media doesn't like the optics of a particular story, they'll put it on the back burner.

Illegal immigrant crimes are met with silence or deceitful headlines to keep the public in the dark. Meanwhile, fake news about so-called Russian election interference floods the airwaves in a desperate attempt to explain away the defeat of Hillary Clinton by our current commander-in-chief.

The fake pandemic of Islamophobia is portrayed as a greater nuisance than Islamic terrorism. Israel is criticized and maligned, while terrorist Palestinians are portrayed as victims. Blatant anti-Semites and terrorist sympathizers are given an open mic, while those exercising an opinion inconsistent with leftist dogma are ostracized entirely.

Money from nefarious sources pours into media institutions, corrupting them and keeping them under the thumb of their leftist sugar daddies who dole out the cash. (I'll share more about this later.) As a result, the agenda of the media has changed dramatically—shifting from what used to be a left-of-center perspective to their modern-day mission of destroying all who hold views opposite to theirs.

KANYE WEST AND THE DEATH OF GROUPTHINK

Love him or hate him, Kanye West is one of the most influential celebrities of the past two decades. His Twitter account commands a following of approximately twenty-eight million people, making him the twelfth most followed male musician in the world for that outlet.[1]

West is known for his musical and fashion endeavors, as well as his unpredictable outspokenness and unique train of thought. He is currently married to another of the most popular yet polarizing celebrities, Kim Kardashian West. The platform shared between these two is astronomical, and younger generations tend to be profoundly enamored by this celebrity power couple.

This in mind, when West recently came out in support of President Trump and against Barack Obama, leftists desperate to maintain their monopoly on celebrity politics nearly lost their minds.

West "broke the internet" when he tweeted out: "You don't have to agree with trump but the mob can't make me not love him. We are both dragon energy. He is my brother. I love everyone. I don't agree with everything anyone does. That's what makes us individuals. And we have the right to independent thought."[2]

The reaction? Hollywood star Kumail Nanjiani called it "the worst day in twitter history."[3] For leftists, that may not be an understatement.

Regardless of what you may think of Kanye West, who has done and said some outrageous things throughout his career, this was a seminal moment for freedom of thought. There has never been a more influential celebrity to come out and attack the church of modern leftism so openly. It was an objectively brave thing for a man of West's influence to do.

West also tweeted a picture of himself wearing a signed Make America Great Again hat and slammed Barack Obama for doing nothing to solve the problem of violence in West's hometown of Chicago,[4] which sent Hollywood and the mainstream media into full-on panic mode!

Obama's former speechwriter Jon Favreau quickly took to Twitter to plead for people to ignore West,[5] knowing the danger of letting others think it's OK to think independently about politics.

Snoop Dogg and Samuel L. Jackson sent tweets indicative of a family member trying to reach out to a loved one hooked on opiates, implying that West had been brainwashed to think "white," supposedly from spending so much time with his white in-laws.

Stephen Colbert, the Left's favorite late-night propagandist, scolded West for getting political. You know, because Colbert never gets political on his show. Except for almost every minute of every show.

Black talk-show host Trevor Noah said that the only reason West would support conservatism was because he was so rich now, implying that black people would have no other legitimate reason to do so. Noah makes a $4 million salary.[6]

Kanye West also expressed support for black conservative Candace Owens, who also threatens the leftist orthodoxy that says blacks are not allowed to stray from the Democratic party.

People magazine wrote a slanderous and unfounded article implying that West's Twitter storm caused an enormous rift with his family, and that it could indicate he was mentally ill.[7] Kim Kardashian West scolded the mainstream media for casually and baselessly discussing whether her husband was mentally ill, simply for expressing his opinion.[8]

In a last-ditch effort to intimidate West into silence, John Legend sent him a text message declaring: "Hey it's JL. I hope you'll reconsider aligning yourself with Trump. You're way too powerful and influential to endorse who he is and what he stands for. As you know, what you say really means something to your fans. They are loyal to you and respect your opinion. So many people who love you feel so betrayed right now because they know the harm that Trump's policies cause, especially to people of color. Don't let this be part of your legacy. You're the greatest artist of our generation."[9]

Impressively West spotted this groupthink intimidation tactic from a mile away and posted the following response online: "I love you John and I appreciate your thoughts. You bringing up my fans or my legacy is a tactic based on fear used to manipulate my free thought."[10]

For those of us who have been familiar with politics for a long time, none of this is surprising, but it became clear that neither West nor the Kardashians had any idea how viciously united the leftist cartel in Hollywood and the media was, nor the lengths they will go to in order to destroy anyone who threatens their political agenda.

The Left's animosity toward Kanye West is understandable, considering how strongly they've dominated the culture war. West may well be the start of a domino effect, the likes of which spell doom for the Left's monopoly on celebrity culture.

Consider this: for years the Left has been able to maintain their political stronghold in the media, Hollywood, and education by infiltrating these institutions themselves and then banishing their opponents from such institutions. Think about it. The Left controls every traditional media outlet with the exception of Fox News. They control CNN, ABC, NBC, PBS, ESPN, etc. They control nearly every Hollywood film studio as well, which allows them to churn out propaganda films as well as push their political agenda at boringly cliché award shows such as the Oscars. They control almost every public and private institution of higher education because they infiltrated from the administration to the classroom to the textbooks.

But there's one problem. Traditional media is dying, along with traditional entertainment and traditional education. A big "uh-oh" just went through the heads of every leftist reading these words, because they know it.

West's support for President Trump may turn out to be short-lived. He could wake up tomorrow and change into a Hollywood leftist. But his tweets are about more than just himself; they're a signal that when it comes to how people retrieve information, they no longer have to or want to get their news from Anderson Cooper or Chris Matthews. They don't have to watch movies only produced by the biggest Hollywood film studios. They don't have to go to college to get an education, because information online is vast, comprehensive, and free. This is why making sure that the internet remains free is the most critical fight of the future with respect to freedom of speech and thought. It's also why Barack Obama is furious that President Trump put an end to net neutrality and took back American control of the internet from foreign entities.

CENSORSHIP ACROSS THE POND

Radical Islamic apologists are not exclusive to American media. They seek to infect the minds of our allies across the pond in the UK as well. The British Broadcasting Corporation (BBC) is the UK's most powerful media outlet, deriving its money from public funding yet remaining anything but objective.

Essentially the BBC is a publicly funded leftist news outlet, which functions more like a propaganda arm than an objective source of information. One such example of the ways in which the BBC seeks to keep British citizens in the dark about the threat Islam poses to the British way of life unfolded as follows.

When a thirty-year-old nursery worker was stabbed in the name of Allah by a Muslim gang of women on her way to work, the BBC censored its television report.[11] Karrien Stevens, a child care center employee, was interviewed after the attack, and time and time again she noted that the assailants were chanting from the Quran and repeating "Allah, Allah" before stabbing her colleague. But in the clip that aired, the BBC cut out Stevens' reference about Islamic chants. The BBC's televised story on the attack described the perpetrators as "dressed in black," but failed to mention what they were shouting before slashing the innocent young woman. Perhaps the BBC wanted its viewers to believe the attackers could've been British nuns.

BBC's Daniel Sandford was confronted on Twitter about the edit and defended the network: "As I explained yesterday, we actually check stories before we publish. Sorry the facts as we can establish them don't fit your narrative." He issued a second tweet that said the police "cautioned against" the version that mentions Allah.[12] Or, as it seems, the facts didn't conform to the BBC's narrative about Islam and violence against women.

Where were all the women's rights groups shouting about BBC's censorship of the attack against an innocent young woman? Crickets. Why? Because Western women will always rank lower on the media's ladder of victimhood than Muslims.

In an enraging example of this from Europe, a seventy-one-year-old Swedish woman, angry over the large number of asylum-seekers who portrayed themselves as children when, in fact, they resembled grown men, referred to Muslim asylum-seekers in a Facebook post as "bearded children" in jest. She went on to discuss how many of these "child" asylees were committing vandalism as well as a large number of rapes throughout Swedish neighborhoods. Her penalty? A Swedish court fined her for "incitement of hatred against an ethnic group."[13]

The court found that she "must have realized that there was an imminent risk that people who read the text would perceive it as an expression of disagreement with other ethnic groups of people in general and the vast majority of single unaccompanied refugees, who, at the time of the comment, had come to Sweden in particular. Despite this, she wrote the comment on Facebook."[14]

Did the mainstream media in Sweden jump to the defense of this elderly woman whose only crime was exercising her human right to freedom of speech out of fear for herself and Western women at large? Hardly. Instead, efforts continued by leftist politicians in Sweden to silence women expressing their fears about refugees committing a staggering amount of rapes.

In America the radical Left would love nothing more than to be able to use taxpayer money to fund media outlets such as NBC, CNN, and ABC, much like they do in Europe. Beware of calls for more "publicly funded" media, or even a new "American News Corporation" that can pump out as much propaganda as it wants, regardless of what the ratings are.

Touting insane headlines such as "Let's Nationalize Fox News: Imagining a Very Different Media," Salon.com is one of many mainstream media outlets that want taxpayer dollars to pay for their propaganda instead of private advertisements.[15] Tech companies are also in the crosshairs of radical leftists who are desperate to stop the spread of information that exposes their lies and biased agenda. This in mind, beware of further propaganda efforts by the media to nationalize tech giants like Facebook, Google, and Amazon.

You better believe that Marxist moneyman George Soros, whose definitive goal is the fundamental transformation and control of the United States, would love to get his hands on these pesky tech outlets, which allow freedom of expression to blossom and combat his lies.

Increasingly, the leftist media is becoming more and more savvy with their plans to control freedom of speech and spread fake news without rebuttal. They dream of days when all speech and ideas contrary to their own can be erased from the public domain instantaneously—an America without Fox

News or talk radio, an America you and I will not recognize, and one in which concepts like freedom of speech are a thing of the past.

FAKE ISLAMOPHOBIA

The American media loves to push a narrative that there has been a sky-rocketing increase in attacks against Muslims since September 11. This is their way of once again changing the conversation and misrepresenting the facts to suit their agenda.

Shortly after President Trump's victory over Hillary Clinton, CNN ran a dreadful article titled "The Secret Costs of Islamophobia," which implied that somehow a Trump presidency would mean a surge in attacks against Muslims. "Muslims live in fear that they will be attacked" the article proclaimed.[16]

The FBI's most recent annual report of hate-crime statistics confirms that the much-hyped reporting of a "backlash" against American Muslims is nothing more than a deceptive myth to carry water for the radical Islamic lobby. Let's take a look at the facts.

In 2015 the FBI changed its method of classification for hate crimes. Ethnic crimes were eliminated as a separate category, and instead they were combined with race to form the race/ethnicity/ancestry category. Anti-Arab was added to this category. Anti-Muslim was already in the religion category and remained there. As a result of adding the anti-Arab classification, incidents targeting Arabs appear to have increased, when in actuality, it was simply the first time they could be classified as hate crimes.

There were 6,121 hate crimes reported in 2016, of which 358 were directed at Arabs or Muslims.[17] Not to belittle any hate crime, but 358 hate crimes in a country of 325 million people doesn't exactly justify the outrageously overblown coverage of anti-Muslim bias we hear so much about in the media today—especially when compared to hate crimes against other ethnicities and religions. Take a look at the following bar graph.[18] The numbers don't lie.

HATE CRIMES

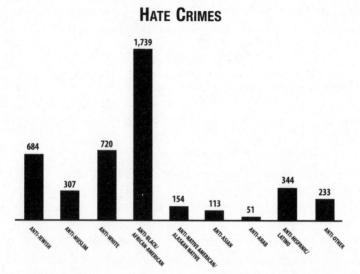

The media's obsession with hate crimes against Muslims while ignoring those against Jews, which are often perpetuated by Muslims, fails to take into account the incentive their own overhyped narrative gives to Islamists to report fake hate crimes. For example, when a Canadian girl claimed her hijab was ripped off of her, Prime Minister Justin Trudeau tweeted, "My heart goes out to Khawlah Noman following this morning's cowardly attack on her in Toronto."[19] Unfortunately for Trudeau, police later determined the girl he publicly supported with no evidence was lying.[20]

Shortly after the election of President Trump, a Muslim student at the University of Louisiana at Lafayette claimed she was attacked and had her hijab ripped off by two white males. The story spread like wildfire, along with the assumption that she was targeted because of her Muslim faith as a result of Trump's election. However, after an investigation by police, the girl admitted that she completely made it up,[21] and the media hasn't spoken of it since. What a surprise.

Question: What would the media's reaction be if, shortly after the election of President Obama, a white girl made up a story claiming she was assaulted by two black males? Do you think we might still be hearing about such a false story even today? I think so too.

A similar fake hate crime was reported by another Muslim woman. Yasmin Seweid said she was attacked on a New York City subway by Trump supporters who tried to rip off her hijab. She was later charged with filing a false police report.[22] Seweid claimed on Facebook that Trump supporters yelled, "Look, it's a f---ing terrorist," and "Get the h--- out of the country!"[23] She even had the nerve to say, "It breaks my heart that so many individuals chose to be bystanders while watching me get harassed verbally and physically by these disgusting pigs."[24]

The *New York Daily News* and BuzzFeed jumped on the story immediately, only to find out they had been conned. But the falsehood doesn't matter to them or to liars like Seweid who later blamed her lie on "family problems."[25] The only thing that matters is that the initial story is reported as fact in support of the overall narrative.

The lamestream media incentivizes these fake hate crimes because they love to champion victimhood. The effort to persuade the public that America is an Islamophobic nation is just the media's latest effort to shift the narrative about terrorism from that of jihad to one in which we are the terrorists and Muslims are the victims.

REPORTING ON ISRAEL

Reporting on the Israeli-Palestinian conflict brings out the absolute worst in the mainstream media. This is a conflict in which there is only one right side, and the media is on the wrong one!

Palestinians encourage their children to become martyrs. A mother poses with her son wrapped in a suicide belt in videos proudly supporting him in his suicide mission. Upon his death she is elevated to the status of hero and is as celebrated as her murderous son. This level of hatred and brainwashing is unmatched. Even the Nazis did not encourage nor celebrate the death of their children.

As I've said many times, the difference between Israel and the Palestinians is the difference between civilization and barbarism, and good versus evil. In my first book, *Because They Hate*, I dedicate a full chapter to this very subject.

Israel affords more rights to its Muslim citizens than any of the Arab nations afford to theirs,[26] yet somehow, every time the Palestinian terrorist organization Hamas lobs rockets into Israel and creates a necessary response, the media portrays Israel as the racist aggressor and the poor Palestinians as oppressed victims.

A BBC headline from February 14, 2016, read "Five Palestinians Killed 'After Attacking Israelis.'"[27] This disgraceful and deceitful tactic of placing quotation marks around the violent acts of Palestinian terrorists is all too common in an attempt to imply uncertainty about whether the terrorist attacks actually happened.

Despite evidence on the ground, the newspaper the *Guardian* put out a similar headline, "Three Palestinian Teenagers Shot Dead on West Bank. Israeli Security Forces allege they were under attack before the killings—though no soldiers were hurt."[28] Even though the article reports that two teens opened fire on Israeli forces and another teen ran at the

> The difference between Israel and the Palestinians is the difference between civilization and barbarism, and good versus evil.

border police with a knife, the headline's use of the word *allege* casts a doubt over these facts. Also, note how the *Guardian* characterized the terrorists as "teenagers," attempting to invoke a sense of childlike innocence on the part of the terrorists and sympathy from the reader.

Allow me to remind you that I am an Arab woman who has lived in both Lebanon and Israel and worked as a journalist. As such, I have no problem calling out this type of bias for what it is: sublimated anti-Semitism.

When President Trump declared that Jerusalem was in fact the capital of Israel and that the United States would be moving its embassy to the city from Tel Aviv, Palestinians responded with a "day of rage," which actually turned into weeks of a violent rampage against Israel. Of course, the media implied that the Palestinian "day of rage" was justified due to President Trump's decision and blamed him for any additional terrorism in the region.

Right, as if Palestinian terrorism toward Israel is something that was created only after President Trump's decision. In fact, at least four days of rage were declared in 2017 by Palestinians prior to President Trump's honorable move, but you wouldn't know it from watching dreadful media coverage such as the following:

- CBS's Seth Doane said, "There are concerns about violence not only here and across the Middle East, but this also could provide rationale for terrorist attacks in the West as well."[29]

- CNN's Aaron David Miller said President Trump was hitting Palestinians "over the head with a hammer" with his decision.[30] Meanwhile, Palestinians were literally throwing rocks and Molotov cocktails at police and Israeli soldiers.[31]

- ABC claimed President Trump was "reversing nearly seven decades of US policy."[32] Except that Congress passed a law in 1995 to recognize Jerusalem as the capital of Israel and to call for the US embassy in Israel to be moved to Jerusalem. But why let facts get in the way of a good narrative?

- MSNBC's Chris Matthews, "By the way, deaths are coming now because of this."[33]

Leftist actor Mark Ruffalo urged Israel not to respond to Palestinian violence saying: "Isreal [sic], please show restraint in the face of these protests. This is a terrible blow to any hope for peace or a life beyond apartheid for your neighbors. Please, all parties, use restraint."[34] If leftists in Hollywood and their comrades in the media had it their way, Israel would respond to every terrorist attack by handing out dandelions.

ILLEGAL IMMIGRATION

Anyone who watches lamestream media coverage knows the full-blown bias shown toward illegal immigrants, even those who commit violent offenses. Stories involving violent crimes committed by illegal immigrants are shoved to the back of the line or are reported with no mention of immigration status.

A study by Media Research Center (MRC) proved the political agenda at ABC, CBS, and NBC with respect to illegal immigration.[35] Their study showed that:

- ABC, CBS, and NBC ignored poll numbers, including their own polls that indicated an overwhelming number of Americans see illegal immigration as a huge problem.

- Networks were also proven to have given amnesty pushers twice as many sound bites as those who opposed amnesty for illegals.

- Cleverly the media used the term *conservative* eighty-nine times when ginning up their narrative, but only used the term *liberal* three times to describe amnesty pushers. This was in order to create the facade that it was "every man's" position to grant amnesty to millions here illegally.

- This unification makes perfect sense considering that illegal immigration should be neither a liberal nor conservative issue, but rather an American issue. However, the media gets it wrong by failing to report that the majority of Americans are united in support of tighter borders, not amnesty.

- CBS and NBC never labeled those pushing for more lenient policies as liberal even one time. Less than 2 percent of stories discussed how illegal immigrants cost more to government than they provide in taxes.

- Networks never once questioned the audacity of illegal immigrants protesting and lobbying on immigration while in violation of federal laws, a blatant disgrace to the rule of law. When Jose Garcia Zarate, the illegal immigrant who was charged with murdering Kate Steinle, was acquitted, CBS Evening News "conspicuously" decided not to mention the outcome of the trial to their viewers. Additionally, of those networks that did report on it, only the Fox News Channel called

> If leftists in Hollywood and their comrades in the media had it their way, Israel would respond to every terrorist attack by handing out dandelions.

Zarate an "illegal immigrant." All the others caved to the PC
police and called him an "undocumented immigrant."[36]

When the media aren't blacking out coverage of stories they don't like,
they're using misleading headlines. This bias was on full display when a gang
of Mexicans were arrested in Richmond, California, for the rape of a lesbian
woman.

Mexican Humberto Salvador bashed the woman on the head with his flash-
light, forced her to strip naked on the sidewalk, and raped her. Other gang
members took her to an abandoned building where they repeatedly and violently raped and degraded her for being a lesbian.[37]

No mainstream media outlets accurately reported that the rapists were
Mexican. News coverage about this particular hate crime described Salvador
as a "Richmond Man," a clever tactic often used by the media to protect
illegals from negative public perception.[38]

Here are a few more examples of the media's deceptive headlining:

- "Richmond Man Convicted in Gang Rape of Lesbian"
  —Associated Press, December 18, 2013[39]

- "Richmond Man Sentenced to 411 Years, Four Months for
  Gang Rape" —Mercury News, May 16, 2014[40]

- "400-Plus Years for Gang Rape of Targeted Lesbian"
  —San Francisco Chronicle, May 19, 2014[41]

- "Man Sentenced in California Gang Rape of Lesbian"
  —Associated Press, May 20, 2014[42]

Had the attackers been white, Christian males, Hollywood would've
already made a movie about the attack and every headline would make
sure to mention the race and religion of the attacker. But I guess protecting
the LGBT community is only advantageous for the media when they can
demonize white Christians in the process.

The media also possesses a particularly interesting ability to mock
Christians about their faith yet remain strangely silent about Islam. Imagine
Joy Behar or any of the other Hollywood hypocrites who mock Vice President
Mike Pence for his traditional Christian beliefs and not eating dinner alone
with a woman other than his wife, making those same comments about a
prominent Muslim. In Islam women are deplorably oppressed, yet oddly,
the only religion that Hollywood elites and mainstream media pundits seem
willing to mock and criticize is Christianity. This double standard could be
explained in two ways. One, the PC worldview of the Left prevents them
from exposing anything that even remotely conflicts with their multicultural
worldview. Two, they're afraid. They're afraid of what will happen to them if

they mock the teachings of Muhammad as they do Jesus. What does that say about Islam? What does that say about the Left?

FAKE RUSSIA COLLUSION

Watching the news on the evening of the 2016 presidential election was one of the most satisfying experiences of my life. I sat cozily on my couch and tossed perfectly buttered popcorn into my mouth while watching the epic meltdown of the mainstream media. I'll never forget the look of disbelief and despair in their eyes and voices as they began to realize that in spite of more than a year of trying to destroy then-candidate Trump, he was going to become the forty-fifth president of the United States of America.

Even more satisfying, the election of President Trump was a monumental public rebuke of the leftist propagandists in the media. It was a signal that times have changed and the days of American citizens buying every word out of their mouths hook, line, and sinker were over.

There has never been a candidate as routinely and disgracefully demonized as President Trump. Equally true is that there has never been a candidate as wildly coddled as Hillary Clinton. In spite of this, both Secretary Clinton and her media cheer squad were defeated.

Realizing what a humiliating public reproach they just received, bitter pundits and journalists needed an excuse to explain away their defeat. Thus, the Russian collusion fantasy made for perfect headlines.

As I write these words, the FBI's special counsel continues to investigate whether or not there was collusion between the Trump campaign and Russian influencers to defeat Hillary Clinton. So far there has been no proof of any so called "collusion" between the Trump campaign and Russia, but the way the media reports on the matter, you'd think that Vladimir Putin was magically able to change the votes of millions of Americans at the request of then-candidate Trump.

The media is desperate to explain away its abysmal failure to install another politically correct ideologue in the Oval Office and continues to cling to this fantasy. An MRC report detailed that in the first nine months of the Trump presidency, media outlets spent a mind-boggling one thousand minutes of coverage on this fake-news fiasco.[43]

> The media possesses a particularly interesting ability to mock Christians about their faith yet remain strangely silent about Islam.

At the same time, just three minutes and twenty-one seconds of evening news coverage was dedicated to the actual fact-based Clinton uranium scandal, which details how then-Secretary Clinton's foundation received over thirty-one million dollars in payments prior to the US State Department granting a Kremlin-controlled company control over US uranium production.[44]

The media's obsessive desire to distract Americans from their humiliating defeat on Election Day in 2017 by chasing a fake Russian collusion story places their blatant bias on full display. It also shows that the American people should not plan for the radical Left to go away quietly. They are willing to fight tooth and nail for control of this nation, and giving up their media stronghold due to one election is not going to happen. Patriotic Americans need to take note of this and consider the motivations behind Russian investigation reporting and any other story that helps them demonize President Trump or anyone else standing in the way of their agenda to control this nation.

GEORGE SOROS

Where does this ideology stem from? Who is pulling the strings behind this propaganda operation? As usual, just follow the money.

Mainstream media sugar daddy George Soros has spent more than $48 million funding mainstream media outlets since 2003.[45] Soros achieves his goal for media control by funneling money from his notorious Open Society Foundations to news corporations, journalism schools, and industry organizations.

Soros is one of the richest men in the world with a net worth of billions. In a December 20, 1998, CBS's *60 Minutes* interview with Steve Kroft, Soros admitted to helping to confiscate property for the Nazis in Hungary during World War II with no guilt. Below is a transcript of Soros' comments.[46]

> KROFT: My understanding is that you went out with this protector of yours who swore that you were his adopted godson.
>
> SOROS: Yes. Yes.
>
> KROFT: Went out, in fact, and helped in the confiscation of property from the Jews.
>
> SOROS: That's right. Yes.
>
> KROFT: That, that sounds like an experience that would send lots of people to the psychiatric couch for many, many years. Was it difficult?
>
> SOROS: Not—not at all. Not at all. Maybe as a child you don't—you don't see the connection. But it was—it created no—no problem at all.
>
> KROFT: No feeling of guilt?
>
> SOROS: No.

KROFT: For example that, "I'm Jewish and here I am, watching these people go. I could just as easily be there. I should be there." None of that?

SOROS: Well, of course I c—I could be on the other side or I could be the one from whom the thing is being taken away. But there was no sense that I shouldn't be there, because that was—well, actually, in a funny way, it's just like in markets—that if I weren't there, of course, I wasn't doing it, but somebody else would—would—would be taking it away anyhow. And it was the—whether I was there or not, I was only a spectator, the property was being taken away. So I had no role in taking away that property. So I had no sense of guilt.

Soros' tentacles have engulfed more than thirty top mainstream news outlets, such as NBC, ABC, the *New York Times*, the *Washington Post*, the Associated Press, and others, while stretching even further into so-called "media watchdogs."[47]

For example, Soros has given $600,000 to the Columbia School of Journalism, which publishes *Columbia Journlism Review* (CJR),[48] which gives him influence over what material gets taught. According to CJR, its mission is to be "the most respected voice on press criticism, and it shapes the ideas that make media leaders and journalists smarter about their work."[49]

In other words, CJR, much like other so-called "watchdogs" such as Media Matters and ProPublica that are also under the financial thumb of Soros, seeks to portray itself as the all-knowing judge of what is considered moral and truthful journalism.

This man has been planning future control of the media as well by brainwashing up and coming journalists.

Soros also funds journalism industry associations such as the National Federation of Community Broadcasters, the National Association of Hispanic Journalists, the Committee to Protect Journalists, and others.[50] This spreads his influence as wide as possible.

Mainstream media propagandist Christiane Amanpour is just one of many examples of journalists who engaged in an explicit conflict of interest by sitting too close to Soros. Amanpour once served on the board of directors for the Center for Public Integrity, a leftist media organization funded by Soros' notorious Open Society Foundations.

Amanpour is the epitome of fake neutrality amongst journalists. While accepting an award at the annual 2016 International Press Freedom Awards following the election of President Trump, Amanpour turned up the leftist hyperbole as high as possible and likened President Trump to the Ayatollah of Iran.[51]

I never thought in a million years that I would be standing up here after all the times I participated in this ceremony, appealing really, for the freedom and the safety of American journalists at home. And ladies and gentlemen, those bits from Donald Trump that were in that, in that video basically show us and remind us of the peril that we face...[52]

Never underestimate the ability of journalists to play the victim and pat themselves on the back for fake heroism. They do this because they want to feel important, like that time Brian Williams falsely claimed he was under fire during the Iraq War, which made for great résumé material at MSNBC who hired Williams after his temporary public hiatus.[53]

Amanpour is no different than Williams; she spews lies and overdramatizes reality in order to continue a narrative consistent with her own warped, ideological worldview. It's a view that Republicans are waging a "war on Moslems," that *Charlie Hebdo* terrorists were "activists," and that President Trump is a dictator.[54]

In her speech Amanpour rededicated herself to wearing her bias on her sleeve, seemingly learning absolutely nothing from the election of President Trump. "I believe in being truthful, not neutral,"[55] she said, displaying not only her ability to dance around her own bias, but also her overinflated ego that believes her perception of politics should be everyone else's. She's everything that the Far Left represents in contemporary America—painfully, deceptively biased, politically correct, and egotistical. It's no surprise that an activist disguised as a journalist like her has such deep ties to Soros.

My organization, ACT for America, was one of the main organizations targeted in the Soros-funded "Fear, Inc." report,[56] which attempted to brand a variety of conservative groups as bigoted, including me personally. The report also defended Sharia law, a barbaric system of oppression and violence in the Islamic world, particularly with respect to women and children.

While the Left loves to fancy itself as the great defender of civil liberties such as freedom of speech, thought, and expression, the reality is they shun such concepts, instead pushing one unified leftist message. They push narratives complaining about the influence that money has over politics, yet all the while taking money themselves from progressive activists. Big money!

If journalists were more up-front, they would have to admit numerous uncomfortable connections with groups that push a liberal agenda, many of them funded by George Soros. Pigs will fly before that happens.

Since the rude awakening of 9/11, journalism, in my view, hasn't kept pace with the bloody growth of terrorism and other threats to our way of life. It needs to catch up.

RISE UP AND ACT

When the media reports on these issues, don't take their word for it. Do your own research. And when you find the truth, don't just change the channel and move on. ACT!

- Put the media on notice. Hold the media accountable by personally writing to the networks and expressing your disappointment in their coverage, even threatening to write their advertisers and cancel your subscription when necessary.

  Pressuring their advertisers through boycott to withdraw their business is key. The Left has perfected this practice and so should we. News agencies that refuse to tell the truth or cover stories that do not fit their narrative should feel the pain where it hurts—in the pockets. This is a strategy that the Right often avoids because the Right sees this form of protest as an act of authoritarianism.

- Put the advertisers on notice too. With the Left being the only side that advertisers hear from, the values of the majority of Americans are perceived as a tiny minority. We must speak up and let these advertisers hear from the real heart of America for a change, instead of the same politically correct ideologues. ACT for America periodically sends action alerts to members with media and advertiser information to take actions as issue arise.

Chapter 10

CAIR AND THE TERRORIST FRONT-SCHEME

Hidden behind the mask of moderation exists an enemy that seeks our total destruction as both a nation and as a civilization. The Muslim Brotherhood, regarded as the oldest and one of the most important Islamist movements in the world, was founded by Hasan al-Banna in 1928 and stated as its mission, "Allah is our objective; the Prophet is our leader; the Quran is our law; Jihad is our way; dying in the way of Allah is our highest hope."[1]

In the West we honor and respect life. In the Islamic world they honor and respect death…in the cause of Allah.

It was a Muslim Brotherhood offshoot that assassinated Anwar Sadat, the former Egyptian president who signed a peace treaty with Israel. They killed him in cold blood because he was a peacemaker.

Osama bin Laden, 9/11 ringleader Mohamed Atta, the head of al Qaeda Ayman al-Zawahiri, and Islamic State head Abu Bakr al-Baghdadi were all members of the Brotherhood.[2] Recognizing this, two of the most powerful countries in the Middle East—Egypt and Saudi Arabia—have designated the Muslim Brotherhood a terrorist organization. When Saudi Arabia considers you a terrorist organization, that is saying something profound.

What makes the Brotherhood particularly dangerous is that in addition to being one of the most influential Islamic terrorist organizations, it is also one of the most educated. Bin Laden was an engineer, al-Zawahiri a surgeon, and al-Baghdadi is a doctor of philosophy. We are not dealing with your average, low IQ, rent-a-jihadist when it comes to the Muslim Brotherhood.

THE PROJECT

In 1982 the Brotherhood wrote a plan for radical Islam to infiltrate and dominate the West and "establish an Islamic power [government] on earth."[3] In counter-terrorism circles it became known as "The Project." This was followed up in 1991 with a memorandum on "the General Strategic Goal for the Group in North America."[4]

The most terrifying aspect of the plan for North America is that it outlines a much more deceptive, long-term approach to infiltrate the West than the blatant calls to "slay the infidels" that we hear from ISIS or chants of "death to America" that we hear from Iran's Hassan Rouhani. The memorandum outlines in crystal clarity the Brotherhood's intentions to destroy America from within. They endeavor to do this by infiltrating the media, government, and educational systems of Western countries. An entire section talks about "settlement" as a means for achieving their end.[5]

They're not talking about a movement dedicated to protecting the Islamic world from perceived Western aggression. What they're talking about is a lifelong mission to infiltrate, attack, and destroy all civilizations that are not Islamic.

> In the West we honor and respect life. In the Islamic world they honor and respect death.

Judging by the events that have taken place in the past two decades across the Western world, "The Project" is advancing rapidly, and so is the memorandum for North America. The Brotherhood has already established successful front groups within the United States, posing as moderate Islamic advocacy groups, most notably the Council American Islamic Relations (CAIR).

CAIR has successfully and deeply embedded itself within our society. Its influence stretches from our schools, to the media, and to the highest levels of government. This happened in spite of the fact that it was named as an unindicted coconspirator in the largest terrorist financing trial in American history and is currently recognized as a terrorist organization by the Islamic, Sharia-abiding UAE.[6]

To understand CAIR's true mission, it is essential to understand how and why it was formed. So how did they go about accomplishing their mission?

THE MEETING

In 1993 members of the Muslim Brotherhood–affiliated Palestinian terrorist organization Hamas held a meeting in Philadelphia to discuss how to prevent peace in the Middle East in opposition to the Oslo Accords.[7]

Remember, it is a fundamentally important concept of the Muslim Brotherhood to keep tensions inflamed in the Middle East, particularly between Jews and Muslims. What they didn't know was that the FBI was recording their nefarious plans to conceal their plot from the federal government.

Those attending the meeting endorsed jihad and discussed the strategic advantages of lobbying in the United States. "We should assist them in this task. This will be an entrance for us to put, through the Islamic community, pressure on the Congress and the decision makers in America," one attendee exclaimed.[8]

They also discussed the importance of sublimating their message and watering it down to fit an American audience. They knew that flying below the radar was crucial to advancing their true agenda. The following are direct statements from a conversation that included CAIR's founders, Omar Ahmad and Nihad Awad, as recorded by the FBI:[9]

Nihad Awad: What is important is that the language of the address is there even for the American. But, the issue is how to use it.

Omar Ahmad: There is a difference between you saying, "I want to restore the '48 land' and when you say, "I want to destroy Israel."

Nihad Awad: Yes, there are different but parallel types of address. There shouldn't be contradiction. Address people according to their minds.

When I speak with the American, I speak with someone who doesn't know anything. As for the Palestinian who has a martyr brother or something, I know how to address him, you see?

CAIR was born less than a year later to fulfill the purposes discussed in this meeting in Philadelphia of pursuing a stealth jihad within the United States. Almost a decade later, both of these men said they couldn't remember having attended the meeting, but their deception was irrelevant given the recordings.

Rafeeq Jaber, one of CAIR's other cofounders, served as president of the Islamic Association of Palestine (IAP). The IAP was dissolved in 2004 after it was shown to have been functioning as a propaganda and fund-raising arm of Hamas. When the Muslim Brotherhood leader in Gaza formally established Hamas in 1987, the IAP became its mouthpiece in North America, much like CAIR is today.[10]

The IAP described itself as "a not-for-profit, public-awareness, educational, political, social, and civic, national grassroots organization dedicated to advancing a just, comprehensive, and eternal solution to the cause of Palestine and suffrages of the Palestinians."[11] How noble.

CAIR describes its current mission as one "to enhance understanding of Islam, encourage dialogue, protect civil liberties, empower American Muslims, and build coalitions that promote justice and mutual understanding."[12] How familiar.

FRIENDS IN LOW PLACES

A decade after the meeting in Philadelphia, federal prosecutors charged the Holy Land Foundation for Relief and Development (HLF), a terrorist front-scheme, with providing material support for Hamas. This trial turned out to be the largest terrorist financing trial in American history and showed that the IAP—CAIR's parent organization—played a central role in the Muslim Brotherhood's Palestine Committee.

In a 2003 civil deposition CAIR cofounder and former IAP president Rafeeq Jaber acknowledged IAP's contract with HLF required them "to promote [HLF] in every way we can."[13] The Holy Land Foundation trial exposed the terrifying Muslim Brotherhood memo on the General Strategic Goal for the Group in North America, which read:

> The process of settlement is a "Civilization-Jihadist Process" with all the word means. The Ikhwan must understand that their work in America is a kind of grand Jihad in eliminating and destroying the Western civilization from within and "sabotaging" its miserable house by their hands and the hands of the believers so that it is eliminated and God's religion is made victorious over all other religions. Without this level of understanding, we are not up to this challenge and have not prepared ourselves for Jihad yet. It is a Muslim's destiny to perform Jihad and work wherever he is and wherever he lands until the final hour comes, and there is no escape from that destiny except for those who chose to slack.[14]

CAIR was also named as an unindicted coconspirator in this trial.

Declining an opportunity to distance CAIR from IAP in September 2003 Senate testimony, CAIR Executive Director Nihad Awad opted instead to defend the group as "a grassroots organization which continues to function legally and has only been 'linked' through allusion and no charge of criminality has been brought against the organization."[15] He can deny it all he wants, but time and time again Awad and his terrorist pals were caught red-handed providing support for terrorism and pursuing civilization jihad through stealthy means within the United States.

When they were asked during a 2003 civil deposition if HLF ever gave CAIR any money, Omar Ahmaad, one of CAIR's founding members, lied and said no.

CAIR's Executive Director Nihad Awad also initially denied having received any money from HLF.[16] But after a copy of HLF's five thousand dollar check was produced at the hearing, Awad was forced to walk back his deception in a supplemental testimony and acknowledge having received money. But you can explain, right Nihad?

CAIR's ties to the Holy Land Foundation were even deeper. They also cosponsored multiple fund-raisers for the terrorist financing organization, even after the US Agency for International Development (USAID) announced plans to terminate HLF's USAID registration due to its shady ties.[17]

CAIR even used 9/11 as a means of raising money for their terrorist pals when they posted a plea on their website shortly after the deadliest terror attacks in world history. Under the heading "What you can do for the victims of the WTC and Pentagon attacks," a link titled "Donate to the NY/DC Emergency Relief Fund" took users to the HLF website.[18] The use of 9/11 to raise money for an Islamic terrorist organization shows how deep their hatred for the United States runs.

Foreign money with extremist ties has flowed into CAIR like the Rio Grande, much of it from Saudi Arabia. Sources include the Islamic Development Bank, which donated $250,000 to CAIR for their headquarters in DC, as well as Saudi Prince Al-Waleed bin Talal, who donated to $500,000.[19]

CAIR has also received money from Saudi-funded organizations with terror ties, such as the International Relief Organization (IRO), which was raided twice by the FBI as part of a terrorist financing investigation, as well as the World Assembly of Muslim Youth (WAMY), whose Washington, DC, office was once headed by Osama bin Laden's nephew Abdullah bin Laden.[20]

WAMY not only committed to supporting CAIR to construct a $3.5 million headquarters in Washington, DC, in 1999, but they worked together on a $1 million public relations campaign in 2002.[21]

In fact, the FBI was investigating bin Laden's family connections to terrorism years before 9/11 but were strangely told to "back off" of the bin Ladens due to political pressure. FBI agents said their investigations into the bin Ladens were "effectively killed."[22] In other words, somebody with big money to spend on Capitol Hill didn't like the investigation of their pals the bin Ladens or the Saudis.

CAIR, being financially and ideologically connected to WAMY, would have a tremendous interest in keeping the FBI as far away from the bin Ladens as possible. With their lobbying headquarters in DC and connections with lawmakers, their power would certainly have been useful had they been asked by the bin Ladens or the Saudi government to help kill the investigation.

What's that they say about the company you keep? That's an awfully lengthy track record of terror-tied alliances to be merely coincidental, don't you think?

IF HE TALKS LIKE A TERRORIST...

CAIR's cofounder and current executive director, Nihad Awad, explicitly stated in a 1994 speech at Barry University in Miami, Florida: "I am in support of the Hamas movement."[23] Hamas had committed multiple terrorist attacks before this ringing endorsement by Awad, including the stabbing of five civilians in Jerusalem in 1989,[24] the kidnapping and murder of a border policeman in 1992, and bus bombings in both 1993 and 1994, which killed at least fourteen people.[25]

Two years prior to Awad's endorsement, the US State Department declared that "various elements of Hamas have used both political and violent means including terrorism, to pursue the goal of establishing an Islamic Palestinian State in place of Israel....Other elements, operating clandestinely, have advocated and used violence to advance their goals."[26]

But CAIR'S official support for Hamas didn't stop there and would continue even after the 1995 executive order by President Clinton, which designated Hamas as a terrorist organization. Then executive director of CAIR-NY, Ghazi Khankan, said in a 2001 speech that "the people of Hamas who direct their attacks on the Israeli military are in the correct position." Considering that virtually every Israeli is inducted into the military or reserves at age eighteen, CAIR-NY was perfectly fine with terror attacks directed at every adult Israeli.[27]

While responding to an Anti-Defamation League request for a statement directly condemning Hamas, CAIR responded by saying, "It's not our job to go around denouncing, that when they say jump, we say how high."[28] How poetic.

Asked in a 2003 deposition whether he supported Hamas, Omar Ahmad, the other CAIR incorporator from the Philadelphia tapes stated, "It depends. Qualify 'support.'"[29] How hard is it to take a position on an anti-Semitic terrorist organization that targets civilians? If you're an official at CAIR, do you need multiple choice?

CAIR even fumbled an opportunity to stand in solidarity with the United States—and humanity, for that matter—by speaking out against the actions of the 9/11 hijackers and those who participated in the deadliest terrorist attack in world history. Immediately after 9/11, CAIR-NY executive director Ghazi Khankan said that "many of the names of the terrorists are people impersonating innocent Muslims and Arabs," peddling a conspiracy theory about a media plot to discredit Muslims.[30]

CAIR's spokesman Ibrahim Hooper shamefully yet unsurprisingly hesitated to blame al Qaeda for 9/11. "We condemn the attacks on the buildings," he told leftist Salon.com in an interview. "If Osama bin Laden was behind it, we condemn him by name." He was then asked why he used the term *if*, and he responded that he resented the question.[31]

Not only has CAIR continually rejected such opportunities to condemn even the most appalling terrorist attacks, they've instead attacked those who do condemn them. In 1997 an Arab American terrorist named Ahmed Hamida deliberately drove his car into a crowd of Israelis at a Jerusalem bus stop. Even after Hamas took credit for the attack, CAIR attacked the US government for failing to "seek justice" for the death of the terrorist, who they described as an innocent "Palestinian-American Muslim."[32]

CAIR also specializes in attacking any and all media outlets that point out their extremist history, even those on the traditional Left. They condemned the leftist magazine *The Atlantic Monthly* after it published an article about the militant Islamic rule and oppression in Sudan, labeling them "anti-Muslim" and accusing them of ignoring "non-Islamic causes of Sudan's turmoil."[33]

They also attacked the *Dallas Morning News* for exposing Hamas infrastructure embedded within Texas,[34] *Reader's Digest* for describing the repression of Christians by Islamists in an article called "The Global War on Christians,"[35] and *The Journal of the American Medical Association* for an article about the victims of terrorism.[36] Right, because we all know how Islamophobic the mainstream press and health care industry are.

CAIR attacked human rights advocate Nat Hentoff for columns written that criticized Louis Farrakhan, Jesse Jackson, and others for failing to speak out against slavery in Sudan. CAIR national communications director Ibrahim Hooper wrote, "Perhaps this hesitancy results from a reluctance to indulge in politically and religiously motivated sensationalism that plays on and amplifies existing Islamophobic tendencies in Western society."[37] In other words, CAIR is keeping well in line with the Muslim Brotherhood playbook to refrain from any statements that could be construed to harm Islam in any way.

CAIR even launched a relentless, two-year campaign targeting Paramount Pictures for originally planning to portray the terrorists in the movie *The Sum of All Fears* as Muslims. Paramount caved and switched the terrorists to neo-Nazis.[38] Whether this was the result of Paramount's penchant for political correctness or executives simply not wanting to have to worry about their studio being bombed while at work, CAIR's cries of Islamophobia were met with surrender.

CAIR continues these same tactics today, with cliché cries of Islamophobia and attempts to silence those who threaten to expose them or stand in their way. In response to a resoundingly patriotic tribute to fallen American soldier and hero Chris Kyle, portrayed in the movie *American Sniper* by Bradley Cooper, CAIR posted a *Guardian*-published story on Facebook called, "The real American Sniper was a hate-filled killer." "Why are simplistic patriots treating him as a hero?"[39]

That's the type of vile poison CAIR likes to peddle about anyone who loves America and applauds our men and women in uniform who fight every day to keep us safe. The story and caption still stand today on CAIR's Facebook page.

AIDING THE ENEMY

Before the 2016 presidential election, US intelligence officials alerted joint terrorism task forces about the possibility that al Qaeda could be planning terrorist attacks for Election Day.[40] CAIR-DFW Director Alia Salem, who had received information that joint terrorism task forces were trying to investigate the matter, took directly to social media to warn the Muslim community.

Salem posted a video advising Muslims to be aware of their civil rights when it comes to talking with the FBI. "The FBI is important and serves an important role in America," she said. "We're not here to inhibit their work, but to prepare the community in how to address [investigators]."[41]

Here's a question, why in the world would anyone who is not a terrorist need specific instructions from CAIR, or anyone else for that matter, about how to talk to terrorist investigators at the FBI? You'd think that normal, moderate Muslims would want to help the FBI in finding out more information, so as to possibly prevent the death of innocent Americans, right?

Apparently, CAIR didn't think so. Salem went on to advise all Muslims not to speak to the FBI without an attorney present and to call CAIR for any additional help, because CAIR would provide them an attorney for free![42] This is exactly the type of dangerous hindrance that can easily result in innocent lives lost, but it's also one of the things CAIR does best.

The FBI was investigating a serious threat to civilians. While you'd think that any reasonable person, regardless of faith, would want to do all they could to help, CAIR was right there to prevent the FBI from obtaining critical information necessary. You don't need a lawyer to give information about a national security issue unless you've got something to hide. It seems for CAIR, their only interest is protecting those who do rather than those who don't.

IF YOU CAN'T BEAT THEM, SILENCE THEM

CAIR issued an open letter to 2016 Republican presidential candidates on diversity, tolerance, and "how to avoid the past mistakes other Republican candidates have made when making remarks about and engaging with the American Muslim community."[43] The letter read in part:

> Promoting Islamophobia and false anti-Muslim conspiracies to prove conservative bona fides and attract support from the GOP base in a presidential bid is a failing strategy....
>
> Making anti-Muslim remarks will not get a campaign the "good" attention it needs to make a run for president. Such remarks do not go unnoticed by watchdogs and turn away independent or undecided voters....
>
> Republican candidates should invest similar resources in courting Muslim voters as they do other minority communities. The American Muslim community is well positioned to impact election results in key swing states such as Ohio, Virginia and Florida.[44]

This is exactly the type of political intimidation CAIR specializes in. The letter went on to warn Republicans:

> CAIR advises that by not giving a platform to Islamophobia, holding accountable those candidates that do use their campaigns to foster anti-Muslim sentiment and making a concerted effort to engage Muslim voters, your campaign and the Republican Party will be closer to its presidential aspirations.[45]

Another CAIR document states:

> Association with anti-Muslim movements or rhetoric discredits those who put themselves forward seeking to earn the privilege of public service.[46]

CAIR also praised New Jersey Governor Chris Christie for speaking out against "Islamophobic criticism of his nomination of Sohail Mohammed as a New Jersey Superior Court judge." At the time Christie said, "This Sharia law business is just crap. It's just crazy, and I'm tired of dealing with the crazies."[47]

The result? Christie barely garnered single-digit support throughout the campaign, while tough, truth-talking, then-candidate Trump steamrolled his way to the nomination and eventually the Oval Office.

The American people are tired of the cliché cries of "Islamophobia" from organizations like CAIR, which have no credibility whatsoever to identify who is and is not an extremist. They lost that privilege upon their inception as a terrorist-front scheme, and their nefarious history is now catching up to them.

It's also no surprise that CNN's *Anderson Cooper 360°*, National Public Radio (NPR), the Southern Poverty Law Center, and the Soros-funded Center for American Progress made CAIR's praise list.[48]

As for Fox News, CAIR launched an attack, quoting results of the Public Religion Research Institute.

> There is a strong correlation between trusting Fox News and negative views of Islam and Muslims. This pattern is evident even among conservative political and religious groups.[49]

You can see where this is going. CAIR knows they don't stand a chance at winning over the minds of Americans without total control of the media. Consequently, they give a pat on the back to those who repeat their talking points almost verbatim and attempt to silence those who challenge them by labeling them "Islamophobic" or "anti-Muslim." As a matter of fact, CAIR has a backgrounder on me personally that they continually, sometimes almost weekly, send to the media. They have perfected the art of shaping the conversation regarding any critic. The media across the board uses CAIR's backgrounder as they write articles about my organization and me, including the SPLC and the ADL. They literally use it verbatim.

While terrorism experts like me who happen to also be survivors of terrorism do not have any budgets, CAIR has millions at its disposal not only from overseas donors, but under the Obama administration from our own government through grants. They've consistently dodged and weaved their way out of their direct ties to terrorism and continued to try to strong-arm their enemies into submission.

For those who do not submit or sit silent, a target will be placed on their backs until they do. In 2013 CAIR made one of many attempts to stop me from speaking at a high school in Minnesota. "As Little Falls High School would not and should not allow a racist or an anti-Semitic speaker to use its facilities, we ask that school and district officials apply the same standard to an anti-Muslim speaker," said CAIR-MN executive director Lori Saroya.[50]

Aside from the irony of this coming from a notoriously anti-Semitic, terror-designated organization, the term *anti-Muslim* is a strategic weapon CAIR likes to use as a defense for Islamic radicalism. "By allowing the school to host this event, the perception is that the school is endorsing hate speech and anti-Muslim views. This perception could have a negative impact on the learning environment for Muslim students."[51]

> As I am a woman, it's offensive to radical Islamists for me to walk around without a hijab, let alone speak my mind in opposition to the spread of global jihad.

CAIR despises me for a whole host of reasons. For one, I'm privy to their terrorist front-scheme and intent on exposing their destructive intentions to all who will listen—most importantly, the United States government and law enforcement.

Secondly, I'm an Arab-Christian woman, hitting the trifecta of animosity amongst radical Islamic men. They despise my Middle Eastern ethnicity because it prevents them from labeling me a racist, as they do to any who are critical of them and do not share the same Arabic mother tongue as most radical Islamists.

Add to the fact that I am not a Muslim but a Christian, which makes me an infidel worthy of death through their radical Islamic lenses. It's the same reason my home in Lebanon was blown up by jihadists when I was a young girl.

As I am a woman, it's offensive to radical Islamists for me to walk around without a hijab, let alone speak my mind in opposition to the spread of global jihad. All of these things make me, as well as the organization I represent, ACT for America, a primary target for CAIR.

I founded ACT for America in the aftermath of 9/11 for the specific purpose of defending America and the Western, Judeo-Christian values on which it was founded and make it the "shining city upon a hill" it was appropriately characterized as by President Reagan. We are now nearly one million members strong, and our organization is far and away the largest and most powerful grassroots national security organization in America.

This in mind, when our organization held a nationwide March Against Sharia in the summer of 2017, CAIR went apoplectic. Sharia law is a system of Islamic law that justifies the killing of innocent women and homosexuals, spousal rape, FGM, and many other human rights atrocities.

CAIR appallingly yet completely unsurprisingly objected to this march. Not only that, they called to have the march shut down in the public forum, exposing themselves for the anti-freedom Islamic extremists that they are. Using a predictable yet baseless tactic, CAIR insinuated that ACT for America is an anti-Muslim, white-nationalist, neo-Nazi hate group.[52] Right, because we all know how well it would go over with a bunch of racist skinheads with swastika tattoos to have an Israel-loving, brown-skinned Arab woman leading their organization.

This is not to mention that we actually had Muslims speaking at our rallies, including one organizing and leading it in Georgia.[53] The truth is, it's CAIR who has all too much in common with neo-Nazis and the Ku Klux Klan, considering they're all terrorist organizations who despise the nation of Israel.

Our March Against Sharia turned out to be a resounding success, despite protests and online intimidation from CAIR and their useful leftist allies.

CAIR's former media stronghold has been steadily evaporating since the creation of Facebook, Twitter, and other forms of information. No longer can they hide so easily behind their victim cards and rehearsed talking points, nor silence those who speak the truth about the threat they pose to America.

PURGING FBI TRAINING MANUALS

CAIR also has led the charge in purging critically necessary national security education manuals of important language regarding radical Islam. It has done so by uniting with other radical Islamic front groups and anti-Semitic Muslim advocacy groups in an effort to put as much intimidating pressure on government agencies as possible.

On February 8, 2012, former FBI director Robert Mueller held a meeting with a variety of radical Islamic front groups with ties to terrorism, including CAIR and others like the Islamic Society of North America (ISNA) and the notoriously anti-Semitic Muslim Public Affairs Council (MPAC)[54]—all Muslim Brotherhood front groups dedicated to destroying our civilization from within. In doing this, they used fools such as Barack Hussein Obama, Eric Holder, and the entire leftist administration.

Mueller assured those attending the meeting that FBI training manuals had been scrubbed of all language that could be considered "offensive" to Muslims. ISNA, along with CAIR, was named as an unindicted coconspirator in the Holy Land Foundation trial prior to this meeting with Mueller.[55]

MPAC bragged about its meeting with Mueller on their website and declared publicly that the FBI's proposed training changes were a "welcomed first step in ensuring that such a mistake does not occur again," and actually had the nerve to demand a formal statement from Mueller "acknowledging the negative impact of these training manuals on the Muslim American Community."[56]

The Department of Defense also purged educational materials when Joint Chiefs Chairman Gen. Martin E. Dempsey ordered the entire US military to review and purge all materials that members of the armed services were studying that could be deemed "disrespectful of the Islamic religion."[57]

MPAC responded with an appalling statement that read, "While we are spending treasures in both lives and finances overseas trying to win hearts and minds, here at home we are training our young servicemen and women to fill their hearts and minds with hate."[58]

Even Mueller himself had previously acknowledged the Muslim Brotherhood is a group that supports terrorism in the US and overseas, yet decided to cater to groups with explicit ties to it.[59] The Mueller FBI investigated a tip from Russia about Boston Marathon bomber Tamerlan Tsarnaev, who attended the Islamic Society of Boston, known to be associated with multiple terrorists, but that apparently made little difference.[60]

Mueller's agent did "outreach" there but said he was not aware that the mosque was started by a prominent terrorist financier.[61] He also refused to allow his agents to receive education on how radical mosques could be promoting and protecting terrorists, which Islamic countries such as the UAE, Jordan, Bahrain, and other countries do regularly to deter terrorism.[62] But perhaps Mueller would say that these are "Islamophobic" nations.

The Mueller FBI's willingness to include radical Islamic groups, even those under current investigation by his own department, gave legitimacy to these groups, and an influential say over what could or could not be taught by law enforcement. Mueller's actions have had a widespread effect because many local law enforcement agencies followed the FBI's lead in allowing Islamic groups like CAIR to dictate what anti-terrorism material could be used to train officers.

Police departments in three Illinois cities—Lombard, Elmhurst, and Highland Park—canceled a counterterrorism course called "Islamic Awareness as a Counter-Terrorist Strategy" over accusations from CAIR that the instructor is anti-Muslim.[63] The New York Police Department has engaged in purging training manuals for law enforcement officers for potentially offensive language toward Muslims.[64] This is what CAIR is systematically doing all across America to prevent law enforcement from cracking down on Muslim extremism.

This is the type of political and legal intimidation that makes CAIR so dangerous to national security. To allow them access to public officials or any government agency is letting the fox inside the henhouse.

In reality CAIR has been and is still currently designated as a terrorist organization by the UAE. The suggestion that attacks against CAIR are racist or Islamophobic are simply an absurd defense for a defenseless and dangerous organization.

Unless allies of CAIR in the media, government, and community are prepared to call the United Arab Emirates government "Islamophobic," they better get smart about the irrefutable ties to terrorism this organization has in both its past and present. In the long run CAIR is going down, along with any of those who stand with it.

RISE UP AND ACT

When you wonder what they're teaching at your community's local school or college, don't just wring your hands and sigh. ACT!

- Call the school and find out if CAIR has a program with the school or has any representative speaking to your children. If they do, make sure you print a backgrounder on CAIR found on our website, www.actforamerica.org, and take it with you to meet with the principal of the school. Tell them that as a concerned parent you want to understand why the school would invite an organization that the FBI has severed relations with for its connection to terrorism. Be polite and respectful.

- Contact your local state legislator and send them a backgrounder on CAIR specifically at the beginning of the legislative session before CAIR has its lobby day or what is now known as "Muslim Advocacy Day" in state capitals.

- Call and email your federal representatives and express to them how disturbed you are that a known Muslim Brotherhood affiliate that has been designated as a terrorist organization by the UAE, has had many of its leaders and members convicted of terrorism charges, and even had the FBI sever its relations with, is still allowed to raise money and lobby politicians on Capitol Hill. Ask them to support the designation of both CAIR and the Muslim Brotherhood as terrorist organizations.

Chapter 11

THE LEFTIST-ISLAMIST COALITION

AS I MENTIONED in an earlier chapter, it has been almost two decades since 9/11, but unfortunately America is no safer. This is due in large part to a treasonous enemy that constantly carries water for those who oppose our very existence. If you think this enemy resides across an ocean or border, think again.

On one hand we are struggling to ward off attacks from radical Islamists who seek to destroy both our nation and way of life at any cost. This enemy is a foreign one and brings its destructive and deadly worldview to our society from abroad.

The other enemy we are fighting is more treasonous in nature due to its American roots. This American enemy, which gives aid to our foreign ones, does so in the name of politically correct terms such as *diversity*, *tolerance*, and *fairness*. I'm speaking, of course, about the radical Left.

This unholy alliance formed between the Far Left and radical Islam has made fighting the war on terror tremendously more difficult, resulting in incalculable loss of life. Far Left groups are regularly working with Islamic organizations such as CAIR, ISNA, and others to prevent almost every common-sense intelligence and security measure that will secure the country from terrorist attacks from taking hold.

These leftists have been colluding with Islamists on everything from cutting human intelligence to monitoring mosques and blocking the training of counter-terrorism agents on signs of Islamic radicalism to smearing their enemies with accusations of "Islamophobia," and the list goes on and on. There is perhaps no greater example of this relationship than that which exists between CAIR and the American Civil Liberties Union (ACLU).

The ACLU functions as CAIR's legal attack dog, filing lawsuits against anyone who gets in the way of CAIR's radical agenda. For example, the ACLU teamed up with CAIR's Washington chapter to have State Department advertisements removed from local city buses that they felt "stigmatized Muslims as terrorists."[1]

The ads were meant to promote rewards for those who were able to help the State Department find wanted terrorists.[2] Something you'd think peaceful, moderate Muslims along with every other patriotic American would want to do. Of course, CAIR is no moderate-Muslim organization, and the ACLU couldn't care less about protecting the homeland.

CAIR didn't like that the ads featured pictures of Muslims, so with the help of their comrades at the ACLU, they threw a fit and the State

Department caved and took down the ads. Wait a minute, we have to take down ads that accurately depict the profiles of most wanted terrorists simply so we don't offend a radical Islamic terror-linked organization?

Is it our fault that the most wanted terrorists happen to be Muslims? Is the ACLU going to sue the next Hollywood film studio who makes a film about 9/11 and depicts the hijackers as Muslims? Maybe in the ACLU-approved version the hijackers can be white supremacists who voted for Trump.

And what about criminal sketch artists? Are they going to sue every police department that accurately sketches and reports the racial and ethnic makeup of a suspect? You can't make this stuff up.

CAIR can always count on the ACLU to help intimidate their opponents legally. That's why CAIR-WA gave the ACLU their "Civil Libertarian Award" for their efforts in helping get the most wanted terrorist ads taken down. It was just one of many times CAIR and the ACLU got together to pat themselves on the back for weakening the nation.

CAIR's Washington chapter worked side by side with the ACLU to try to prevent the FBI from properly investigating terrorist recruitment. The executive director of CAIR's Washington state chapter, Arsalan Bukhari, has been quoted as saying, "There's nothing to gain from talking to law enforcement."[3] Encouraging Muslims to say nothing to the police is par for the course with CAIR, which is on constant lookout nationwide to make sure authorities cannot do their job properly.

For example, CAIR repeatedly railroaded a Somali community leader from Minnesota named Abdirizak Bihi after he began to warn law enforcement about the dangers of radicalization within the Minnesota area.[4] When al-Shabaab terrorists launched a terror attack on a mall in Nairobi, Kenya, it was determined that Minnesota residents (Somali Americans) were among those who participated in the attacks.

Bihi was particularly outraged because he had been warning law enforcement for years about this threat but was silenced and slandered by CAIR's go-to "Islamophobia" defense. That's right, CAIR accused a Somali community leader—whose nephew joined the Islamic terrorist organization al-Shabaab—of being Islamophobic, and it worked!

The FBI and Justice Department, whom Bihi had been working with to stem radicalization, cut ties with him during the Obama administration. Bihi told the Daily Caller in an interview:

> They lie about my life most of the time and try to destroy my character, my capability, and my trust in the community.[5]

This is exactly what CAIR and their leftist cohorts at the ACLU do to anyone who stands in their way, even Muslims.

It's good that not all Muslims agree with CAIR and the ACLU's effort to protect Islamic extremists, but how can these moderate voices ever be heard when smear merchants at the ACLU, who are supposed to support the civil liberties of all citizens, bully them into silence? Former Muslim Brotherhood member Abdur-Rahman Muhammad said it best when he noted:

> This loathsome term [*Islamophobia*] is nothing more than a thought-terminating cliché conceived in the bowels of Muslim think tanks for the purpose of beating down critics.[6]

When they're not intimidating law enforcement agencies and moderate Muslims, CAIR and the ACLU enjoy raising money together. Jameel Jaffer, director of the ACLU's Center for Democracy, served as a keynote speaker at a fund-raiser for CAIR's Michigan chapter along with a man named Kifah Mustapha, who has direct ties to both the Muslim Brotherhood and Hamas.[7] The result? The event brought in a whopping $130,000 for CAIR.

When the US government designated CAIR as unindicted coconspirators in the Holy Land Foundation trial, the ACLU came running and sued in their defense. The ACLU even had the nerve to complain to the court that the terrorist designation of the Holy Land Foundation caused CAIR's "good name to be dragged through the mud."[8] That tends to happen when you are explicitly linked to financing terrorism, but maybe CAIR should've thought of that before they exchanged money with terrorists.[9]

Now you can see why CAIR is fighting so hard today to prevent the Muslim Brotherhood from being designated as a terrorist organization. Even if CAIR wasn't simultaneously designated by the US government along with the Muslim Brotherhood, their donations would dry up like the Sahara.

When Congress expressed concern over CAIR's close involvement with various government agencies given their ties to terrorism, the ACLU was there to provide backup. The ACLU, along with over forty other Far Left groups signed a letter attacking several members of Congress—Rep. Michele Bachmann, Rep. Trent Franks, Rep. Louie Gohmert, Rep. Tom Rooney, and Rep. Lynn Westmoreland—for their inquiry, noting in the letter that the evidence against CAIR was minimal and that their suspicion was highly inappropriate.[10]

It wasn't "tenuous evidence,"[11] it was explicit, and unless every Muslim has connections to Hamas, it's more than just the fact that CAIR was a Muslim group that congressional representatives had serious concerns. If only the Obama administration had some.

Be that as it may, the ACLU's dedication to defending CAIR has had deadly consequences. The ACLU, CAIR, and their radical allies like fake-feminist Linda Sarsour signed an open letter demanding an end to the NYPD's undercover terrorist surveillance program, which kept the city safe in the aftermath of 9/11.[12] The nature of the program was to identify Islamic extremism in the local community using undercover agents as resources. But that went too far for the Islamist-Leftist coalition.

The result? Eventually Mayor Bill de Blasio, who is, in my opinion, the biggest misfortune to ever befall New York City's mayoral office, disbanded the program in the name of politically correct insanity.

And get this, the ACLU's lawsuit even resulted in the creation of a civilian position to act as a watchdog against, get ready for it—unwarranted spying by the NYPD.[13] The NYPD! Not as a watchdog against terrorists, but against those watching the terrorists!

Ladies and gentlemen, I give you the ACLU.

> We now live in a backward society where oppression of women is protected by so-called "feminists," while those fighting to liberate women from the oppression of Sharia law are portrayed as bigots.

This catering to the objections of radical leftists and Islamists would prove to have fatal consequences after a man named Sayfullo Saipov, an Islamic immigrant from Uzbekistan, drove into unsuspecting civilians on a Manhattan sidewalk, mowing down cyclists and runners along a New York City bike path and leaving eight people dead.

After being shot and arrested, police found an ISIS flag in Saipov's truck. Later, while receiving medical treatment at the hospital, the terrorist bragged about those he had killed.[14]

Saipov's mosque was under surveillance by the New York Police Department starting in 2005 as part of the program that CAIR, the ACLU, and Sarsour helped to disband.[15] The surveillance program was discontinued in 2014. There are deadly consequences to catering to these anti-American forces, and this tragic case illustrates it all too well.

LINDA SARSOUR

While self-important celebrities like Madonna marched on Washington, DC, wearing hats meant to symbolize female genitalia, Ayaan Hirsi Ali and I were fighting to prevent girls from having their genitalia removed. Astoundingly, an anti-Semitic Sharia supporter like Linda Sarsour, whom I mentioned in chapter 8, can posture herself as a feminist without so much as a peep from leftists who market themselves as the great defenders of women.

We now live in a backward society where oppression of women is protected by so-called "feminists," while those fighting to liberate women from the oppression of Sharia law are portrayed as bigots. Leftist organizations and their pals in the media are active participants in this web of deception and have given Sarsour, a woman with unmistakable connections to terror and blatant racism against Jews, all the legitimacy she needs to secure the title of "feminist."

The ACLU even features a special Linda Sarsour section on their website, helping her spread the message that President Trump is a racist bigot who hates all Muslims and continuing the narrative that America is an oppressive nation. Her ACLU website commentary reads as follows:

> This Administration has kept their promises and unleashed racist inhumane policies targeting communities of color, making previously targeted communities increasingly vulnerable in this new environment. Amidst the chaos, I have held on to an image that fills my heart with hope—the thousands of people who showed up at airports across the country demanding that we let in Muslim immigrants and refugees from countries placed on a ban by Trump. As a Muslim American who has been working to defend the rights of Muslims in the post-9/11 era, this act of solidarity was especially important and meaningful.[16]

The Southern Poverty Law Center (SPLC) is another organization trying to legitimize Sarsour. In response to criticism over her support for Saudi Arabia's treatment of women and support for Sharia law, the SPLC tweeted:

> Islamophobes have been attacking #WomensMarch organizer @lsarsour. We stand with her against this type of hate and bigotry. #IMarchWithLinda[17]

Both Ayaan Hirsi Ali and myself have darker skin than Sarsour and speak fluent Arabic just as she does, but in the eyes of Far-Left outfits like the SPLC, we might as well have white sheets over our heads and be cross-burning Klansmen, simply because of our willingness to speak truthfully about the dangers of Islamic extremism.

That's also why the Far Left holds Sarsour up to be a pioneering feminist, despite her declaring that Ayaan Hirsi Ali and I should have our female reproductive parts removed. On March 8, 2011, Sarsour tweeted this:

> Brigitte Gabriel=Ayaan Hirsi Ali. She's asking 4 an a$$ whippin'. I wish I could take their vaginas away - they don't deserve to be women.[18]

How poetic. She's like an Islamic Robert Frost.

Aside from the fact that I lost my childhood trying to survive relentless Islamic terrorist attacks and Ayaan Hirsi Ali is a victim of FGM herself, in what universe could anyone who tweets such filth about another woman be considered a feminist? Only in the Twilight Zone or the mainstream media bubble.

Glamour Magazine, which you'd think would be focused on things like…glamour, instead decided to jump face-first into the arena of social justice when they named Sarsour, along with the other Women's March organizers, one of their 2017 Women of the Year.[19] Because apparently, nothing says feminism like threatening to remove another woman's reproductive organs, supporting Sharia law, defending Saudi Arabia's treatment of women, spouting anti-Semitism, and hanging out with terrorists.

If she's a feminist, I'm a professional hockey player.

Sarsour is being funded by leftist groups like the SPLC and ACLU to continue spreading her poisonous propaganda. An excerpt from an interview with *Glamour* noted:

> GLAMOUR: Do you feel like there has been enough support from larger institutional bodies for the people doing reactive organizing? I know the rally in downtown Manhattan was put together by some amazing grassroots groups, but most people are focusing on larger organizations like the ACLU. Do you think there will be greater coordination and support coming from the larger groups, or do you feel like you're on your own?

> LS: I haven't seen coordination like this in my 16 years of doing community organizing, both locally and nationally. We absolutely have the support of groups like the ACLU, the Human Rights Campaign, and Planned Parenthood. I was the head of fundraising for the Women's March, and I chose not to take money from corporations. This really worried people on my team, but what we found was that these big organizations really came through for us. Planned Parenthood, for example, was the premier sponsor of the Women's March. And other groups—like the National Resource Defense Council, NARAL, Pro-Choice America, MoveOn.org, the Human Rights Campaign, and even labor unions like 1199, SEIU, and the American Federation of Teachers—came out in support.[20]

Sarsour's response reveals a dangerous web of alliances between Far-Left groups and radical Islamists like her, who have teamed up to fight a mutual enemy, the United States and its Judeo-Christian culture. They raise money together, repeat each other's talking points, and defend one another whenever the other is exposed.

This in spite of the fact that Sarsour has a disgracefully proven track record of anti-Semitism and Islamic radicalism. Following Hurricane Harvey, Sarsour teamed up with a leftist organization called the Texas Organizing Project Education Fund to solicit donations from unsuspecting donors.[21] While people thought they were donating to Hurricane Harvey relief efforts, they were actually giving to a social justice activist organization.

From the fund's website:

> Together we will organize and advocate for our devastated communities, shining a spotlight on inequalities that emerge in the restoration of lives, livelihoods, and homes, amplifying the needs of hard-hit communities, and providing legal assistance for residents wrongfully denied government support.[22]

Not one cent of the money Sarsour solicited went toward lost cars, or other possessions, including devastated homes. Nor did it go toward diapers, food, water, or blood. Instead, the donations went toward leftist community organizing and further dividing the country over race, which both Sarsour and leftists know how to do very well.[23]

Sarsour also discouraged people from donating to the Red Cross, suggesting instead that they contribute to radical leftist organizations.[24] The media predictably said little about this shameful and borderline criminal solicitation to defraud unsuspecting relief donors.

But for those who know her history, Sarsour's actions are not the least bit surprising. On December 9, 2017, the "feminist trailblazer" took to her Facebook account to justify Palestinian terrorism against Israelis:

> Nobody gets to tell an occupied people how to respond to their own oppression and the continued stripping of their humanity, agency and land whether they are Palestinians or not. Nobody. Oppressed people determine how, when and where to resist. They set the parameters. You don't have to agree ...[25]

That's right, Linda. You tell them! No one's going to tell you who you can and can't kill! Of course, not a peep about this from the mainstream media, who seem to have a seizure every time President Trump tweets something they deem even remotely controversial.

But we shouldn't be surprised, given that Linda supports the Nation of Islam and even spoke at the same event as it's anti-Semitic leader, Louis Farrakhan, a man she defends.[26] Speaking at an annual conference for the terror-linked Islamic Society of North America, another unindicted coconspirator in the Holy Land Foundation trial, the Farrakhan fan-girl Sarsour called for jihad against President Trump.

> I hope that we, when we stand up to those who oppress our communities, that Allah accepts from us that as a form of jihad. That we are struggling against tyrants and rulers, not only abroad in the Middle East or on the other side of the world, but here, in these United States of America, where you have fascists, and white supremacists, and Islamophobes reigning in the White House.[27]

Who would have thought after 9/11 we'd have a media-celebrated Islamist calling for jihad against our own president? And yet Sarsour's calls for jihad should not have been surprising, considering she led off her speech by paying tribute to Siraj Wahhaj, her "favorite person in the room."[28] Wahhaj was an unindicted coconspirator in the 1993 World Trade Center bombing and has explicit jihadist ideology.[29]

Equally appalling, Sarsour continued to fan the flames of divisiveness and anti-Westernization by scolding anyone who might try to assimilate or cooperate with law enforcement in weeding out extremism.

> We gotta stay in our lanes. If you are not a communications specialist, then you are not to be advising our community on how to communicate with the rest of the public.[30]

Wait, what does she mean, "the rest of the public"? I thought Muslims were supposed to be part of our American communities? It's almost as if Sarsour is suggesting that they're a separate community that doesn't share our values. She also amped up the animosity even further, implicitly inciting violence to an applauding audience.

> We have to stay outraged. Do not criticize me when I say that we as a Muslim community in these United States of America have to be perpetually outraged every single...when I wake up in the morning, and I remember who's sitting in the White House, I am outraged. This is not normal, Sisters and Brothers. Those people sitting in the most powerful seats in this country is not normal. So, do not ever be those citizens that normalize this administration, because when the day comes that something horrific happens to us or to another community, you will be responsible for normalizing this administration.[31]

Sarsour is also friends with Islamic terrorist Rasmea Odeh and former Hamas operative Salah Sarsour. She also has relatives in prison in Israel on terrorist charges.[32] One of her cousins has spent over twenty-five years in prison in Israel. Her brother-in-law has also been imprisoned for his ties to the terrorist organization Hamas.[33]

What's that they say about the company you keep? Sarsour certainly shares Hamas' hatred for Israel. She once tweeted, "Nothing is creepier than Zionism," and stated that one cannot support Israel and still be considered a feminist.[34]

Of course, in Sarsour's warped mind, one can support Sharia law and still hold the title. Why? Because Israelis are depicted are oppressors by Sarsour and many of her leftist enablers.

A lengthy history of palling around with terrorists and spouting anti-Semitism akin to that of Palestinian terrorists indicates why it's unsurprising that the NYPD eventually opened a "terrorism enterprise investigation" on Sarsour's Arab American Association of New York and even attempted to get an informant on its board.[35]

Sarsour has so many connections to terrorists and their sympathizers that it's almost impossible to keep up with them all. She specializes in attacking the US government as oppressive against Muslims simply for trying to prevent future terrorist attacks. When complaining about the NYPD's surveillance program, she stated:

> We believe that the NYPD informants actually manufacture these cases so they can justify the funding that comes to the NYPD.[36]

And an Al Jazeera article she cowrote with Khaled Beydoun states,

> The value of Arab life—whether nameless Palestinian children bombed by American-funded fighter jets or American youth profiled, questioned and incarcerated for frequenting a particular mosque—is spiraling downwards rapidly in the US and at a more accelerated rate in the Arab World.[37]

As discussed earlier, leftists like Mayor de Blasio caved to pressure from Sarsour and her band of leftist enablers and legal advocates, resulting in the disbanding of the program that was surveilling the mosque of an Islamic terrorist. But according to Sarsour, perhaps that was simply a "manufactured" case of terrorism.

That's not the first time Sarsour used paranoid conspiracy theories to prevent government officials from doing their jobs. When a member of al Qaeda plotted to blow up an airliner using a bomb in his underwear, Sarsour tweeted that she believed the operative was a CIA agent.[38]

But who could blame the poor girl for spouting conspiracy theories? After all, if you spend enough time fangirling over a conspiratorial anti-Semite like Louis Farrakhan, a man who blamed 9/11 on the Jews, you're going to learn a thing or two.[39]

The Left cannot continue to carry water for Islamic extremists and still hold itself up as a defender of human rights and civil liberties.

Whether it's her terrorist relatives, connections to Hamas, blatant anti-Semitism, or preventing law enforcement from doing their jobs, there is absolutely no logical reason for Linda Sarsour to have any type of public legitimacy. The fact that a woman with a track record as damning as hers is allowed to posture herself as a feminist, speak on college campuses, and run activist organizations can only be explained through her allegiances in the media and leftist organizations. Switch her ties to Islamic terrorist groups for ties to white supremacist groups and her anti-Semitism for anti-black racism, and Linda Sarsour would be one of the most notoriously despised individuals in America, and rightfully so.

The Left cannot continue to carry water for Islamic extremists and still hold itself up as a defender of human rights and civil liberties. They must make a choice between radical Islam and the Western world. Given their lengthy history of aligning themselves with radical Islamists, it seems to me they already have.

RISE UP AND ACT

When you hear about extremist theology in your community, don't bury your head in the sand. ACT!

- Write emails and send tweets to any media outlets who give a platform to Linda Sarsour. Reference her proven track record of extremism, which I've outlined in this chapter, and ask why they feel it's appropriate to legitimize her.

- Keep an eye out for any schools hosting Linda Sarsour as a speaker and ask why they feel it's appropriate to host an Islamic extremist with explicit ties to anti-Semites and terrorists.

  Ask your local school board if it is working with any groups to help combat extremism in your community. If they mention partnerships with CAIR, Linda Sarsour, or other radicals, be sure to express your concern that the schools are giving a platform to people linked to terrorism and radical views and explain why such partnerships are so dangerous.

- Support and thank moderate-Muslim voices who reject CAIR, Linda Sarsour, and other radicals, and who speak out against them. We must continue to show moderate voices that they have allies in this fight to rid their communities of extremist ideology.

Chapter 12

THE BUSINESS OF FAKE HATE

O NE OF THE most pervasive and menacing leftist organizations aligning with our nation's enemies in recent years has been the Southern Poverty Law Center (SPLC). This group of terror enablers specializes in smearing and silencing any organization or individual who dares to stray from their politically correct worldview, particularly when it comes to radical Islam.

The SPLC is a vehemently anti-Western attack dog that worships at the altar of multiculturalism yet attempts to portray itself as a neutral arbiter of bigotry. The SPLC was cofounded by a leftist named Morris Dees, who typically solicited donations from top donors seeking to fight the Ku Klux Klan in the Dixie Democratic south.[1] Now that the KKK and white-supremacist groups have such tiny membership levels and Islamic terrorism threatens the free world as we know it, the SPLC needs a new boogeyman to attack in order to raise money.

The SPLC has a particularly dangerous relationship with CAIR, regularly serving as one of their foremost defenders. The most consistent tactic for attacking those they seek to destroy is by falsely labeling their enemies as a "hate group."[2]

The SPLC has a self-identified "hate group list" and "hate map" that it puts out on a regular basis and that it uses to slander those it disagrees with from media to the halls of Congress. In doing this, the SPLC hopes to blacklist its enemies from legitimacy in the public forum of open ideas.[3]

The SPLC knows that the biggest threat to its agenda and that of its radical Islamic allies is information and ideas. Therefore, its only hope is to intimidate its enemies into silence or, if necessary, slander them into it. Essentially the SPLC lives by the motto "By any means necessary" when it comes to destroying their enemies.

We're not simply talking about notable conservatives here. The SPLC is willing to attack anyone, even those who claim to align with them on a majority of issues, if they stray far enough away on the most important ones. Here is the SPLC's Mission Statement:

> The Southern Poverty Law Center is dedicated to fighting hate and bigotry and to seeking justice for the most vulnerable members of our society. Using litigation, education, and other forms of advocacy, the SPLC works toward the day when the ideals of equal justice and equal opportunity will be a reality.[4]

Allow me to translate that with alternate, more truthful wording.

The Southern Poverty Law Center is dedicated to fighting non-leftists and to seeking justice for the most dangerous members of our society. Using litigation, misrepresentation, and intimidation, the SPLC works toward the day when the ideals of equal justice and equal opportunity will only be a reality for those we agree with politically. But truthfully, we hope that day never comes because then we would be out of money.

The SPLC lists a group called White Lives Matter (WLM) as a hate group on its notorious "hate group list." While the label could be fitting for WLM, an organization almost no one has ever heard of before, it is most certainly true about the group Black Lives Matter (BLM), which almost everyone has heard of. But strangely, BLM seems to have escaped the all-knowing SPLC's hate list, further exposing them as a biased and untrustworthy source.

> The SPLC is a vehemently anti-Western attack dog that worships at the altar of multiculturalism yet attempts to portray itself as a neutral arbiter of bigotry.

BLM members have explicitly called for dead cops and the lynching of white people, and they explicitly endorse racial segregation.[5] SPLC President Richard Cohen stated:

> There's no doubt that some protesters who claim the mantle of Black Lives Matter have said offensive things, like the chant "pigs in a blanket, fry 'em like bacon" that was heard at one rally.[6]

First of all, that's not just offensive, it's a death chant, but go ahead, Richard...

> But before we condemn the entire movement for the words of a few, we should ask ourselves whether we would also condemn the entire Republican party for the racist words of its presumptive nominee— or for the racist rhetoric of many other politicians in the party over the course of years.[7]

This desperate attempt by Cohen to explain away his bias and that of his organization is beyond absurd. What this really demonstrates is the soft bigotry of low expectations that radical leftists like Cohen have for minorities. They stand on their heads to excuse the inexcusable, because they don't assign the same standard of moral decency to minorities as they do to whites.

But minorities who object to its agenda are another story. You'd think that an organization like the SPLC, which claims to stand up for the most vulnerable, would be sympathetic to minorities who have accomplished tremendous feats in life, despite suffering from prejudice. But you'd be wrong.

Take the case of Dr. Ben Carson, a black, world-renowned, pediatric brain surgeon. When running for president in 2016, the SPLC placed Carson on its Extremist Watch List because of what the SPLC called "anti-LGBT" views.[8]

Normally when one thinks of an extremist watch list, he'd probably think of Islamic extremists or other domestic terror groups. Bear in mind, Dr. Carson literally spent most of his life removing cancerous tumors from the brains of children.

The SPLC exposed themselves for the frauds that they are when they placed a man with Dr. Carson's character on their useless Extremist Watch List. After receiving epic backlash for their absurd attack on Dr. Carson, the SPLC took Dr. Carson off the list and issued a half-baked apology.

> In October 2014, we posted an "Extremist File" of Dr. Ben Carson. This week, as we've come under intense criticism for doing so, we've reviewed our profile and have concluded that it did not meet our standards, so we have taken it down and apologize to Dr. Carson for having posted it.

But the SPLC still attacked Dr. Carson by placing former statements of his in their equally useless "Extremist Files."

> We've also come to the conclusion that the question of whether a better researched profile of Dr. Carson should or should not be included in our "Extremist Files" is taking attention from the fact that Dr. Carson has, in fact, made a number of statements that express views that we believe most people would conclude are extreme.[9]

Here's one of the quotes made by Dr. Carson that the SPLC found worthy enough for its Extremist Files:

> If you look in the writings of a lot of the neo-Marxists, when they talk about the New World Order, they say there's only one stick in the mud: the United States. How do you get them out of the way, or how do you change them? And they said there were two fundamental things, their Judeo-Christian faith and their strong families. Those were the things that had to be attacked and those things have been systematically attacked over the last several decades.[10]

How "extreme."

For the record, the SPLC makes no mention of terror-tied groups such as CAIR or their anti-Semitic executives on their Extremist Watch List or Extremist Files. (In fact, the SPLC's hate group categories don't even include anti-Semitic.[11]) That's because to the SPLC, anti-Semitism and true hatred is tolerated, as long as it's perpetrated by the right minority group with leftist leanings. But should a minority stray from their PC worldview, the SPLC will rain down on them with extra scrutiny because their ideology contradicts their skin tone.

Take the case of Maajid Nawaz for example. A British Muslim and outspoken critic of President Trump, Nawaz is hardly what one would consider a right winger. However, Nawaz made a critical error in the eyes of the SPLC for his outspoken identification of radical Islam and its anti-human rights atrocities.

The consequence? The SPLC did the bidding of CAIR and attacked Nawaz as a hateful bigot, and their cliché accusations of Islamophobia were served.[12] That's right, accusations of "Islamophobia" about an Arab Muslim who, ironically, was once imprisoned in Egypt for his involvement in a group linked to supporting the establishment of an Islamic caliphate.

Nawaz responded by filing a lawsuit against the SPLC for defamation, which was settled for $3.3 million.[13] He also took to the left-wing HBO program *Real Time With Bill Maher* to address the target put on his back by the SPLC. He told Maher that he was "sick to death...of well-meaning and liberal left-wing, usually white men," who don't allow him to criticize his own religious heritage without being labeled an "anti-Muslim extremist."[14]

Nawaz rightly pointed out that the SPLC is supposedly pro-gay rights, labeling virtually anyone who opposes concepts such as gay marriage a hateful bigot. But they are hesitant to point out that Sharia law allows gays to be thrown off buildings in certain Muslim-majority Middle Eastern countries.[15]

In other words, the SPLC is a fraud that pretends to stand up for human rights, and particularly, the rights of the most oppressed. In reality, it's merely a Far-Left smear machine dedicated to attacking anyone who holds different political views.

> **The true fighters of freedom are being portrayed as haters, while the true haters are held up as freedom fighters.**

Nawaz believes that Islam needs to reform itself and that a fundamentally important part of that is acknowledging the problem in the first place. Jihadists identify anyone who strays too far from radical interpretation of scripture as heretics.[16] So it seems that the SPLC has a lot more in common with jihadists than it realizes.

Another victim of the SPLC's slander is former Muslim Ayaan Hirsi Ali, another advocate of Islamic reformation and a survivor of FGM. Hirsi Ali grew up in Somalia, an Islamic country, which legitimizes FGM and other appallingly oppressive human rights atrocities.

After moving to Europe as an adult, Hirsi Ali rejected Islam and began speaking out against its brutality. Consequently, jihadists put a fatwa on Hirsi

Ali (a declaration for her to be killed for insulting the prophet Muhammad and Islam).[17]

While working on a movie in the Netherlands exposing the truth about Islam's brutality, the director of a film Hirsi Ali was helping with, Theo van Gogh, was assassinated in cold blood on the streets of Amsterdam.[18] The jihadists who shot him stuck a knife in his bloodied body with a note declaring that Hirsi Ali would be next. This killing preceded the later *Charlie Hebdo* killings in Paris, another fatwa-inspired massacre.

In the same way that jihadists want to shut Hirsi Ali up through violence, the SPLC wants to do so through false labels. In her response to the SPLC identifying her as a bigot in their "Field Guide to Anti-Muslim Extremists," Hirsi Ali said:

> In that guide, the S.P.L.C. claims that I am a "propagandist far outside the political mainstream" and warns journalists to avoid my "damaging misinformation." These groundless smears are deeply offensive, as I have dedicated much of my adult life to calling out the true extremists: organizations such as Al Qaeda and ISIS. Yet you will look in vain for the S.P.L.C.'s "Field Guide to Muslim Extremists." No such list exists.[19]

Imagine the tragic irony of Hirsi Ali having to respond to a bunch of rich, mostly white, leftist males who call her a bigot for bravely risking her life to expose this evil ideology so that one day maybe girls in Somalia won't have to endure what she did anymore. It's too bizarre to even be in an episode of the *Twilight Zone*.

While the SPLC seems obsessed with combating so-called "white supremacy" in the United States, it goes to great lengths the defend Islamic extremism, which poses a much more significant threat to every country on the face of the earth. The SPLC has also placed me, along with my organization, ACT for America, on its dubious hate watch list.

It's ironic that those who seek to lecture Ayaan Hirsi Ali and myself—two ethnically Arab women who grew up in Islamic countries—about bigotry do so from their cushy offices, having never walked a single step in our shoes. I know full well the danger and unspeakable evil that radical Islamic ideology legitimizes, having grown up in war-torn Lebanon.

As a woman, I find it particularly appalling that an organization pretending to stand up for the rights of the oppressed would smear anyone who attempts to take on the real "war on women." The true fighters of freedom are being portrayed as haters, while the true haters are held up as freedom fighters.

Southern Caribbean Investment Center

The name "Southern Poverty Law Center" is ironic, considering the SPLC is anything but poor and does remarkably little litigation with their massive bankroll. That's why Charity Watch, which monitors nonprofits for their economic efficiency, gave the SPLC an F for sitting on an enormous amount of assets.[20]

But it's not just that the SPLC is sitting on hundreds of millions of dollars as a "nonprofit"—it's where that money is being kept. The SPLC reported over $50 million in fund-raising in 2015 and had $328 million in net assets on its 2015 tax form and transferred millions to offshore accounts in the same year![21] Talk about red flags!

It is widely considered unethical for any US-based charity to invest large sums of money overseas because these are virtually unregulated accounts. Isn't it interesting that a "nonprofit" supposedly dedicated to fighting poverty in the deep southern United States would be hoarding millions in offshore accounts? I think so too.

As a side note, Alabama locals where SPLC is based like to refer to its headquarters as "Poverty Palace." Thus, another reason for the SPLC to continue pumping out smear campaigns and label just about everyone it disagrees with politically as a "hate group" is because there's an awful lot of money in fake hate.

Unreliable Sources

The mainstream media still cites the Southern Poverty Law Center as a reliable source of information about hate groups, despite proven bias. In a *Washington Post* article titled "Federal Government Has Long Ignored White Supremacist Threats, Critics Say," an SPLC official ginned up fears of Far-Right groups as an underestimated threat.[22]

Of course, the article didn't bother to give any background about the SPLC or its political and financial interests in making this claim, hoping the reader would never catch on, a familiar and all-too common media strategy. This is par for the course, given the media's dreadful bias toward leftist groups and outright hatred for conservative organizations.

The election of President Trump gave the SPLC an even greater opportunity to spout fake hate. The SPLC and media enablers are constantly warning of an increase in hate crimes against Muslims, directly in line with the talking points of CAIR. Thus, the SPLC finds a very mutually profitable relationship with the terror-tied group.

Every time the SPLC publishes misleading reports and smears those it disagrees with, the media reports on it, and CAIR gets to sit back and play the victim. It's quite the arrangement. The SPLC benefits because its white, leftist donors get to feel good donating to an organization dedicated to fighting a

Far-Right boogeyman, the media gets to report more fake news that aligns with their ideology, and CAIR gets to play the "Islamophobia" card like always.

Time magazine published an article in September of 2017 titled "Read the List of the 917 Hate Groups Identified by the Southern Poverty Law Center." The article had a giant photo of a Klansmen with a white sheet over his head just underneath the title.[23]

In the article it mentioned the SPLC's designation of my organization, ACT for America, as well as myself. Bear in mind, I am a Lebanese-born-and-raised Arabic woman who immigrated to the US from Israel, a country to which I am wholeheartedly devoted, and *Time* magazine publishes an article linking me with the Ku Klux Klan.

If any group bears similarity to the Ku Klux Klan, it's groups like CAIR, which share a mutual hatred of Israel and the Jewish people. I don't need lectures from white leftists about hatred. Unlike them, I've seen true hatred with my own eyes.

- True hatred is what caused Islamic terrorists the blow up my home as a child.

- True hatred is what caused a group of men in their twenties and thirties to fly planes into skyscrapers, killing themselves and thousands more in the process.

- True hatred is what causes Palestinians to kidnap and kill Jewish children.

But the SPLC isn't interested in true hatred; its interest is in protecting its delusional worldview and raking in donations. The SPLC's latest hate group stats claimed that the number of anti-Muslim hate groups nearly tripled in 2016. They dramatically called 2016 "The Year in Hate and Extremism."[24] Who are these haters?

For one, a sign outside a bar in Kmart Plaza in Allegheny County, Pennsylvania. That's right. A sign outside the bar had been listed as a hate group by the SPLC for years.[25] The bar, Casa D'Ice, had a sign outside that almost always had a politically incorrect statement on it, so the SPLC bravely took action.

Again, the SPLC listed the "sign" as a hate group—not the bar or its owner who put up the sign, which would've been embarrassing enough for the SPLC, the actual sign. Casa D'Ice has since been sold and inevitably, the sign was then removed. Chalk up another victory for the noble hate fighters at the SPLC.

The SPLC claimed that the number of anti-Muslim hate groups shot up from only 34 in 2015 to 101 in 2016.[26] Why such a dramatic rise? More signs? Actually the SPLC decided to count forty-seven individual chapters of my organization, ACT for America, as separate groups.[27] When you suddenly classify forty-seven chapters of one group as completely separate groups, it's not very hard to falsify the numbers. ACT for America was only listed as one group in the 2015 SPLC list,[28] but magically turned into forty-seven overnight.

Furthermore, ACT for America has over one thousand chapters nationwide, so why just count forty-seven? For one, if it listed any more than that, it would be obvious how deceptive its numbers are, though the cat is out of the bag on that one anyway. Two, it can keep increasing the number of hate groups each year for the next decade, by simply adding more from ACT for America each year.

The SPLC obviously picked 2016 to do this because it wanted to raise money off the election of President Trump. Once President Trump took office, the SPLC has been swimming in cash from leftist celebrities and corporations.

In fact, the SPLC raised millions of dollars in one weekend alone after a protester was killed by a domestic terrorist in Charlottesville, Virginia, during a white-nationalist march. One million of that came from George and Amal Clooney,[29] another million from Apple,[30] and MGM Resorts went one step further, agreeing to match any and all employee contributions to both the SPLC and its terror-linked partner in crime CAIR.[31] The SPLC truly lives by the motto of Obama pal and Chicago mayor Rahm Emanuel, "You never want a serious crisis to go to waste."[32]

DEADLY DECEPTION

The SPLC's fund-raising strategy is to conflate all groups it opposes with the most heinous groups in existence in order to sell a perceived danger to potential donors. Assigning credibility to the SPLC's false claims of hatred isn't just immoral, it's dangerous. After the SPLC designated the conservative Family Research Council (FRC) as a hate group and attacked it viciously on its website, a deranged man named Floyd Corkins II walked into FRC headquarters in Washington, DC, and started shooting.

In a confession to the FBI, Corkins said he was specifically motivated by the so-called "hate map" on the SPLC's website and incensed by its propaganda. When the FBI asked Corkins how he found out about FRC and where its headquarters were located, Corkins said:

> Southern Poverty Law lists…anti-gay groups. I found them online, did a little bit of research, went to the website, stuff like that.[33]

Can you even imagine if this had been a conservative who walked into a leftist nonprofit headquarters and began shooting, only to then specifically cite a conservative group as the motivational mechanism for the attack? Anderson Cooper and Don Lemon would've led with the story every day for the next year on CNN. Every single mainstream media paper would have front-page coverage of the attacker, his ideology, how he became so incensed, which candidates he voted for, which campaigns he donated to, what his favorite color is, etc.

Instead, the media buried the story, probably in large part because they had cited so much of the poison that the SPLC promoted, which pushed this leftist nut over the edge. But Corkins isn't the only leftist wacko who tried to kill conservatives that has been linked to the SPLC.

James T. Hodgkinson, the unhinged leftist who shot and nearly killed Republicans at a congressional baseball practice, was an avowed supporter of the SPLC.[34] Hodgkinson liked the SPLC on his Facebook page, along with other leftist groups, such as George Soros' Media Matters and MoveOn.org, that similarly spread falsehoods against their political opponents. As was the case with the Family Research Council shooting, the SPLC had repeatedly attacked Rep. Steve Scalise, who nearly died of his wounds.

Tragically the SPLC's dehumanizing of its political opponents and linking everyone who holds opposing views to actual hate groups like the KKK and neo-Nazis is bound to get more people attacked. But with all that money it's comfortably rolling around in thanks to its smear campaigns, the SPLC probably won't be changing its tactics anytime soon. It will continue to endanger the lives of its political enemies, while actively defending those of this nation's, such as CAIR and other Islamic extremist groups.

This unholy alliance is one that must be exposed and destroyed before it is too late. CAIR must be properly designated as a terrorist organization, just as it has been by the UAE, so that organizations that align with CAIR, such as the SPLC, will be forced to pay a heavy price for their treasonous alliance. Until then, the SPLC will continue to pump out poisonous and dangerous lies for wads of cash, while true hate groups like the ones it defends continue their plans to destroy this country from within.

RISE UP AND ACT

When you hear about the agendas of organizations like the SPLC and CAIR, don't daydream about heading for the border. ACT!

- The next time you see a news publication reference the SPLC as a source of information for identifying "hate groups," contact them via email or social media and ask why they're using such a biased and unreliable source. Reference the fact that the FBI has severed ties with the SPLC for its absurd bias and tell them to stop masking a political attack dog as an objective and accurate source of information.

- There are many videos on YouTube exposing the SPLC and its political agenda. Be sure to share these videos on your social media to help spread the truth about this nefarious organization. John Stossel, PragerU, myself, and others have all produced viral videos exposing these frauds. We need your help to tell the American people what the mainstream media will not.

Chapter 13

THE DEATH OF FREE SPEECH

Freedom of speech is the most fundamental pillar of Western, Judeo-Christian society. Increasingly, this fundamental civil right afforded to all Americans through the First Amendment to our Constitution is being eroded by the Islamist-leftist coalition in an effort to assert control over "we the people."

The unholy alliance between radical Islamists and radical leftists has resulted in a modern-day America our founders would not recognize. America, despite being known for its protection of free speech, is now a country where speaking the truth will leave you labeled a bigot or the new attack word *Islamophobic*.

The key date in history was 9/11. The whole world began to take seriously the very real threat that radical Islam posed to the free world. That's what happens when Islamic savages use commercial airliners as human missiles to kill themselves and over three thousand innocent civilians in a matter of hours while yelling "Allahu Akbar!"

As a result of 9/11, the West began asking questions about Islamic ideology in trying to understand and solve the problem of terrorism. The Islamic world had to come up with a clever way not only to silence criticism but also continue playing the victim card, something they have perfected for centuries.

Playing the victim card would allow them to silence Westerners who began to expose the evil nature of Islamic ideology and the nefarious intentions of those who seek to wage jihad. Thus, the sly new term *Islamophobia* was born and the Islamist-leftist coalition began their assault on freedom of speech.

THE OIC AND THE UNITED NATIONS: ISLAMOPHOBIA AND "DEFAMATION OF RELIGION"

The Organisation of Islamic Cooperation (OIC) is an international coalition of Islamic nations with a permanent delegation to the United Nations and a permanent observer in the European Union. Formed in 1969, the OIC is comprised of fifty-seven countries that are predominantly Muslim, many of which are beholden to Sharia law, and thirteen of its member nations currently sit on the United Nations Human Rights Council.

The OIC's purpose when it was founded back in 1969 was for Muslim countries to create a more powerful, unified force and promote Islamic interests over Westernization. The OIC says its purpose is to "safeguard and protect the interests of the Muslim world in the spirit of promoting international peace and harmony."[1] Of course, it's hard to promote international peace and harmony when almost all your members have atrocious human rights records and/or have supported terrorist movements.[2] But maybe that's just me.

Freedom House, an independent watchdog organization dedicated to defending human rights around the world, publishes an annual Freedom in the World survey of 195 countries and 15 territories, scoring them on issues such as freedom of expression and belief and personal autonomy and individual rights. Based on their scores, countries are given a status of free, partly free, or not free. Only four of the fifty-seven member states of the OIC had a status of free in 2016.[3]

This is why I think it's patently insane that this collective body holds thirteen of the forty-seven seats on the United Nations Human Rights Council. I know more about playing quarterback for the New England Patriots than these countries know about promoting human rights. Islamic countries who make up the OIC do not take kindly to those insulting their prophet. In many of these countries the penalty for blasphemy is death.[4] To say that they're opposed to freedom of speech is the understatement of the century.

Things escalated after 9/11, when Westerners began trying to understand what drove educated and sometimes wealthy people such as Mohamed Atta, the ring leader of the 9/11 hijackings, to kill themselves. In order to get to that answer, Westerners started scrutinizing the Quran and debating it in public forums, otherwise known as exercising freedom of thought and expression, a big no-no in the Muslim world.

The Bible says, "Come now, and let us reason together" (Isa. 1:18, NKJV). Jews have religious schools where all they do all day long is debate scripture. However, in Islam there is no questioning the word of Allah, and those who dare will be dealt with accordingly.

According to the Libyan representative to the UN, freedom of speech is not the issue, but rather, "misuse" of that right.[5] What a coincidence; that's exactly how the leftist mainstream media feels!

In 1999 Pakistan, on behalf of the OIC, brought the first resolution about the defamation of Islam before the UN (Commission of Human Rights at the time, now the Human Rights Council).[6] The UN changed it to "Defamation of Religions" before the resolution was adopted. Similar nonbinding resolutions were passed in the years between 1999 and 2010.

In 2011 the first resolution seeking to criminalize those who made offensive comments about Islam was introduced (16/18).[7] When confronted by Western nations about this absurd idea of criminalizing one of our most fundamental values, nations like Iran said that it was a necessary move in the fight against terrorism. In other words, Islamists would stop trying to kill us if we would just stop talking. How rich is that? They need to criminalize your right to speak out against the cause of terrorism in order to combat terrorism!

Sure enough, a later version of this resolution 16/18 sought to criminalize speech that incites violence against others on the basis of religion, race, or national origin. Naturally this won the approval of the Obama administration.[8] How interesting. President Obama and Secretary of State Hillary Clinton were signing you up for Sharia compliance without you even knowing it. Then Secretary of State Hillary Clinton said:

> The United States strongly supports today's resolution, which rejects the broad prohibitions on speech called for in the former "defamation of religions" resolution, and supports approaches that do not limit freedom of expression or infringe on the freedom of religion.[9]

Dr. M. Zuhdi Jasser, a physician, an American Muslim, and the founder of the American Islamic Forum for Democracy, properly outlined the dangers of this proposal when he noted:

> Beginning to categorize speech as "incitement" is a slippery slope that could open the floodgates for any post-tragedy analysis to indict what would otherwise be free speech absurdly as incitement in some far-fetched cause-effect analysis that would depend on proving that speech causes violence.[10]

Islam does not allow freedom of speech and brings barbaric brutality—including death—to those who exercise it. Naturally, as the massive migration of Muslims into Europe and, increasingly, the United States has unfolded, there has been a precipitous drop in freedom of expression.

I'm not just talking about political correctness here or the mainstream media silencing voices they disagree with—though we'll get to that as well. I'm talking about the fact that simply because I have written this book and spoken the words I have spoken in my life, I am marked for death in the eyes of an Islamist.

One of the most tragic realities of Islamist opposition to freedom of speech has been those who have been killed for simply speaking up in criticism of Islam, such as filmmaker Theo van Gogh producing a video criticizing Islam's treatment of women or a newspaper publishing editorial cartoons of the prophet Muhammad.[11]

Most Muslims view depictions of prophet Muhammad as strictly forbidden and therefore consider them to be blasphemy, and under Sharia law blasphemy is punishable by death. Consider that for a moment. What does it say about a religion if simply characterizing its prophet justifies the murder of another human being? What does it say about the values of someone who believes in such inhumane barbarism?

Of course, the Left will inevitably read this and say that it's religion in general that's the problem, and that all religions are equally dangerous and inhumane in their own ways. They will cite the Crusades and passages from the Bible and Torah to justify their desperate attempt to resist offending anyone from a different culture, because for the Left, cultural relativism is their religion.

> Simply because I have written this book and spoken the words I have spoken in my life, I am marked for death in the eyes of an Islamist.

Here's where the Far Left gets it wrong, even when it's smacking them directly in the face. When Christians hear about a movie or TV show that expresses what they feel to be anti-Christian messaging, their response is to vehemently voice their opposition and boycott the programming. This goes for Jews, Buddhists, atheists, and even Westernized Muslims who believe in the First Amendment right to free speech, the Constitution, and the Enlightenment.

When leftist playwrights on Broadway decided to demean and mock Mormons for their religion with the musical dubbed *The Book of Mormon*, you didn't see Mormons staging worldwide protests and calling for the death of the producers, as Islamists did when a Danish cartoon depicting the prophet Muhammad was published back in 2005.[12]

The same can be said for Christians who find the Broadway musical *Jesus Christ Superstar* offensive. You don't see Christians or Mormons storming the offices of the producers in broad daylight with AK-47s and slaughtering them for their perceived blasphemy, as Islamists did when the French magazine *Charlie Hebdo* published a perceivably "offensive" depiction of their prophet in 2015.[13] You don't see Christians or Mormons attending these shows, only to stand up and begin shooting at audience members for their attendance and participation in such offensive events.

You don't see these things because, as opposed to the Islamic world where such actions are considered heroic, for those of us who believe in freedom of speech, the Magna Carta, the Bill of Rights, and Western civilization, such actions are considered barbaric.

In fact, the creators of the musical told NPR that they "had faith" that the church would not respond with anger.[14] Try making a Broadway musical called *The Quran* and see what happens.

You know what's tragically ironic about the lie that Obama and Susan Rice cooked up about Benghazi being the result of an internet video? They thought the public would believe it because, well, Islamists certainly would kill someone over a video they didn't like.[15] In the Western world, we use words. In the Islamic world, they use swords.

THE SATANIC VERSES

Islamist opposition to free speech and leftist enabling of their opposition is not a new problem. One of the first and most profound examples of Islam attempting to suppress freedom of speech within the Western world was when the Ayatollah Khomeini issued a fatwa against British journalist Salman Rushdie on February 14, 1989, for his then newly released book, *The Satanic Verses*.[16]

Rushdie's novel was perceived by many Muslims to be an insulting depiction of the prophet Muhammad. This was a crime Islamists felt worthy of death.

Iranian organizations have offered an almost $4 million bounty for anyone who killed Rushdie for his publication. As recently as 2016, Iranian media outlets added $600,000 to the bounty. You know, to keep up with inflation.[17]

Naturally the book was banned in many Islamic countries and caused deadly protests around the globe, so much so that Rushdie and his family had to be put under British police protection for the next several years.

The Ayatollah of Iran stated the following while issuing his fatwa against Rushdie:

> We are from Allah and to Allah we shall return. I am informing all brave Muslims of the world that the author of *The Satanic Verses*, a text written, edited, and published against Islam, the Prophet of Islam, and the Qur'an, along with all the editors and publishers aware of its contents, are condemned to death. I call on all valiant Muslims wherever they may be in the world to kill them without delay, so that no one will dare insult the sacred beliefs of Muslims henceforth. And whoever is killed in this cause will be a martyr, Allah willing. Meanwhile if someone has access to the author of the book but is incapable of carrying out the execution, he should inform the people so that [Rushdie] is punished for his actions.[18]

It wasn't just Rushdie whose life was endangered, but everyone who was selling the book as well. Many bookstores around the world who sold Rushdie's novel were firebombed by angry Muslims. Muslim communities in several Western nations rose up with vicious protests, calling for Rushdie to be killed and burning copies of his book in the streets.[19]

Muslims bombed two bookstores in what is arguably the leftist capital of the World—Berkeley, California.[20] The New York news outlet *The Riverdale Press* was bombed after an editor made the unforgivable mistake of standing up for freedom of speech and declaring the right of all human beings to read the novel, while also criticizing those who pulled Rushdie's work out of intimidation.[21]

Back in the UK, London bookstores, Penguin, Collets, and Dillons, were bombed by Muslims as well, with several others targeted but foiled due to faulty explosives.[22] Those who did carry Rushdie's book did so under the counter for safety.

The massive violence stretched across the globe, and at least twelve people were killed when Muslims started a riot in Bombay, India, in response to the novel.[23] The Union of Islamic Students' Associations in Europe pledged allegiance to the Ayatollah Khomeini and encouraged the killing of Rushdie for insulting their prophet.[24]

A prominent Muslim property owner in London declared:

> If I see him, I will kill him straight away. Take my name and address. One day I will kill him.[25]

How's that for cultural diversity?

George Sabbagh, who was the director of the Near East Studies Center at UCLA at the time, said that Khomeini was completely within his rights for issuing the fatwa against Rushdie.[26] How would you like to have him educating your children?

President Jimmy Carter also threw Rushdie under the bus when he said of the novel:

> It is a direct insult to those millions of Moslems whose sacred beliefs have been violated and are suffering in restrained silence the added embarrassment of the Ayatollah's irresponsibility.[27]

Carter went on to imply that Rushdie had it coming because he knew what this would provoke in the Muslim world.[28] In other words, the soft bigotry of low expectations on steroids. Since Islamists can't possibly be held to the same standards of behavior of Westerners, even Western children for that matter, the onus falls on Rushdie to show restraint.

The reaction of leftists in education and in the media to the Rushdie controversy was the first major warning sign that the Left didn't really believe in liberalism; they believed in multiculturalism masked in liberalism.

THE REGRESSIVE LEFT

There's nothing liberal about cowering and submitting to Islamic fascists while simultaneously throwing your fellow man under the bus simply for exercising the most basic freedoms as recognized by Western civilization for centuries.

Any religion that advocates killing another human being for simply offending you is a religion stuck in the seventh century. Therefore, we must resist calling those on the Left who seem hell-bent on apologizing and excusing such barbaric beliefs "progressives," and instead call them "regressives."[29]

One of the most objective minds in modern media I have come across in recent years is Dave Rubin, a self-identified classical liberal. I use the term *classical*, since many who identify as liberal today have absolutely no idea what true "liberalism" really is.

Classical liberalism is more similar to what we think of today as libertarianism, while modern "liberalism" and "progressivism" have morphed into an ideology that prefers cultural relativism above any and all rational thought.

Rubin has very appropriately identified this segment of society as the "regressive left."[30] The regressive Left doesn't have the same appreciation for the freedoms and human rights that Western civilization secured for us, because they hate the West to begin with.

They see Western civilization as nothing more than an evil empire formed by colonialism, built off the backs of slaves and aboriginals. They believe that the only reason radical Islamists commit terrorism today is because of the colonial sins of the past.

Few have understood and confronted regressive leftist ideology better than the late Christopher Hitchens. Once a self-identified Marxist, Hitchens moved away from his leftist comrades after 9/11, when he realized that all the ideals he held dear, most notably, freedom of speech and expression, were actually under attack by the very people he once identified with.

Regressive leftists routinely blamed 9/11 on American foreign policy and characterized the Iraq War as just another attempt to colonize brown people and steal their oil. While taking questions from an audience at the leftist Freedom From Religion Foundation convention in 2007, a standard regressive leftist confronted Hitchens about his support for the Iraq War.

> I'm wondering how you can possibly say that it is Western civilization, the civilization of the colonizers, and the oppressors, who do it all of course in the name of liberation and democracy, how this is not the fundamental problem, rather than what you call, the jihad, of what I consider to be the response to the crimes of US and European Imperialism.

Hitchens was having none of this and responded:

> Well, there you have it, ladies and gentlemen, there you have it. You see how, you see how far the termites have spread and how long and well they've dined, when someone can get up and say that, in a meeting of unbelievers, that the problem is Western civilization, not the Islamic threat to it, that's how far the termites have gotten.[31]

Hitchens, a devout atheist, was routinely baffled by the idiocy of his former allies on the Left who couldn't see the insane hypocrisy of attacking Christianity and Judaism while carrying water for radical Islam.

But once you understand the animosity the Left has for Western civilization, it becomes clear how they possess the same hatred for the freedoms it solidified.

The Left knows that most Americans—and all sane human beings— would oppose their borderless, kumbaya vision for the future. That's why the Left and their radical Islamic allies decided that the only way to potentially achieve that future is to silence voices of opposition.

This concept of finding useful allies to manipulate is directly spelled out in the Muslim Brotherhood plan to overtake the West, in which they outline the necessity to work with like-minded Islamist and progressive organizations that share similar goals for defeating the West.[32] Thus, a strategic, all-out war on freedom of speech has been launched by the Islamist-leftist alliance.

INSTITUTIONS OF HIGHER CENSORSHIP

There is perhaps no better example of the all-out assault leftists have launched against freedom of speech than on college campuses. Leftists have progressively taken over American universities and, just as quickly, systematically eroded freedom of speech and engagement for the students. Not only are voices that leftist faculty members disagree with prevented from speaking, but voices espousing violent, anti-Semitic, and radical Islamic rhetoric are welcomed with open arms.

One of the most active Islamic organizations on college campuses is the Muslim Students' Association (MSA). They have nearly six hundred chapters on college campuses in the United States and Canada, making them the most visible and influential Islamic student organization in North America. The MSA is mentioned in the Muslim Brotherhood memorandum for North America as one of their front organizations to destroy America from within.[33]

In May 2010 Jewish author David Horowitz was taking questions from an audience at University of California San Diego, when a female MSA student stood up to confront Horowitz about his views.[34] When Horowitz asked the young woman if she supported the terrorist organization Hamas, she replied: "If I say something I'm sure that I will be arrested. For reasons of Homeland Security."

In other words, of course she supported Hamas, but she didn't want to be arrested or investigated on terrorism charges if she essentially admitted that she was a terrorist. But Horowitz pressed further. "I'm a Jew. The head of

Hezbollah has said that he hopes that we will gather in Israel so he doesn't have to hunt us down globally. For it or against it?"

After a pause, the Muslim student leaned into the microphone and with a cold, calculating voice stated, "For it."[35]

If that doesn't send chills up your spine, nothing will. It shows how much of a dangerous breeding ground for terrorists our college campuses have become. When a student can stand up and declare herself a supporter of Jewish genocide with absolutely no consequence and the terrorist-linked organization she's a part of can still function openly on campus, we're way past the tipping point.

Of course, adding to the absurdity of allowing terrorists and anti-Semites to openly flourish on campus, conservatives are shunned and accused of "hate speech." In response to a scheduled appearance by Milo Yiannopoulos at leftist haven University of California, Berkeley, Antifa and their leftist comrades started a violent riot, smashing store windows, causing over $100,000 in damage, and injuring innocent civilians.[36]

Keep in mind that Yiannopoulos is a proud and particularly flamboyant gay man. But to the Left, his conservative views deprive him of his VIP membership to the club of victimization. More to it, the fact that he's espousing conservative viewpoints as an openly gay man makes him a traitor in the eyes of the Left and a particularly important voice to silence.

Black-masked leftists threw large rocks, commercial fireworks, and Molotov cocktails at police, in response to Yiannopoulos setting foot on campus to say things they didn't like. Over fifteen hundred angry leftists formed a mob and chanted, "No safe space for racists," and "This is war," but were strangely missing their pitchforks.[37]

One innocent woman who is a Trump supporter was pepper-sprayed in the face while being interviewed on live television by an ABC affiliate.[38] That's strange; I thought the Left was supposed to be fighting for the rights of women.

Embarrassed by the national disgrace, administrators at Berkeley tried to play defense, while at the same time letting the violent mob know they support them in spirit.

> We condemn in the strongest possible terms the violence and unlawful behavior that was on display and deeply regret that those tactics will now overshadow the efforts to engage in legitimate and lawful protest against the performer's presence and perspectives.[39]

See, it was all peaceful until fifteen hundred trouble makers showed up. They continued:

> While Yiannopoulos' views, tactics and rhetoric are profoundly contrary to our own, we are bound by the Constitution, the law, our

values and the campus's Principles of Community to enable free expression across the full spectrum of opinion and perspective.[40]

There's the continued attack on Yiannopoulos, an openly gay man, whose biggest crime was that he attempted to speak at a public university. When it comes to free speech, the aggressors are almost exclusively on the Left.

Isn't it interesting that when radical leftist speakers or even terrorists get to speak on college campuses, and in many cases, even teach on college campuses, you never seem to see violent mobs of conservatives firebombing the building or throwing deadly objects at police. Years of pampering and propaganda have caused late Generation X, millennial, and Generation Z leftists to feel entitled to such behavior. They feel their right to not be offended trumps your right to speak your mind.

It isn't just conservatives who are being attacked by regressive leftists on college campuses. Long-time liberal comedian and political commentator Bill Maher ran into this issue when he was scheduled to give a commencement address at Berkeley. Muslim and leftist students argued his views on Islam were dangerously Islamophobic and that he did not deserve to speak.[41]

Students then put together a petition on the site change.org to prevent Maher from speaking.[42] The petition referenced certain statements Maher had made in the past that the precious student snowflakes simply couldn't handle. These included:

"Islam is the only religion that acts like the mafia that will...kill you if you say the wrong thing."

"Talk to women who've ever dated an Arab man. The results are not good."

"The Muslim world has too much in common with ISIS."

"You have to understand, you have to embrace the values of Western civilization. They're not just different, they are better."

"For a lack of a better term I would say the feminine values are now the values of America, sensitivity is more important than truth, feelings are more important that facts."

Over six thousand people signed the petition to have Maher canceled.[43] Addressing the issue on his HBO show *Real Time With Bill Maher*, Maher confronted the spoiled brats "Whoever told you you only had to hear what didn't upset you?" he rightly asked.[44] When Berkeley rescinded an invitation to Ann Coulter, he called it the Left's version of book burning. "Berkeley, you know, used to be the cradle of free speech. And now it's just the cradle for...babies."[45]

The attacks launched on Maher were a clear warning sign to any other leftist celebrity: if you step out of line, the regressive Left will come for you, just as we did Maher. Of course, this is always done to protect society from hearing dangerous and provocative speech.

It's ironic that those who claim to be fighting fascism at every turn are, in fact, fascistic themselves. (Antifa stands for "Anti-Fascist.") Of course, it's hard to convince people you're genuine in your opposition to fascism when you're wearing black masks over your head while you violently attack innocent civilians simply for wanting to hear a speaker you do not agree with.

Remember, at multiple rallies then-candidate Trump spoke at during his presidential and primary campaign, countless interruptions of crazed leftists arose, as they screamed mindless babble at the top of their lungs to try to silence him. They knew that if the American people heard his message about putting America first and speaking truthfully about the threats of open borders, he would win. So they tried desperately to silence him. But their plans failed, and President Trump won handily over Hillary Clinton.

How many times were Hillary Clinton's speeches interrupted by conservatives during her campaign? Did she ever have Secret Service agents rush the stage during one of her speeches after a crazed conservative tried to attack her, as a crazed leftist did President Trump?[46]

No.

Did she ever have an actual rally in a major city canceled due to a violent domestic terror mob taking over the arena, as was done to President Trump in Chicago?[47]

No.

Clinton didn't confront those issues for the same reason that an anti-Semitic terror sympathizer like Linda Sarsour can speak at City University of New York, and a domestic terrorist like Kathy Boudin can teach a class at Columbia because the Left has a monopoly on violent anti-free speech radicalism.[48]

Unfortunately this trend of attacking free speech is not exclusive to college campuses or to younger generations. CNN's Chris Cuomo, the younger, better-looking, and more ignorant brother of leftist New York Governor Andrew Cuomo, embarrassed himself on Twitter after getting into a debate with another user who said, "Too many people are trying to say hate speech does not equal free speech."[49]

"It doesn't," Cuomo replied, in pure ignorance. "Hate speech is excluded from protection. Don't just say you love the Constitution. Read it."

Of course, nowhere in the Constitution does it mention hate speech, but that didn't stop Cuomo from digging himself an even deeper hole and stating that those challenging him were simply "drinking haterade."[50] As a general rule, when a grown man uses terms like *haterade*, he's probably not someone you should be listening to, particularly on matters of constitutional law.

Cuomo brought on the exchange when he criticized the organizers of a "Draw Muhammad" event in Garland, Texas, which resulted in two Islamic terrorists trying to shoot everyone in the conference center. Leave it to leftists to attack the victims of Islamic terror, rather than the actual terrorists. Is there any clearer example of the soft bigotry of low expectations?[51]

The Supreme Court already ruled in an 8–1 verdict in *Snyder v. Phelps* that outrageous speech cannot be censored, but Cuomo, in his own ignorance, persisted. Cuomo eventually walked back his claims and admitted to making "clumsy" statements. Nevertheless, the ignorance shown by a major media host with respect to our most fundamental of rights is beyond alarming.[52]

POLITICAL ENABLERS

On April 20, 2017, failed Democratic presidential candidate Howard Dean tweeted: "Hate speech is not protected by the first amendment."[53] Keep in mind, this man was once considered the Democratic front-runner in the 2004 Democratic primary race. Now you know how John Kerry was able to secure the nomination. It wasn't exactly a bright field of competitors.

Dean's tweet would be comically ignorant if so many holding power didn't agree with him. Unfortunately, spineless Republicans are becoming increasingly hostile toward free speech in order to prevent themselves from being labeled "racist" by the *Washington Post* and *New York Times*.

In 2017 Republicans introduced H.R. 257, which supposedly attempted to combat hate crimes but, in reality, achieved nothing but potentially eroding our First Amendment rights.[54] This particular legislation was merely a formal statement by a legislative body. But those who helped write the resolution provide very alarming insight into the true intentions of the move by lawmakers.

We've seen this before when the Obama administration worked with the OIC on UN Resolution 16/18, which sought to suppress free speech offensive to Islam.[55] That's probably why groups like the Muslim Political Affairs Council (MPAC) were so happy to work hand in hand with Rep. Barbara Comstock on this particular legislative language.[56]

Though sponsored by twenty-three Republicans and a predictable laundry list of Democrats, the House resolution, introduced by Republican Congresswoman Barbara Comstock of Virginia, was actually drafted by two Islamic terrorist-linked groups.[57]

Rep. Comstock herself has a disturbing pattern of kowtowing to some of the most dangerous Islamists in America. Immediately following the electoral landslide of President Trump, Rep. Comstock went on an apology tour that would make actions by President Obama look Reaganesque. Why?

To comfort Muslims who were frightened after the election of President Trump.[58]

And even more unbelievable, Rep. Comstock chose the terror-linked All Dulles Area Muslim Society (ADAMS) Center as the right place for Islamic outreach. With Republicans in Congress like this, who needs Democrats?

Six months after 9/11, the ADAMS Center was raided during an FBI investigation into support for terrorist groups.[59] ADAMS Center Chairman Ahmad Totonji was named in the affidavit in support of the search warrant.[60] Totonji was also assistant secretary general of the World Assembly of Muslim Youth, whose Virginia chapter was founded by Osama bin Laden's nephew Abdullah bin Laden.

> The reality is freedom of speech, the most fundamental pillar of our Constitution and Western civilization at large, is under attack by two relentless enemies: radical Islam and the radical Left.

Rep. Comstock worked with two terror-linked groups on the House resolution: EMGAGE and MPAC.[61] The Department of Homeland Security (DHS) recently decided not to give MPAC the Countering Violent Extremism (CVE) Grant that was approved in the last days of the Obama administration. According to a spokeswoman, "DHS utilized its discretion to consider other factors and information when reviewing applicants. The Department considered whether applicants for CVE awards would partner with law enforcement, had a strong basis of prior experience in countering violent extremism, [or] had a history of prior efforts to implement prevention programs targeting violent extremism." The DHS spokeswoman explained that after these considerations were applied, top-scoring applicants remained as awardees while others did not. In other words, given MPAC's links to terrorism, their application was denied. So Republicans like Comstock thought to themselves, "Hmm, seems like a great group to write a resolution for us!"[62]

Over the years, EMGAGE held a number of events at terror-linked mosques, such as Darul Uloom in Pembroke Pines, Florida, where al Qaeda global operations chief Adnan el-Shukrijumah once worshipped![63] EMGAGE has also sponsored anti-Semitic speeches made by various Muslim extremists, such as Sayed Ammar Nakshawani, who has called for the destruction of Israel.[64]

The reality is freedom of speech, the most fundamental pillar of our Constitution and Western civilization at large, is under attack by two relentless enemies: radical Islam and the radical Left (and now even ignorant Republicans only interested in votes and not the security of our nation). Both are working together to shut you up and prevent your children and grandchildren from exercising the same rights that every American since the nation's founding have had the privilege of doing.

Unless Americans take hold of this increasingly dangerous threat, our ability to fight back with truth could be gone forever. We must not take this most crucial freedom for granted, for if we do, it's only a matter of time before the enemy takes it away. We must make sure those who represent us in Washington understand that freedom of speech is an absolute right, and that we will not be silenced.

RISE UP AND ACT

When you notice an infringement on someone's freedom of speech, don't just pray for a miracle. ACT!

One particular legislation ACT for America has introduced is a bill titled "Free Speech Defense ACT," which we have passed in eleven states so far. The bill protects freedom of speech, freedom of the press, and free expression by shielding authors, journalists, bloggers, radio hosts, and artists from foreign libel judgments originating in jurisdictions that do not afford the same protections as the First Amendment of the US Constitution. (Beyond the Free Speech Defense ACT, we are involved in passing legislation all over the country on an ongoing basis. Please sign up to receive our action alerts so you will always know the latest legislation that needs your involvement.)

- Action item: Check to see if your state has passed this legislation. If not contact your state legislator in either the House or Senate and ask if they will cosponsor this legislation.

- Let your elected officials know how concerned you are about how the term *hate speech* is being used as an excuse to curb your First Amendment rights. Let them know that you will be watching their actions very closely to ensure their commitment to freedom of speech is not in any way compromised.

  A sample script might read:

Hello Senator/Congressman,

My name is John Smith, and as a constituent of yours I want to express how troubled I am about the recent trends I'm seeing toward using so called hate speech as a means of eroding freedom of speech. The First Amendment must never be compromised, and I will be watching your actions very closely to ensure you also embrace this concept. I would appreciate your leadership on this critical issue and look forward to seeing what actions you take to address it in the future.

Chapter 14

OPERATION INDOCTRINATION

It's no secret that America's younger generations lack the fundamental patriotism and appreciation for the freedoms they enjoy that previous generations largely held. They're starved of even a very basic knowledge of the Constitution, the Founding Fathers, and American heritage.

Taking it a step further, in September 2016 students at Kellogg Community College were actually arrested for handing out copies of the Constitution! The administration accused them of obstructing student education by asking fellow students on their way to class, "Do you like freedom and liberty?"[1]

Although this sounds like something that would happen to students in Cuba, it's happening right here in our own backyard. And with the continued indoctrination of our youth, the problem is bound to get even worse.

We shouldn't be surprised then that a seventy-five-year-old leftist like Bernie Sanders could ride a tidal wave of youthful support to the very end of a Democratic presidential primary, and he probably would've won if Hillary Clinton and the DNC hadn't colluded to fix the whole thing.[2] But older generations watched in disbelief as young people, many of them not even old enough to vote, wore T-shirts supporting the devout socialist Sanders.

The truth is, many of our young people have been taught to admire historical political figures that make Sanders look like Reagan. Walk around any college campus in America and you're bound to encounter at least one student, and possibly a professor, wearing a Che Guevara T-shirt.[3] Che was a terrorist killer and a fundamental communist figure in the Cuban Revolution during the 1950s.[4]

In fact, if you turn on the television, you might even catch a glimpse of an athlete donning a Fidel Castro T-shirt. That's what former NFL quarterback Colin Kaepernick did when he wore an ode to Castro during an official press conference in November 2016.[5]

Bear in mind, Castro is a man who tortured and killed tens of thousands of his own people (estimates range from 35,000 to 141,000) without remorse.[6] Kaepernick, being someone whom young athletes aspire to be like, chose to honor this tyrant on live television for all to see.

And what was the NFL's reaction to Kaepernick romanticizing a terrorist? Much like their punishment for him wearing socks to a team practice depicting police officers as pigs—nothing. No suspension, no fine, nothing.

An SB Nation contributor seemed to particularly love the socks, even putting a link in his column where others could buy the socks with "piggies" as police officers.[7] These are the voices our young people are listening to.

They're not reading the Founding Fathers; they're reading social media posts from anti-American leftists who seemed to endorse the idea of disarming all police officers after the school shooting in Parkland, Florida, in February 2018. You know, because of their racism and oppression.

Most adults have no idea what their children are learning, and more importantly, who they're learning it from. Not only are children influenced by their teachers and their leftist school environment, they continue to digest information from an unlimited number of leftist sources after they get home.

The radical Left today controls Hollywood, social media sites such as Facebook and Twitter, as well as youth-driven outlets such as MTV, which is where our young people derive their political knowledge and overall worldview. God, help us all!

These outlets are a constant leftist propaganda machine, pushing racial tribalism, denigrating the historical heritage of the United States, and stumping for socialism, communism, fascism, and Islamism. They sell young people on the idea that groupthink is somehow rebellious, and that freedom and liberty are oppressive and outdated. Anyone who doesn't buy into this warped PC nonsense is shunned.

Remember the two doctors in Michigan who were charged with genitally mutilating seven-year-old and nine-year-old girls? When my organization, ACT for America, launched a nationwide March Against Sharia to stand up for human rights—specifically girls' rights—in the wake of this shocking event, *Teen Vogue* released a particularly dreadful article titled "What the 'March Against Sharia' Protests Teach Us About Countering Hateful Speech."[8]

> If children grow up learning that their country was founded on racism, bigotry, oppression, and genocide, we cannot expect them to fight for the freedoms it gave to them.

In other words, standing up for a woman's rights not to wear a hijab, not to have her genitalia mutilated against her will, and not to be subjected to the oppression of Sharia law is "hate speech" to the leftists at *Teen Vogue*. These are the voices shaping our young people's views and beliefs.

Most parents have no clue what their kids are soaking up. Ask mothers about *Teen Vogue*, and 99 percent probably think it's about makeup, nail polish, and clothing for teenage girls. Almost none of them know it as the political activist and social justice magazine that it really is. I am a mother of two daughters. The only reason I knew about the article is because it involved me personally.

Given how absorbent and easily influenced children are, particularly by adults they look up to as trusted sources of information, it is all the more critical that we scrutinize what our children are being taught in their schools. Hitler, the most evil dictator the world has ever known, once stated, "He alone, who gains the youth, gains the future."[9] You don't have to be as deadly as Hitler to understand why he said that.

If children grow up learning that their country was founded on racism, bigotry, oppression, and genocide, we cannot expect them to fight for the freedoms it gave to them. Add to this the fact that our current teenagers weren't even born yet on September 11, 2001, and no one under the age of twenty-one has any firsthand recollection of the evil that was done to our nation and all of humanity by radical Islam that day.

That's exactly why those who wish to destroy the United States of America from within are doing so through the textbooks your children are consuming. They know that societies are not transformed overnight, but by a slow, incremental, and generational shift in ideology.

Western parents are far too trusting of those who teach their children as well as the material they are assigned to read. This is largely because when baby boomers and, to a large extent Gen Xers, went to school, they were not being systematically indoctrinated with anti-American propaganda.

PROFESSORS OF HATE

Isn't it interesting to hear radical leftists in academia constantly lecture Americans about tolerance, when in fact they themselves profess the most abominable hatred imaginable and get away with it?

Following the passing of our beloved former first lady Barbara Bush, a professor of creative writing at Fresno State University, Randa Jarrar, showed off her vitriol by tweeting how overjoyed she was about Mrs. Bush's death.

"I'm happy the witch is dead. can't wait for the rest of her family to fall to their demise the way 1.5 million Iraqis did." Jarrar said. This followed her initial statement that Barbara Bush was an "amazing racist who, along with her husband, raised a war criminal."[10]

When she faced immediate backlash from just about everyone who had a soul, Jarrar blamed criticism of her tweet on the fact that she is "an Arab American Muslim American woman with some clout."[11] She must've taken debate lessons from CAIR.

Naturally, in response to calls for her to be fired for her unimaginably evil tweets, Jarrar arrogantly proclaimed, "I work as a tenured professor. I make 100K a year doing that. I will never be fired."[12]

The worst part? She's not wrong.

Fresno State President Joseph Castro issued a statement saying that Jarrar's comments, though offensive, "are protected free speech under the First Amendment of the US Constitution."[13]

True, but what does the First Amendment of the US Constitution have to do with forcing a taxpayer-funded institution to continue employing someone no matter how offensive their comments? Nothing, of course. Fresno State, like all leftist institutions, only references the First Amendment when it can aid their political purpose.

I, for one, find it hard to believe that Fresno State would have taken the same action if one of its professors tweeted that they wished Michelle Obama had died instead of Barbara Bush. Would Fresno State President Joseph Castro have issued the same cop-out response to that type of vile tweet? Let's not kid ourselves.

One year prior, a history lecturer at Fresno State tweeted, "To save American democracy, Trump must hang. The sooner and higher the better," while also calling for "the execution of two Republicans for each deported immigrant."[14] This lecturer was placed on leave but was not fired. He should have been thrown in jail for issuing death threats against the president of the United States, in addition to losing his job.

Think this is exclusive to leftist California? Think again.

A Rutgers University professor in New Jersey named Michael Chikindas displayed how acceptable anti-Semitism is in leftist academia when he posted on social media that Jews want to "exterminate" Palestinians but were so far unsuccessful because so many Jews in Israel are gay.[15] He also added vile anti-Semitic images on his Facebook page, as if his words weren't despicable enough.

His punishment? Rutgers patted themselves on the back for removing the professor from teaching required courses, but the tenured professor got to keep his job and his massive pension, courtesy of New Jersey taxpayers.

Leftists don't care about racism; they care about politics. They despise Israel for political purposes, so filth like this professor's tweet is entirely acceptable in the high offices of liberal academia.

Racism against white people is another favorite of the Far Left, demonstrated perfectly when a professor at Drexel University in Philadelphia tweeted, "All I Want for Christmas is White Genocide." After obvious backlash from non-racists, the self-admitted communist George Ciccariello-Maher said he was just joking. Of course, that's hard to believe given that Ciccariello-Maher also tweeted that he wanted to "vomit" when he saw someone giving up their first-class seat on an airplane to a uniformed soldier.[16]

Drexel placed Ciccariello-Maher on leave but did not fire him. After having been exposed as a racist, the communist professor would eventually resign from Drexel, blaming "white supremacist media outlets" for endangering him and his family, saying he no longer felt safe teaching on campus.[17]

Upon his resignation, Drexel publicly thanked Professor Ciccariello-Maher for his contributions "to the field of political thought and his service to the Drexel University community as an outstanding classroom teacher."[18]

Really? What kind of contributions? Communist indoctrination of students? Racist tweets? Is that what an outstanding classroom teacher embodies for Drexel University?

The sad response to those questions is a resounding yes, just as it is for the majority of American universities after decades of incessant leftist infiltration. They oppose racism but support anti-Semitism. They oppose sexism but support Sharia law. They oppose hate speech but speak hatred.

Today this is exactly what is happening in universities and high schools all across America. If you find it hard to believe, I encourage you to ask your child about what their teachers are preaching in the classroom and ask them to bring home their American history textbooks to see for yourself what they are being forced to read.

TEXTBOOK PROPAGANDA

George Orwell once said, "The most effective way to destroy people is to deny and obliterate their own understanding of their history."[19] There is a concerted effort on behalf of American leftists to indoctrinate unsuspecting minds through the very books they are assigned to read in class. Much of this brainwashing effort by the Far Left goes unnoticed and unchallenged.

Howard Zinn's textbook *A People's History of the United States* has had a major impact on how history is taught in schools today and has shaped the minds of many young Americans.[20] This book has sold over two million copies since it was published and is still required reading from high school to college.[21]

Zinn's book is even mentioned in the classic Hollywood film *Good Will Hunting* by Matt Damon's character as a "real history book" worth reading.[22] The entire book is an attempt to prove that America is an evil empire based on white supremacy and the oppression and genocide of minorities.[23] It mentions absolutely nothing of American exceptionalism!

Zinn was open about the fact that his goal in writing the book was to start a "quiet revolution."[24] That is, one that transforms society and leads to the eventual overthrow of American institutions of power from those who consume his poisonous propaganda and would then turn against their country. The election and reign of Barack Obama was, in fact, Howard Zinn's dream becoming reality.

> There is a concerted effort on behalf of American leftists to indoctrinate unsuspecting minds through the very books they are assigned to read in class.

Zinn was once vice president of a group investigated by the FBI for alleged communist infiltration in Brooklyn,

New York, and attended meetings almost every single day of the week.[25] He was so respected amongst the Communist Party that he actually taught a class on Marxism to his fellow comrades.[26]

Initially Zinn lied repeatedly about his Communist Party membership in order to continue his "quiet revolution" unbothered. But FBI documents on him released in 2010 prove otherwise.[27]

A People's History of the United States was specifically written to promote the downfall of America and to rob children of their ability to take pride in being American.[28] In truth, it's nothing more than pseudo-history invented by a man who despised America and did everything he could to bring it to its knees. Although Zinn's work is the most notorious amongst leftist propaganda books, his work has no doubt inspired others.

The issue of textbook brainwash has gotten so dire that Arizona actually had to pass a law to stop schools from teaching classes that "promote the overthrow of the United States government; promote resentment toward a race or class of people; are designed primarily for pupils of a particular ethnic group; or advocate ethnic solidarity instead of the treatment of pupils as individuals." That is, until radical leftist Ninth US Circuit Court of Appeals Judge A. Wallace Tashima imposed an injunction against Arizona's efforts to treat every student equally rather than based on skin color, as well as to prevent blatant racial animosity from being taught.[29] In other words, "Judge" Tashima felt that Arizona should take a lesson from the Jim Crow South and its days of "separate but equal" treatment of students.

Arizona's Superintendent of Public Instruction, Tom Horne, said that Tucson School District propaganda courses often promoted the idea that Latinos were "victims of a racist American society driven by the interests of middle- and upper-class whites."[30] On classroom walls hung seemingly worshipful pictures of Fidel Castro and Che Guevara. Both were terrorists and mass killers, but they were portrayed as "heroes" to the students. Tucson divided students based on race for the African American and Native American courses that they taught.[31] Leftist administrators literally brought back the segregation policies of the racist Jim Crow South.

In 1954 one of the most famous court cases in American history, *Brown v. Board of Education*, drove a stake through the racist policy of segregating schools. The Supreme Court in *Brown v. Board of Education* ruled that racial segregation violates the Equal Protection Clause of the Fourteenth Amendment, only to have leftist administrators bring it back in the name of "social justice."[32]

Martin Luther King Jr. famously declared:

> I have a dream that my four little children will one day live in a nation where they will not be judged by the color of their skin but by the content of their character.[33]

Segregating students in a public school is not only unconstitutional, it's a slap in the face to everything a man like Martin Luther King Jr. stood for. It's a direct betrayal of everything that binds us together through our common humanity and nationality.

A Tucson teacher named John Ward was shamefully removed from teaching a class for Mexican Americans and was reassigned because he questioned this racist, anti-American propaganda campaign. Ward was called a racist and, since he himself is of Mexican heritage, he was also called *vendido* (Spanish for *sellout*).[34]

Of course, Spanish is a language from Europe, a "white country," but that irony was lost on those who attacked Mr. Ward.[35] The only reason Latin Americans speak Spanish is because of European colonialism. If the radical leftists who organized these racist courses and attacked Mr. Ward wanted everyone to truly revert back to their native culture, which seemed to be the general theme, they should've taught the courses in ancient Mayan.

Textbooks in class also referred to Americans as "Anglos" or "Euromericans" instead of just "Americans."[36] Mr. Ward wrote:

> It justified teaching that the Southwestern United States was taken from Mexicans because of the insatiable greed of the Yankee who acquired his values from the corrupted ethos of Western civilization.[37]

The books also led students to believe that the United States was not actually a country, and Arizona is part of "Aztlan, Mexico," even though the Aztecs never lived in current United States territory.[38] Leftists have found a very creative way to legitimize racism under the veil of tolerance, and our children are the direct victims.

ISLAMIC PROPAGANDA

The textbook *History Alive! The Medieval World and Beyond* reveals a troubling pattern, consistent with many educational textbooks written about world religions. The book bends over backward to portray Islam as a religion of peace, while giving overblown and inaccurate scrutiny to other religions.[39]

Sharia-legitimized practices, such as forced marriage, pedophilia, domestic violence, beheadings, and stonings, were not mentioned at all.[40] Additionally, Muhammad was given an entire chapter of entirely positive dedication, while Jesus received just one sentence throughout the entire book.[41] One sentence about Muhammad read:

> He preached tolerance for Christians and Jews, as fellow worshipers of the one true God.[42]

Of course, it's hard to make that argument with actual verses from the Quran such as:

> And fight them until there is no more Fitnah [disbelief and worshipping of others along with Allah] and worship is for Allah alone.
> —QURAN (2:191–193)

By contrast, it doesn't mention any of Christ's teachings, and dedicates a lengthy list of examples of Christians oppressing others.[43] Why the double standard? This is what it looks like when leftist educators and the radical Islamic lobby work together to brainwash your children.

The Muslim group Council on Islamic Education (CIE), which changed its name to the Institute on Religion and Civic Values (IRCV), collaborates frequently with educational publishers for grades K–12 to push their propaganda into the minds of unsuspecting children.[44] IRCV is run by a man named Shabbir Mansuri, who has himself stated that he's waging a "bloodless revolution" inside American classrooms to promote Islam in a positive light.[45]

Judging by the current state of our educational system, the bloodless revolution has been going well for Mansuri. Who would have thought that in 2018 American children would have to celebrate Hijab Day, where young American girls would be segregated from boys, covering their heads with Muslim garb, all while young girls in Iran are fighting for the right to show their hair.[46]

More on that later.

Textbook publishers such as Houghton Mifflin, McGraw Hill, and Prentice Hall have allowed Mansuri and his radical organization to review and edit their books for anything they find offensive.[47] According to the American Textbook Council, "Textbook publishers court the Council on Islamic Education and other Muslim organizations—or at least try to appease them. This legitimacy is bestowed in spite of longstanding questions about sources of funding and degree of control over publishers."[48]

The American Textbook Council goes on to say,

> Textbook editors try to avoid any subject that could turn into a political grenade. Willingly, they adjust the definition of *jihad* and *sharia* or remove these words from lessons to avoid inconvenient truths that the editors fear activists will contest. Explicit facts that non-Muslims might find disturbing are varnished or deleted. Textbooks pare to a minimum such touchy subjects as Israel and oil as agents of change in the Middle East since 1945. Terrorism and Islam are uncoupled and the ultimate dangers of Islamic militancy hidden from view....Islamic organizations, willing to sow

misinformation, are active in curriculum politics. These activists are eager to expunge any critical thought about Islam from textbooks and all public discourse.[49]

In the past, most K–12 textbooks gave no more than a few pages to Islamic history, and the material was far more objective. But now, thanks to powerful Islamic lobbying forces like IRCV, text dedicated to Islam has exploded.[50]

It would be troubling enough to have supposedly historical textbooks whitewash the violent truth about Islam, but to have them actively promoting Islam is beyond absurd. This is being done in conjunction with classroom activities.

After students are done being brainwashed with lies about the religion of peace, they'll be treated to lectures demonizing Judaism and Christianity in a nation founded on Judeo-Christian values and principles. Our schools have moved from education to indoctrination in a blatant attempt to soften our children's opinions of Islam, and in the most egregious cases, to even convert them.

Textbooks written under the powerful and influential voices of Islamic pressure groups such as CAIR, IRCV, or other radical Islamic propagandists often portray Christian and Jewish traditions as simply stories attributed to some human source, as opposed to Islamic traditions, which are presented as indisputable facts.[51]

- For example, the textbook *McDougal Littell World Cultures and Geography* states that Judaism is a "story," and that Christians only "believe" that Jesus was King, which would be fine if not for the fact the same book states that the Quran actually "is the collection of God's revelations to Muhammad."[52]

- Another book *Holt World History* cleverly states that Moses "claimed" to receive the Ten Commandments directly from God, while Muhammad, simply "received" the Quran directly from God.[53]

- One textbook *Across the Centuries* waters down the meaning of jihad to simply an "internal struggle" for Muslims.[54] So 9/11 was just an internal struggle then?

Over 90 percent of Muslim interpretation refers to jihad as a holy war against infidels to either kill them or subjugate them. Only a select few describe it as an internal struggle. But why let facts get in the way?

As a child growing up in Lebanon, I always knew that jihad meant fighting for Allah. In the Islamic Middle East it is a given that dying while killing infidels is the highest form of jihad. But holy war is not in the definition of *jihad* in the *Across the Centuries* textbook.[55] "An Islamic term that is often misunderstood is jihad," it says, adding, "The term means 'to struggle,' to do one's best to resist temptation and overcome evil." One of IRCV's teacher guides actually had the nerve to list giving up cigarettes as an example of jihad.[56]

In a San Francisco–area school fed up parents sued the school over a required project for students to "become Muslims" for two weeks.[57] The project, which IRCV helped write, required children to analyze at least one verse of the Quran, memorize five Islamic proverbs, and give up things such as watching TV or eating lunch in honor of Ramadan fasting![58]

The instructions for the project literally stated, "From the beginning, you and your classmates will become Muslims."[59] The teaching module also implemented "suggestions" by a man named Yousef Salem, who has an explicit history of praising terrorist groups like Hezbollah and calling Israelis terrorists.[60]

The course on Islam even had students learning about the Shahada, the Islamic prayer equivalent to the salvation prayer in Christianity. As a part of studying verses from the Quran, here is what Johnny and Sally are asked to recite and "analyze" in public schools. From the Islam Simulation materials:

> Your task is to analyze one of the verses and be able to explain what the verse means in relationship to life, today, to meet the Salaat (prayers) activity requirement.
> The Exordium
> In the name of Allah, the Compassionate, the Merciful
> Praise be to Allah, Lord of Creation,
> The Compassionate, the Merciful,
> King of Judgement-day!
> You alone we worship, and to You alone we pray for help.
> Guide us to the straight path
> The path of those whom You have favoured,
> Not of those who have incurred Your wrath,
> Nor of those who have gone astray.[61]

Teachers even warned students against saying anything negative about Islam during the project and told them that dressing as Muslims and trying to be involved will increase their chances at earning an excellent grade and having more fun.[62] Did I mention this is in a public school, paid for by tax dollars?

Can you imagine if a teacher was teaching students a course on Christianity and encouraging students to adopt Christian names, recite and memorize verses from the Bible, and go to a church on a field trip to understand what it is like to be a Christian? What would the ACLU say? What would the media say?

Yet this is exactly what has been happening in our schools since the publication of this Islam course in 1991. I suppose we can call this "Muslim privilege." These are the same schools where students cannot sing Christmas songs at Christmas. Oops, I forgot—you can't even call it Christmas! It's now called "Winter Break," and the songs must be about Santa and gift-giving without ever mentioning the reason for the holiday itself.[63]

Yet at the same time, young students in our country are being taught to actually recite the Quran! The Islam course was introduced in California schools in 1991, ten years prior to September 11. But in actuality, this "civilization jihad" of Islamic infiltration into American schools has been occurring for over forty years. In chapter 10 of my first book, *Because They Hate*, I explained how the Saudi royal family has spent close to $70 billion worldwide to further the teaching of Wahhabism through Islamic madrassas and to spread anti-American and anti-Israel sentiment. Much of this money is spent deceptively on US universities, which have been undermining the education system in America for more than four decades while unsuspecting parents had no clue.

As a result, the education system in America has been reengineered to disproportionately highlight Islam's ideology in history and social studies textbooks nationwide. In *Because They Hate*, I talk specifically about how the Saudis have used Title IV of the National Defense of Education Act to build Muslim student associations and support Saudi "mercenaries" on campuses. I also discuss this problem in my second book, *They Must Be Stopped*. I encourage you to read both of these books if you haven't already done so.

As a mother, I want my children to have an overview of all major religions, Christianity, Judaism, Buddhism, Hinduism, and Islam, from an informative and objective perspective. But neither I nor most of you reading this book should want our children indoctrinated into any religion. It's up to parents to instruct their children about their own faith and why they value it personally. This is not for public schools to push on students, particularly when other religions are held to such a strict standard.

The problem was so out of hand that my organization, ACT for America, worked with other like-minded patriots nationwide and shined a light so bright on the issue that the Texas State Board of Education passed a resolution that warned publishers against printing textbooks filled with Islamic propaganda.[64]

Students at Friendswood Junior High in Houston were actually required to attend an "Islamic Awareness" presentation featuring representatives from none other than terrorist-designated CAIR during physical education class.[65] During the presentation, students were taught things such as "there is one God, his name is Allah" and "Adam, Noah, and Jesus are prophets."[66] They were also taught how to pray five times a day and wear Islamic religious garb properly.[67] Clearly, the phys ed teacher did not organize this presentation as a way to get students to run during class. Parents were not notified about it until after the story blew up in the local media.

This problem is not exclusive to any one part of the country; it is a nationwide indoctrination epidemic. In Amherst, New Hampshire, students were placed in a "Saudi Arabian Bedouin tent community."[68] They were segregated based on sex, with the girls hosting hijab and veil stations and handing out oppressive Muslim garb to be worn from head to toe. The boys hosted Arabic food-tasting stations and dancing because, as was explained to them, "the traditions of Saudi Arabia at this time prevent women from participating in these public roles."[69] The Islamic religion station even had a prayer rug with Quranic verses for students to cite and a compass conveniently pointing toward Mecca.

Can you even imagine if a public high school made young girls dress up as nuns and boys as priests? What if they had the Catholic stations of the cross set up and instructed students how to say a "Hail Mary"? How about Pentecostal stations where students could all learn to speak in tongues? You know what might also be fun? A baptism station where students could all practice baptizing each other in water. Do you think Muslim parents would be comfortable with their children learning to dress as Orthodox Jews or being told how to recite the Torah? CNN would be running wall-to-wall coverage, and the ACLU would be on the doorstep of the school district at lightning speed to sue for a violation of the civil rights of atheists and other religions.

Curiously, the leftists in education, who always claim to stand for human rights, particularly women's rights, are completely silent, or worse, actually glorify oppression of women in Islam to young children. On February 1, 2018, also known by some as "World Hijab Day," students and teachers at Leonardo Da Vinci High School in Buffalo, New York, celebrated by donning the hijab as a "social experiment," along with many others all across the country.[70]

Interesting, I wonder what would happen if Muslim students were asked to wear yarmulkes for "World Kippa Day"? Or a cross to celebrate "World Cross Day"? Do you think there might be some outrage on the part of Muslim parents?

Do you think the media might not treat the story as favorably as the *Buffalo News* did?[71] The mainstream press reported that the event was held to "foster tolerance at a time when hijabs have made Muslim women a visible target for ridicule or even violence."[72]

I vote we try "World Kippa Day" at Leonardo Da Vinci High School, since no religious group has been the target of hate crimes more than Jews have in recent history. Don't hold your breath. We wouldn't want to cross the always-guarded leftist line between separation of church and state. That privilege is held exclusively by Muslims who get special treatment in the name of "tolerance," "inclusivity," and "fairness."

Another example: in October of 2017 in Newton, Massachusetts, high school students were told to pretend to be Muslims as part of an assignment on the Israeli-Palestinian conflict.[73] One father was rightfully upset when he discovered his daughter had been assigned an anti-Semitic, pro-Palestinian article. The principal callously responded to the father's outrage by telling him that lessons next year would be even more upsetting to him. Courtesy of your tax dollars, ladies and gentlemen.

The class assignment, "Cities: Connecting the Islamic World," was excerpted from a book by CAMERA, the Committee for Accuracy in Middle East Reporting.[74] Students were told to talk about the heritage of their assigned "Islamic hometowns."

Except for one little problem.

One of the eight "Islamic hometowns" was Jerusalem, the capital of Israel. Can you imagine how young Jewish students must have felt to have to endure this assignment? Can you even begin to imagine the media apocalypse that would ensue if a public school taught Muslim students that Mecca was actually Jewish land?

In January 2018 an outraged mother in New Jersey filed a federal civil rights lawsuit against her daughter's school district. According to the mother, Chatham Middle School administrators and teachers made students view Islamic propaganda, including an explicit call to convert to Islam.[75]

The video lessons featured the prayer "May God help us all find the true faith, Islam. Amen,"[76] as well as Quranic verses that stated Islam is "perfected" and is the only religion for mankind. Students were then required to complete an Islamic conversion creed and prayer on a fill-in-the-blank worksheet, which also had a link to a website that would help them easily convert to Islam.[77]

Of course, Christianity and Judaism were not covered in the class, because that would be crossing the line between church and state. Let's be honest, if the videos had involved Christianity or Judaism, there would have been a reporter from every mainstream media news outlet on the doorstep of the superintendent's home demanding a comment. The Council on American-Islamic Relations would have tried to strong-arm the school into submission, and all we would hear about is how we need to respect the secular nature of public education.

And yet, when it's one particular religion that crosses the boundary between mosque and state, not only is it tolerated, but it's even celebrated. In May 2017 parents in the San Diego School District sued the district over their ties with CAIR. Parents were outraged that CAIR's "Anti-Islamophobia" initiative was focused on giving special privileges to Muslim students while indoctrinating all students to view Islam with a pro-Muslim perspective, leaving out the aspects of jihad and Islamic terrorism. CAIR said their aim was to combat bullying, but in reality they used the anti-bullying theme as a front to push their radical indoctrination curriculum.[78]

CAIR was also teaching students about the dangers of "Islamophobia" as well as attempting to brainwash them on concepts such as jihad. To add to the aggravation amongst parents, taxpayer dollars were used by the district to purchase material prepared by CAIR to hand out in classrooms.[79]

> As the most powerful nation on earth, our downfall will be incremental in nature. It will come from generations who were never taught the true value of America or the true nature of its enemies.

Under pressure from parents in July 2017, the school board voted to sever ties with the terror-designated group. But when documents obtained in a public-records request showed that the school district's officials, including Superintendent Cynthia Marten, met with CAIR officials to continue the relationship on the same day the board voted to end it, parents decided to sue. CAIR's efforts in San Diego are just a microcosm of a much broader goal of conquering each and every American school.[80] The wall between church and state has never been higher, and the leftist love affair with Islam never stronger.

The destruction of America will not happen overnight. As the most powerful nation on earth, our downfall will be incremental in nature. It will come from generations who were never taught the true value of America or the true nature of its enemies. It will come from those who seek its destruction, filling the minds of future generations with poison and lies.

We owe it to our children to educate them about America's heritage, where our values come from, what made us the greatest nation on earth, what contributed to our growth, and the growth of humanity in modern history. If we do not instill within our children these critical values through their K–12 education, they will not have any context for why they're so lucky to live in this country, nor the invaluable sacrifices made by those before them to give them the priceless gift we call home today.

THE GOOD NEWS

Here's the good news for patriots and the bad news for leftists. The rapid advancements in technology over the past decade have made it much harder for brainwashing academics to maintain their propaganda monopoly. Recent polling done on Generation Z (also called iGen and centennials) suggests a positive trend for freedom of thought.

Generation Z is the generation after millennials (Generation Y), and they are typically classified by sociologists as anyone born between the mid- to late

1990s. Hard as it is to believe, some Gen Zers have already graduated from college, and some millennials are already in their late thirties. Compared to millennials preceding them, Generation Z avoids student loans like the plague, which means they're exercising much better scrutiny over the value of higher education. With propagandist professors running rampant, it's easy to see why! A study by the Center for Generational Kinetics also found that Gen Z students plan to "work during college, keep clear of any personal debt, and start saving for retirement."[81]

Amazingly, 12 percent of Gen Zers have already started saving for retirement, and a huge 21 percent of them had their own savings account since before the age of ten! Right now, 77 percent of Gen Z earn their own spending money doing "freelance work, a part time job, or earned allowance."[82] This is likely due to the fact that this generation grew up during the financial crash of 2008 and are far more prudent about how they spend their money, so leftist indoctrinators may face a tougher future than they think.

A *Harvard Business Review* study suggests that "Gen Z is more conservative, more money-oriented, and more entrepreneurial than the millennials, and that nearly 70 percent of Gen-Z teens were 'self-employed' (e.g., teaching piano lessons, selling goods on eBay) vs. just 12 percent that held a 'traditional' teen job (e.g., waiting tables)."[83]

Why does this matter? Because Gen Z is showing signs of independent thought and thinking outside the box, which is the antithesis of leftism.

Get Ready for Conservative Gen Z.

Category	Percent
ALREADY SAVE FOR RETIREMENT	12%
HAVE SMOKED (COMPARED TO 55% OF TEENS IN THE '80s)	18%
HAVE A SAVINGS ACCOUNT	21%
HAVE HAD A DRINK OF ALCOHOL (COMPARED TO 62% OF TEENS IN THE '80S)	38%
ATTEND CHURCH	41%
ARE SELF-EMPLOYED	70%
EARN THEIR OWN SPENDING MONEY	77%

It's not just economics either, Generation Zers are ten times less likely to get tattoos, participate in underage drinking or illicit drug use, or smoke cigarettes than millennials. One study found that in the mid-1980s, 55 percent of eleven- to fifteen-year-olds had smoked a cigarette and 62 percent had drunk alcohol at some point.[84]

Compare those statistics with Gen Zers today, where only 18 percent have smoked a cigarette and 38 percent have had a drink of alcohol. Despite the ongoing opioid epidemic, the problem seems to be massively concentrated in preceding generations, as opposed to Gen Zers, as illicit drug use amongst early teens has been cut in half since 2001.[85]

Another startling statistic comes from a 2016 US study, which found that 41 percent of Gen Zers attended church during young adulthood, compared to 18 percent for millennials, 21 percent for Generation X, and 26 percent for baby boomers. This is great news for a society that was founded on Judeo-Christian principles.[86]

These are all promising signs for the freedom movement in the United States, as leftists who specialize in groupthink will predictably have a harder hill to climb with Gen Z indoctrination than they did with millennials or Gen Xers before them. Research data from Wright State University in Ohio, which polled twelve hundred Generation Z students at fifteen different colleges, found that Gen Z likes and trusts their parents far more than any generation before them, and are not as impressed with fame, celebrities, athletes, or politicians as millennials.[87]

> We owe it to the next generation to tell them the wonderful truth about America and the cold, hard truth about its enemies. We owe it to them so that they too can know what it's like to be proud of their country and preserve the freedoms and opportunities it gave them for future generations.

Since fame and celebrity have come easier to Gen Zers than any other generation with the social media revolution, this makes perfect sense, and it is another blow to the leftist indoctrination movement. I for one can't wait for the day when anti-American speeches given by cliché celebrities at Hollywood events such as the Oscars, Grammys, or Golden Globes will be completely ignored by America's largest voting bloc.

Still, these figures should not let us lose sight of the fact that right now our children are in danger and being led down the road of deceit and destruction by those they trust. It is our responsibility, those of us who know what a priceless treasure this country is, to give our young people the same opportunity to love it—to wave the American flag with pride instead of viewing it as a symbol of oppression or "white supremacy," as many have shamefully been led to believe.

We owe it to the next generation to tell them the wonderful truth about America and the cold, hard truth about its enemies. We owe it to them so that they too can know what it's like to be proud of their country and preserve the freedoms and opportunities it gave them for future generations.

RISE UP AND ACT

If you have children or grandchildren in your life, don't sit around wishing you could do something to protect them. ACT!

- If you have a child or grandchild, check what they have been learning. Become as invested as you need to be in their education, because if you don't, you may lose them. Children spend more time at school than they do at home, so the influence teachers have over them is profound. It is essential for parents to monitor potential efforts to indoctrinate their children.

- If possible, join your local school board. Local school boards have autonomy over education and can make a huge difference in weeding out potential attempts to indoctrinate students by leftist teachers, principals, and superintendents.

- If you are a parent considering paying for your child to go to college, be very mindful that you may be paying for their indoctrination. Consider sending them to an institution that embraces academic freedom, and do not believe that just because a university is Catholic, Baptist, Jewish, or religious, that they embrace those values. Do your own investigation. This is a huge investment, and you deserve the right to know whether it will be worth it or not.

Chapter 15

ACTIVISM FOR OUR NATION

Our nation is at a crossroads, the consequences of which are irreversible. We will either be destroyed and reshaped by leftist and Islamist forces, or our national identity will be preserved and restored to that which our Founding Fathers intended.

Today we are the deciding factor.

We decide what direction our ultimately takes.

We can either honor and preserve our Judeo-Christian heritage and the freedoms it has bestowed upon us, or we can sit idly by as our nation becomes the leftist utopia about which politicians like Barack Obama, Bernie Sanders, and Elizabeth Warren have always dreamt.

I firmly believe that each one of us has a calling, a destiny, and a purpose in this life. We all play a role in shaping history, whether we're aware of it or not.

Even our inactions shape history. In 2012 those who stayed home because they didn't want to vote for Mitt Romney left the door wide open for Barack Obama to walk through. Believe me, there are a lot of things Mitt Romney could improve upon as a politician, but at least he doesn't hate America.

I was bitten by the activism bug after a defining moment for America and the world: 9/11 changed all our lives forever. It changed the way we think, the way we act, the way we travel, the way we vote, and the way we viewed the rest of the world.

Americans of every race, religion, class, and creed were glued to our TV sets, watching in horror as images of the World Trade Center collapsing were shown over and over. It was like something out of an apocalyptic movie. After the shock wore off, we were left with broken hearts and feelings of helplessness in the face of such evil.

We couldn't bear to think about the children who would never see their parents again, the parents who would never see their children again, and the children onboard the airplanes who would never have a chance to grow up. "What kind of soulless monsters would commit such an atrocity?" we thought to ourselves. Not only did they kill thousands of innocent civilians, but they thought they were going to paradise for doing so.

We were united on that day, not only as Americans but as human beings. Nothing else mattered in those moments of horror except seeing our loved ones again and grieving for those who wouldn't have the chance. Political affiliation didn't matter. Race didn't matter. Gender didn't matter. None of the things that our enemies use today to divide us mattered. We were all united under the same flag of freedom.

For me, 9/11 brought back memories I wish I never remembered. While I watched on television as family members rushed to the scene, I could hear my parents' voices screaming my name as I laid trapped and wounded under my bedroom wall after Islamic terrorists blew up my home. I could still smell the smoke from the explosion that nearly killed me as I watched smoke engulf half of Manhattan. It sent chills down my spine as my worst nightmares were resurrected.

My two daughters, both young at the time but old enough to understand what was happening, came home from school that day and found me sitting in front of my TV crying my eyes out. My youngest daughter, who was around ten years old at the time, looked at me and asked, "Mommy, why did they do this to us?"

I couldn't believe I was answering her exactly the way my father answered me when I asked him that same question from a hospital bed in Lebanon twenty-five years earlier. "They hate us because we are Christians, and they consider us infidels," I said to her.

I was a ten-year-old Lebanese girl who spoke Arabic; she was a ten-year-old American girl who spoke English. Eight thousand miles and twenty-five years apart, yet both attacked by the same evil enemy for the same evil reason.

> You are one step away from becoming an unstoppable force of influence in your community.

That day was a defining moment in my life. I vowed right then and there that I would do everything I could to make sure that my daughters would never ever have to look into their children's eyes and tell them what both my daddy and I had to say. That day I was reborn as an activist.

Realizing how misinformed most Americans were about the root cause of Islamic terrorism, I knew I had to speak up as loud as possible. That desire to sound the alarm for my fellow countrymen was the motivational mechanism behind starting ACT for America.

I started ACT for America, the nation's largest grassroots national security advocacy organization, with the specific purpose of mobilizing average citizens concerned about our nation's security and turning them into one unified force for freedom.

Now that you know what we're up against as a nation, I hope today is your defining moment to stand up for our country and push back against America's enemies and their all-out assault on our most treasured freedoms and the Western, Judeo-Christian values they were founded upon. Having read all you have throughout this book, you are one step away from becoming an unstoppable force of influence in your community.

Today ACT for America has almost a million members nationwide, and when we stand united, we make a noise so loud that it can't be ignored—not by the DC swamp, and not by the mainstream media. Originally started out of my guest bedroom, ACT for America has exploded into the largest, most powerful national security–focused grassroots advocacy machine in the nation.

As of this writing, we've helped pass almost one hundred bills, with thirteen at the federal level and eighty-three on the state level, in thirty-two separate states. All of this from an organization started by a mother of two young girls in her spare time. Don't let anyone tell you that you can't affect real change. Especially yourself!

Remember, 2 percent of the passionate will always rule 98 percent of the indifferent. Choose to be part of the 2 percent of trailblazers like our nation's founders, and turn your passion, your drive, and your desire for change into an unstoppable force.

I strongly encourage you to join us at www.actforamerica.org and become a member and an activist. Start a chapter in your own community, or take this knowledge and use it to implement positive change on your own by starting a small group of your friends and neighbors. Either way, we need as many patriots as we can in this fight to defeat the radicals trying to destroy this nation from both abroad and within. Their side is active and mobilized. We need to be too. If you do choose to join us, we will provide you with enhanced training information as well as support, and connect you with like-minded patriots right there in your own backyard.

I'll tell you this, this fight is going to come down to who wants it more. The mighty British Empire was defeated by farmers, blacksmiths, and even preachers who were willing to die for the right to life, liberty, and the pursuit of happiness. The British couldn't replicate the American determination, and thus they were defeated, despite their enormous advantage on paper.

Grassroots activism is no different. The following is detailed information on how to build a strong activist network in your community, plan and execute activism initiatives, help fellow citizens get registered to vote, lobby for change in your state and federal government, and inform your peers about the most critical national security initiatives. All the bills mentioned in this chapter are given as examples; you should substitute whatever current legislation or issues are relevant.

I've seen it happen far too many times to not believe it: you *will* enact

> Remember, 2 percent of the passionate will always rule 98 percent of the indifferent. Choose to be part of the 2 percent of trailblazers like our nation's founders, and turn your passion, your drive, and your desire for change into an unstoppable force.

meaningful change within your community if you follow this proven blueprint. Start today. Our nation needs you.

KEEPING YOUR EYES ON EDUCATION

Universities have become centers of liberal indoctrination, but even more alarming than the one-sided political bias that exists is the strain of anti-Semitic and anti-American propaganda being pushed by faculty.

We are also seeing these views permeate into high schools and even elementary schools.

Leftists and Islamists are poisoning the minds of our youth with lies. You can play a crucial role in holding these administrators and faculty members accountable for their actions.

Here's what you can do when you hear about a concerning assignment, textbook, or activity occurring.

- Step 1: Select a professor or teacher at a school nearby who has been proven to espouse anti-American or anti-Semitic bias in the classroom. You can find examples of professors on Professorwatchlist.org and canarymission.org/professors.

- Step 2A: Organize a phone call campaign with your group to call the school administration about the professors troubling behavior. For universities, this could be the dean, or in high schools and/or elementary schools, try the principal and the superintendent. Contact information for these individuals can normally be found right on the school website, or you can call and ask the school secretary.

  If you have to leave a message, do so yourself, rather than hoping someone else will pass it on to them later. Be firm, direct, but respectful toward the administration. Often times administrators are consumed with so many other things, they are not aware of what the situation is, and you will catch more bees with honey than you will with vinegar.

- Step 2B: Organize a social media campaign from your group to tweet and post on Facebook about the professor's comments or actions.

- Step 2C: Have key members of your group write Letter to the Editor notes for all the local and statewide publications.

- Step 2D: Organize a letter-writing campaign to the university president or principal, calling for action against the faculty member in question.

- Step 2E: Email the proper administrator about the issue. Be sure to rally as many people as possible to do this. The more emails, the more impactful!

  Below is a sample email:

  President [Last Name],

  I am reaching out to you because, your student/faculty member/administrator at _____ [university/college] recently _____ [person-in-question's bad action/statement]. I am horrified to hear that someone who acts in such a disgraceful manner is [enrolled/employed] at your institution.

  [Professor/student/administrator name] is a(n) _____ [anti-Semite, anti-American, threat to campus safety, etc.] and should be removed from your campus immediately. Do the right thing for the [safety, integrity, etc.] of [the students and faculty, your university] you are responsible for.

  Outraged,
  [Your Name]

- Step 3: If your phone call campaign is not successful with triggering a reaction from the university (a statement, termination, suspension, etc.) or you are not satisfied with the university's reaction, it's time to organize a protest on the campus *only* if it is a public university, otherwise, on a public sidewalk close to the private university. If it's a high school or elementary school, request an in-person opportunity to address the school board.

  You will enact meaningful change within your community if you follow this proven blueprint.

  If you are hosting a protest, you will need to coordinate with your group to pick the best time/day to attract the most attendance. You will need to prepare signs on poster boards for group members to hold and either print in large font or use bold markers. The message on the poster boards should be very clear and focus on what outcome your group is looking to receive. Here are two clear examples: "Fire (professor's name)" or "Expel (student's name)."

  If your university protest doesn't trigger the university to respond appropriately, your next and final step will be to reach

out to your state's Board of Regents. The Board of Regents is
the governing body for public universities in every state. If you
are unfamiliar with how to find your regent or get in touch
with them, you can go to www.actforamerica.org or email us for
more information.

ACT for America sends out periodic "ACTION ITEM" emails focusing
on biased and radical educators nationwide. Be sure to sign up for these
emails on www.actforamerica.org and be on the lookout for these calls to
action!

KNOW THY LEGISLATOR

Besides meeting with your congressional representatives in DC or local
office, town halls are a great way to hear from your legislators in person.
More importantly, it's an opportunity to ask them questions and get those
answers on record.

Materials needed
Questions written on note cards or on your phone. (See a sample question
below. Topics and issues will change, but this will give you an idea of how to
ask a question.)

- The Muslim Brotherhood is a terrorist organization that
  funds Hamas. How do you feel about this issue?

- We must have merit-based immigration reform. Will you sign
  on as a cosponsor for the Reforming American Immigration
  for Strong Employment (RAISE) Act?

At least two volunteers

- One volunteer to ask the congressperson questions
- One volunteer to film the other person asking questions, as
  well as take pictures

How to attend a town hall

- Find a town hall near you at www.townhallproject.com.
- Mark your calendar and make a plan to attend your local
  town hall.
- Ask a friend to come with you.
- Designate one person as the questioner and the other to film
  it and take pictures.

- Email your friends, post on Facebook, and/or tweet that you'll be attending the town hall, providing all the location details.

- Email pictures@actforamerica and share your experience, as well as your film and pictures.

Helpful tips

- The more friends you have come with you, the better.

- Make sure each person has a copy of the questions mentioned above.

- Have people sit away from one another in different areas of the room.

- Remember: your goal is to film the response to your questions so it's on record.

LOBBYING

Congress works for us, not the other way around. One of the most important things you can do is call, email, and meet with your legislators.

People tell me all the time, "Brigitte, what is my voice going to do? My congressman needs to hear from forty thousand people in order to listen and do something." Wrong! I talk to elected officials all the time. Here is the science behind the numbers.

One phone call on an issue represents a thousand voters. That's why anytime you call a congressional office, the staff have to either pick up the phone and write down everything you say or transcribe the message you left on paper and send it to the Washington, DC, office. The more people who call on an issue, the more voters the elected official will be afraid of losing when it comes time to vote. Emails are great too but can be easier to ignore than phone calls.

Meeting face to face with a congressperson or staff member is one of the most effective ways to keep our legislators accountable. The more

> **Congress works for us, not the other way around.**

people you bring to the state capitol with you, the more powerful your voices will be.

PHONE CALLS

- The congressional switchboard to reach any member of Congress is 202-224-3121.

- Sample scripts might be:

My name is _____ and I'm asking for Senator _____ to sign on as a cosponsor for Senate Bill S.68, the Muslim Brotherhood Terrorist Designation Act of 2017. Thank you for delivering my message.

My name is _____, and I'm asking for Senator _____ to do what is necessary to protect this nation, and vote to appropriate funding for an impenetrable wall on our southern border. If we don't have borders, we don't have a country. If the senator does not vote to appropriate funding for a wall, I will not vote for him/her in the next election. Thank you, and I look forward to watching the senator's actions toward this issue.

Emails are not as effective as in-person meetings or phone calls, but if you choose to write to your legislator, mail them a handwritten letter, and it will make a much greater impact!

Remember, just forty phone calls are counted as forty thousand voters, so your group, or even you as an individual, *can* make a difference.

Letters to the Editor (LTE)

Writing letters to the editor of your local newspaper helps to bring awareness to an issue and allows you to define the narrative. Remember, perception is reality.

Helpful tips

An LTE is usually 250 words; some publications ask for 200 or fewer.

Your goal is to persuade or inform the reader about an issue.

Back everything up with facts from reputable news sources or research. Remember, your LTE will be scrutinized heavily by the opposition.

You want to make a difference, not just a statement, so it's incredibly important to stay on message and never write something you cannot verify is 100 percent accurate.

General format

- Make a statement.
- Back up the statement with three supporting facts.
- Conclude your LTE with an emphasis on persuading the reader why your initial statement is correct.

Example

Designating the Muslim Brotherhood as a terrorist organization is not anti-Muslim. The Muslim Brotherhood has been designated as a terrorist organization by several Muslim-majority countries, including Egypt, the Kingdom of Saudi Arabia, Syria, and the United Arab Emirates. Therefore, designating the Muslim Brotherhood as a terrorist organization cannot be anti-Muslim, as several Muslim-majority countries agree with the policy.

Where to Send LTEs

- This website provides you with the top one hundred online and print publications across the country: www.theoped project.org/submission-information.

Below is an example of a Muslim Brotherhood LTE

Did you know that Egypt, the Kingdom of Saudi Arabia, Syria, and the United Arab Emirates have all designated the Muslim Brotherhood as a terrorist organization?

Yes, these are all Muslim-majority countries. America should follow suit and has the opportunity thanks to Senator Ted Cruz's proposed bill, the Muslim Brotherhood Terrorist Designation Act of 2017 (S.68).

On November 24, 2008, a federal jury in Dallas, Texas, convicted five leaders of the Holy Land Foundation (HLF) charity for providing material support to Hamas, a terrorist group.

The US government provided evidence that the Muslim Brotherhood set up the HLF with the intent to fund Hamas. Even worse than the HLF donating $12.4 million to terrorism is that the Muslim Brotherhood's goal is to destroy Western civilization from within.

A federal judge also listed the Council on American-Islamic Relations (CAIR), a Muslim Brotherhood front group, as an unindicted coconspirator in the HLF trial. CAIR's president, Nihad Awad, is a professed Hamas supporter.

With Muslim Brotherhood groups in the US, like CAIR, it is clear we must designate the Muslim Brotherhood as a terrorist organization. Please call your senators and ask them to sign on to the bill as cosponsors.

Below is an example of a Back the Blue LTE

Police officers are our brothers, sisters, and neighbors, and are woven into the fabric of society. In 1955 the Los Angeles Police Department adopted "To Protect and Serve" as the official motto of its Police Academy.

There are many instances of cops risking their lives to protect and serve us, and we should back the blue.

Norbert Ramon is a twenty-four-year veteran of the Houston Police Department. During Hurricane Harvey, Ramon helped rescue fifteen hundred victims from the fatal floods. He did all of this despite having stage 4 colon cancer, which spread to his liver and lungs, and despite being given six to eight years to live.

Similarly, Officer Gene Taylor, Monroe County, Michigan, risked his life to save a fourteen-year-old girl. The girl ran onto railroad tracks, while a train sped toward her, and Officer Taylor pulled her to safety.

These police officers are both heroes. They put themselves in danger and truly live by the motto of "To Protect and Serve." We must never forget the bravery of officers like Ramon and Taylor, and we must always back the blue.

SOCIAL MEDIA ACTIVISM

Leftists and Islamists are experts at defining and controlling a narrative about their opponents, no matter how absurd or baseless. Radicals at the SPLC, CAIR, and leftist media outlets tried to shut down our "March Against Sharia" by attacking me and ACT for America relentlessly on social media, claiming that I was the leader of a white supremacist group.

Bear in mind, there aren't many white supremacy groups led by a tan-skinned, Arab woman who's a passionate supporter of Israel, but that doesn't matter in the eyes of our enemies. All that matters to them is spreading falsehoods and smears as far and wide as possible, hoping the average person will not do any investigating.

Part of defeating false narratives and defining true ones is engaging on social media.

This is the outlet that helped President Trump battle his way past the mainstream media lies and directly into the hearts and minds of the American voters.

Here's how to get a large amount of people to see what you have to say on high-profile Twitter accounts.

Goal

Select a group or individual on Twitter you want to oppose, such as the SPLC, CAIR, Linda Sarsour, etc. Once you have your target, make sure you and your fellow members or friends sign up for notifications of tweets on Twitter or posts on Facebook.

The next time this group tries to spread falsehoods or push radical propaganda, you can respond in a timely manner.

Instructions

Follow @lsarsour, @splcenter, @CAIRnational, and/or another account on Twitter.

1. While on one of these pages, click on the button that looks like a vertical ellipsis.
2. Click "Turn on mobile notifications."
3. Whenever one of these groups tweets, you will receive a text message.
4. As soon as you receive a text message, go to their most recent tweet.
5. Take the respective suggested tweets below and copy/paste a reply.

Suggested tweets

- @lsarsour is an anti-Semite who said that a victim of female genital mutilation should have her genitalia taken away from her. #LoveTrumpsLinda
- @CAIRnational is known by the FBI to be a Muslim Brotherhood front group. Muslim-majority countries, such as the UAE, have designated the Muslim Brotherhood as a terrorist organization, and the United States should do the same.
- Why hasn't the @splcenter designated @lsarsour as a hate leader, who is not only an anti-Semite, but also worked with Rasmea Odeh during the Women's March? Rasmea Odeh is a convicted terrorist who murdered 2 Israeli students

LOCAL POLITICS

Remember, even today all politics is local, and though ACT for America is the largest grassroots national security organization in America, we still know the importance of maintaining a presence at school board and city council meetings. Relationship building is key. Be proactive about potential threats to your community before they even get started.

You can attend a school board meeting and city council meetings, or assign a group member or friend to do so. If you start a group or chapter, each member should take notes during the meeting of any potentially concerning issues.

Some potential issues to listen for include discussion on textbooks, zoning and any new buildings, immigration or refugee resettlement, parents complaining about religious homework, amongst others.

Pay close attention to who speaks at these meetings and what their beliefs are. If they feel similarly on your issues, be sure to introduce yourself to them before leaving the meetings and ask them to join you in your activist mission. There is strength in numbers.

Follow up with them every so often and invite them to your chapter meeting if you have one or a casual get-together to stay in touch.

Simply establishing a presence at these meetings can allow you to not only learn about potential issues before they take root, but also to establish rapport with school board and city council members. They pay attention to who speaks at and attends these meetings as well and will listen more closely to those who have stuck in their minds due to regular attendance.

ELECTIONS MATTER

We're living in a time of increasingly important elections. Sure, we've been hearing for decades about how every election is the most important of our lifetime, but this time it's no exaggeration. Since 2008 the Democratic Party has gone from the Center-Left party of Bill Clinton to the anti-American party of Barack Obama.

There were serious questions about President Clinton's moral decency, but I view him as more of a political opportunist than a leftist. If we compare his views and actions with those taken by Obama, the Clinton administration comes out looking like a bunch of Republicans. Did Clinton have serious character flaws? Yes. But I don't believe Bill Clinton hated America or its founding principles as much as he was just apathetic toward them. Sadly, I can't say the same for Barack Obama.

Since Obama's rise to power, the Democratic Party has been transformed to the party of lawlessness and anti-Americanism. It's embraced anarchist groups such as Antifa and Black Lives Matter, calling them "peaceful protesters," even after such groups call for the death of police officers. It's trotted out anti-Semitic Islamist and 9/11 conspiracy theorist Rep. Keith Ellison from Minnesota as a front-runner in their election for DNC chairman.[1] It's even discussed adding reparations for slavery as one of its official platform issues in the next presidential election.[2] This happened during a recently held donor meeting in Atlanta attended by Rep. Tom Perez, who edged out Farrakhan-favorite Keith Ellison by a hair for DNC chairman. It's embraced George Soros' vision for an "open society," embracing lawlessness and sanctuary cities for illegal immigrants.

In fact, the Democrats' support for sanctuary cities, which intentionally subvert federal immigration law in order to harbor illegal aliens, is proof that local elections can be just as paramount to the survival of this nation as federal elections. When the leftist

> We cannot continue to give power to those who have no respect for this country, the Constitution, its founding principles, or human rights.

mayor of Oakland, Libby Schaaf, got wind of an Immigration and Customs Enforcement (ICE) raid to be conducted in the area, she took matters into her own hands and tipped off illegal residents by tweeting about the raid in advance to warn them.[3] When a locally elected mayor can put the lives of federal immigration officers in danger and play a key role in illegal aliens—some of whom are violent—evading arrest, you know things are out of hand.

Don Rosenberg, an "Angel Dad" whose son, Drew, was killed when an illegal-immigrant driver from Honduras hit him on his motorbike, correctly pointed out that Schaaf and every other sanctuary city mayor should be prosecuted.[4] Shockingly to me, the Justice Department did nothing to Schaaf and continues to allow sanctuary cities to flourish throughout our nation. The way you can help change this is from the ground up. We've got to focus our energy not just at the federal level, but at the state and local level as well.

The sanctuary city issue is just one of many examples of how local politics can have a federal impact. Recently in Maine the Democratic Party amended a bill that bans FGM and holds perpetrators accountable for their barbaric actions. The result? Maine House Democrats removed penalties in the bill for accomplices to the crime, leaving them to get off scot-free.[5] Yet another example of how radical one party has gotten and how local politics can profoundly impact the fabric of our American society.

These are important truths to keep in mind for the next local, state, and federal elections. We cannot continue to give power to those who have no respect for this country, the Constitution, its founding principles, or human rights. America needs your activism on this issue, and without your voice and your vote, those who seek to, in the words of Barack Obama, "fundamentally transform this nation" will have every opportunity to do so.

9/11 REMEMBRANCE

We said we would never forget, but in many ways our nation has. Rarely do we ever even see images of the World Trade Center anymore or videos of the horror that took place that day. Allowing families to grieve is important, but we also must remind ourselves of this infamous day, so we can honor those lost and fight to prevent anything even close to this level of catastrophic attack from reoccurring.

Remember, anyone under the age of twenty-one today (Gen Z) does not even remember 9/11. They grew up in a post-9/11 world, where Islamophobia was portrayed as more of a threat than Islamic terrorism. We must continue to remember that which we said we always would and educate our young people about the threat that Islamic terrorism still poses to our country and Western, Judeo-Christian civilization as we know it.

It may not sound like much, but some possible activities to organize in your community and keep the spotlight on this important historical event might include holding a candlelight vigil at your local city council, spelling out "Remember 9/11" or "Never Forget Means Never Again" at a local park with chalk, holding signs with similar messaging at a busy intersection, or even just sharing your stories on social media and asking others to do the same.

Be sure to take pictures and/or videos and send them to pictures@actforamerica.org with a caption so we can share what you did with our nearly one million members and hundreds of thousands of followers on social media.

No matter who you are, where you reside, what your age, or how busy you are, make no mistake: everyone reading this can truly change their country and community for the better. Having worked side by side with patriots just like you for almost two decades, I've seen truly remarkable change enacted at the local, state, and federal levels because of the actions of a few.

The suggestions I shared in this chapter are just the tip of the iceberg of what we provide with ACT for America. I encourage you to join us as a member, as an activist, or if you're really determined, as a chapter president. We have extensive information and everything you need on how you can be a tremendously effective activist at www.actforamerica.org.

America is calling each and every one of us to protect it from harm. We are the instruments of change, writing history with our actions and inactions. What we do today will forever shape the future of this nation and leave our footprint in the canvas of freedom.

I believe every single one of us is prepared in life to fulfill a mission, to be an instrument of change to make this world a better place than when we found it. Every single trial and tribulation we go through is nothing more than preparation for the great work we are destined to do. Nothing happens by chance. Everything happens for a reason. You are reading this book today for a reason. Ask yourself, "What am I being called to do? What is my destiny? How can I be an instrument of change for my country? How can I honor our Judeo-Christian heritage and secure its future at least in my time and my children's lifetime?" Some people are called to become leaders, some to become part-time volunteers, and some to become financial supporters of the cause if they do not have the time to be involved. Let this day be your defining moment.

What we have here in America is truly exceptional, regardless of what the mainstream media will tell you. All cultures are not equal. Western, Judeo-Christian civilization is one of the greatest gifts humanity has ever known. I can't speak for anyone else, but I want that same shining city upon a hill that President Reagan referenced to be there long after I am gone.

I want my children, grandchildren, and generations following to grow up in a society that allows freedom of expression, the right to protect oneself from harm, the right to disagree without being labeled a bigot, the right to say "Merry Christmas" when it's Christmas, the right for young girls not to have to hide under a burka in shame or have their genitalia removed, the right to get on an airplane without fear of terrorism, the right to equal treatment under the law, and all the other rights that Western, Judeo-Christian civilization has afforded all of us.

We cannot continue to sit idly by as our community, country, and civilization continues to be attacked from both abroad and within, without any pushback.

It may be too late for Europe, but it's not too late for us.

It's time to take the fight to our enemies, both abroad and right here at home, and toss off the politically correct chains that have been crippling us for decades.

It's time to secure our borders once and for all and restore rule of law in this country.

It's time to teach our young people how to love this country again and be proud of their national identity.

It's time to show the anti-free speech bullies that we will not be silenced.

It's time to show the media that we will not buy any more of their lies.

It's time to show our elected officials that we will vote them out if they do not represent and protect this nation.

It's time to restore the tight-knit, God-loving, American family that saved the world from tyranny and pioneered the cause of liberty for the rest of the world to parallel.

It's time to rise.

NOTES

INTRODUCTION

1. Abraham Lincoln, "The Perpetuation of Our Political Institutions: Address Before the Young Men's Lyceum of Springfield, Illinois," January 27, 1838, http://www.abrahamlincolnonline.org/lincoln/speeches/lyceum.htm.

2. "Glenn Beck: Rome's Rise and Fall," December 1, 2010, FOX News Network LLC, http://www.foxnews.com/story/2010/12/02/glenn-beck-rome-rise-and-fall.html.

CHAPTER 1—OUR NATION DIVIDED

1. "September 11th Hijackers Fast Facts," Cable News Network, updated August 28, 2017, https://www.cnn.com/2013/07/27/us/september-11th-hijackers-fast-facts/index.html.

2. Ed Vulliamy, "'Let's Roll...,'" *Guardian*, December 1, 2001, https://www.theguardian.com/world/2001/dec/02/september11.terrorism1; Francie Grace, "White House Was Flight 93 Target," CBS Interactive Inc., May 20, 2002, https://www.cbsnews.com/news/white-house-was-flight-93-target/.

3. Sam Webb, "Cleric Crackdown," *The Sun*, January 2, 2017, https://www.thesun.co.uk/news/2517413/saudi-arabia-executed-more-than-150-prisoners-last-year-as-hardline-islamic-leaders-use-sharia-law-to-justify-tough-punishments/.

4. Anthony Castellano and Michael Rothman, "How Baseball Helped New York Heal Post 9/11," ABC News, accessed April 4, 2018, http://abcnews.go.com/US/fullpage/baseball-yankees-helped-york-heal-post-911-president-33663881; gregtassone, "President Bush's Opening Pitch at Yankee Stadium After 9-11," YouTube, September 6, 2011, https://www.youtube.com/watch?v=bxR1tZ08FcI.

5. Nicole Knight Shine, "American Flag, Others Banned in UC Irvine Student Area," *Los Angeles Times*, March 6, 2015, http://www.latimes.com/local/lanow/la-me-ln-american-flag--ban-uc-irvine-20150306-story.html.

6. Shine, "American Flag."

7. Martha Schick, "Mass. College Removes American Flag After Flag Burning, Race Concerns," *Boston Globe*, November 21, 2016, https://www.bostonglobe.com/news/politics/2016/11/21/mass-college-stops-flying-flag-after-becomes-focus-dispute-over-trump/3zo5w4tqw4AQbjRhth1g9I/story.html.

8. Schick, "Mass. College Removes American Flag."

9. Ron Dicker, "TV Host Mike Rowe Slams College That Removed American Flag," HuffPost, December 2, 2016, https://www.huffingtonpost.com/entry/tv-host-mike-rowe-slams-college-that-removed-american-flag_us_58414da6e4b0c68e04803a34.

10. "Roger Goodell 'Proud' How NFL Responded to President Trump's Comments," September 25, 2017, ESPN.com, http://www.espn.com/nfl/story/_/id/20814437/roger-goodell-reaction-proud-our-league.

11. Josh Peter, "Head of Police Organization: Colin Kaepernick's Socks 'Disrespectful' and NFL at Fault," *USA Today*, September 1, 2016, https://www

.usatoday.com/story/sports/nfl/49ers/2016/09/01/police-reaction-colin-kaepernick
-pig-socks-san-francisco/89715672/.

12.   Armando Salguero, "Unrepentant Hypocrite Colin Kaepernick Defends
Fidel Castro," *Miami Herald*, updated November 28, 2016, http://www.miami
herald.com/sports/spt-columns-blogs/armando-salguero/article117033883.html.

13.   Brandon George, "Flashback: NFL Wouldn't Allow Cowboys to Wear
Decal Supporting Dallas Police on Their Helmets," SportsDay, updated August
11, 2016, https://sportsday.dallasnews.com/dallas-cowboys/cowboys/2016/08/10
/nfl-allow-dallas-cowboys-wear-arm-arm-decal-helmets-games.

14.   Jason Wolf, "NFL Squashes Titans Linebacker Avery Williamson's Plan
to Honor 9/11 Victims," *Tennessean*, September 9, 2016, https://www.tennessean
.com/story/sports/nfl/titans/2016/09/09/nfl-squashes-titans-linebacker-avery
-williamsons-plan-honor-911-victims/89956128/.

15.   Clark Mindock, "Taking a Knee: Why Are NFL Players Protesting and
When Did They Start to Kneel?," *Independent*, September 25, 2017, http://www
.independent.co.uk/news/world/americas/us-politics/taking-a-knee-national
-anthem-nfl-trump-why-meaning-origins-racism-us-colin-kaepernick-a7966961
.html.

16.   Dan Cahill, "64 Percent of Americans Agree With Trump About
NFL—Study," *Chicago Sun-Times*, September 26, 2017, https://chicago.suntimes
.com/sports/trump-nfl-poll-anthem-respect-study/.

17.   Maghen Moore, "Watch: Shannon Sharpe 'Unimpressed' With NFL
Protest," *Atlanta Journal-Constitution*, accessed April 4, 2018, https://www.ajc
.com/sports/watch-shannon-sharpe-unimpressed-with-nfl-protest/Qja90AMfxl
Th2PYAkEV7ON/new.html.

18.   "Shannon Sharpe: Alejandro Villanueva 'Wrong' to Stand for National
Anthem Against Team Vote," Newsround, September 25, 2017, http://newsround
.io/pop/shannon-sharpe-alejandro-villanueva-wrong-to-stand-for-national-anthem
-against-team-vote/23670.

19.   Joe DePaolo, "Skip Bayless Criticizes Steelers' Villanueva for Being Only
Steeler to Honor Anthem," Mediaite LLC, September 25, 2017, https://www
.mediaite.com/online/skip-bayless-criticizes-steelers-villaneuva-for-being-only
-team-member-to-come-out-for-anthem/; Sean Gentille, "Alejandro Villanueva: 'I
Feel Embarrassed' by Anthem Foul-Up," *Pittsburgh Post-Gazette*, September 25,
2017, http://www.post-gazette.com/sports/steelers/2017/09/25/alejandro
-villanueva-steelers-national-anthem-protest/stories/201709250175.

20.   James Dator, "Alejandro Villanueva Has the Steelers' No. 1-Selling Jersey
After Going Out for Anthem Without Teammates," Vox Media Inc., September
25, 2017, https://www.sbnation.com/lookit/2017/9/25/16360882/alejandro
-villanueva-steelers-no-1-selling-jersey-anthem.

21.   Lisa Respers France, "Snoop Dogg 'Shoots' Trump Clown 'Ron Klump'
in New Video," Cable News Network, updated March 15, 2017, https://www
.cnn.com/2017/03/14/entertainment/snoop-dogg-donald-trump-video/index.html;
Nick Vadala, "Philly Man Who Directed Snoop Dogg's Trump 'Assassination'
Video Says He 'Click-Baited the President,'" *Inquirer*, updated March 20, 2017,
http://www.philly.com/philly/blogs/entertainment/celebrities_gossip/Philly-man

-who-directed-Snoops-Trump-assassination-video-says-he-click-baited-the
-president.html.

22.   Tom Kludt, "FCC Won't Take Action Against Colbert Over Trump
Joke," Cable News Network, May 23, 2017, http://money.cnn.com/2017/05/23
/media/stephen-colbert-fcc-donald-trump/index.html.

23.   Tim Hains, "Maxine Waters: 'God Is on Our Side,' If You See a Member
of Trump Cabinet, 'Push Back,'" RealClearHoldings LLC, June 25, 2018, https://
www.realclearpolitics.com/video/2018/06/25/maxine_waters_god_is_on_our_
side.html#!.

24.   Adam Shaw, "Angela Merkel Admits That 'No-Go Zones' Exist in Germany," FOX News Network LLC, March 1, 2018, http://www.foxnews.com
/world/2018/03/01/angela-merkel-admits-that-no-go-zones-exist-in-germany.html.

CHAPTER 2—THE COST OF TERROR

1.   Kevin Sieff, "Boko Haram Kidnapped 276 Girls Two Years Ago. What
Happened to Them?," *Washington Post*, April 14, 2016, https://www.washington
post.com/news/worldviews/wp/2016/04/14/boko-haram-kidnapped-276-girls
-two-years-ago-what-happened-to-them/.

2.   Hilary Matfess, "Three Years Later, A Look at the #BringBackOurGirls
Catch-22," The Daily Beast Company, April 14, 2017, https://www.thedailybeast
.com/three-years-later-a-look-at-the-bringbackourgirls-catch-22.

3.   "Lashkar-e-Taiba," Stanford University, accessed April 4, 2018, http://
web.stanford.edu/group/mappingmilitants/cgi-bin/groups/view/79.

4.   "Ansar al-Sharia in Libya (ASL)," Counter Extremism Project, accessed
April 4, 2018, https://www.counterextremism.com/threat/ansar-al-sharia-libya-asl.

5.   "Ansar al-Sharia," Counter Extremism Project.

6.   Mike Opelka, "Video Montage Shows Obama, Hillary, Susan Rice and
Jay Carney All Blaming Benghazi on the Video," TheBlaze Inc., May 2, 2014,
https://www.theblaze.com/news/2014/05/02/video-montage-shows-obama
-hillary-susan-rice-and-jay-carney-all-blaming-benghazi-on-the-video.

7.   David Daoud, "Meet the Proxies: How Iran Spreads Its Empire Through
Terrorist Militias," *The Tower*, March 2015, http://www.thetower.org/article/meet
-the-proxies-how-iran-spreads-its-empire-through-terrorist-militias/.

8.   Radhika Chalasani, "A Look Back at the Deadly 1983 Marine Barracks
Bombing in Beirut," ABC News, October 23, 2017, http://abcnews.go.com
/International/back-deadly-1983-marine-barracks-bombing-beirut/story?id=
50663026; Erica Pearson, "1983 United States Embassy Bombing," *Encyclopedia
Britannica*, accessed April 4, 2018, https://www.britannica.com/event/1983
-United-States-embassy-bombing; Erica Pearson, "Khobar Towers Bombing of
1996," *Encyclopedia Britannica*, accessed April 4, 2018, https://www.britannica
.com/event/Khobar-Towers-bombing-of-1996.

9.   Mark Mazzetti and Thom Shanker, "Arming of Hezbollah Reveals U.S.
and Israeli Blind Spots," *New York Times*, July 19, 2006, https://www.nytimes
.com/2006/07/19/world/middleeast/19missile.html; Anthony H. Cordesman,
"Iran's Rocket and Missile Forces and Strategic Options," Center for Strategic &

International Studies, October 7, 2014, https://csis-prod.s3.amazonaws.com/s3fs
-public/legacy_files/files/publication/141007_Iran_Rocket_Missile_forces.pdf.

10. Lizzie Dearden, "Hamas Declared a Terrorist Organisation by the European Court of Justice," *Independent*, July 26, 2017, http://www.independent.co.uk
/news/world/europe/hamas-terrorist-organisation-ecj-european-court-of-justice
-eu-uk-palestinian-israel-a7860301.html; Tamara Qiblawi, Angela Dewan, and
Larry Register, "Hamas Says It Accepts '67 Borders, But Doesn't Recognize
Israel," Cable News Network, updated May 3, 2017, https://www.cnn.com
/2017/05/01/middleeast/hamas-charter-palestinian-israeli/index.html.

11. Patrick Worrall, "Does Hamas Use Civilians as Human Shields?,"
Channel Four Television Corporation, July 24, 2014, https://www.channel4.com
/news/factcheck/factcheck-hamas-civilians-human-shields; "The Lead With Jake
Trapper," Cable News Network, July 15, 2014, http://www.cnn.com
/TRANSCRIPTS/1407/15/cg.02.html.

12. Ronn Torossian, "CNN Anchor Constantly Defends Hamas, Attacks
Israel and Jews," Algemeiner.com, December 14, 2015, https://www.algemeiner
.com/2015/12/14/cnn-anchor-constantly-defends-hamas-attacks-israel-and-jews/.

13. "Legal View With Ashleigh Banfield," Cable News Network, November
18, 2014, http://www.cnn.com/TRANSCRIPTS/1411/18/lvab.01.html.

14. "'The New York Times' Uncovers How ISIS Recruits From Afar," *All
Things Considered*, NPR, February 6, 2017, https://www.npr.org/2017/02/06
/513769884/the-new-york-times-uncovers-how-isis-recruits-from-afar.

15. Kimberly Amadeo, "War on Terror Facts, Costs, and Timeline," The Balance, updated March 31, 2018, https://www.thebalance.com/war-on-terror
-facts-costs-timeline-3306300.

16. Gillian Kiley, "U.S. Spending on Post-9/11 Wars to Reach $5.6 Trillion
by 2018," Brown University, November 7, 2017, https://news.brown.edu
/articles/2017/11/costssummary.

17. Neta C. Crawford, "United States Budgetary Costs of Post-9/11 Wars
Through FY2018," Watson Institute, November 2017, http://watson.brown.edu
/costsofwar/files/cow/imce/papers/2017/Costs%20of%20U.S.%20Post-9_11
%20NC%20Crawford%20FINAL%20.pdf.

18. "Costs of War," Watson Institute, accessed April 4, 2018, http://watson
.brown.edu/costsofwar/.

19. Crawford, "United States Budgetary Costs"; "Estimated Cost to Each
U.S. Taxpayer of Each of the Wars in Afghanistan, Iraq and Syria," Department
of Defense, July 2017, https://comptroller.defense.gov/Portals/45/Documents
/defbudget/fy2018/Section_1090_FY17_NDAA_Cost_of_Wars_to_Per_
Taxpayer-July_2017.pdf.

20. "Aid to Pakistan by the Numbers," Center for Global Development,
accessed April 4, 2018, https://www.cgdev.org/page/aid-pakistan-numbers.

21. Ishaan Tharoor, "Pakistani Leaders Knew Osama bin Laden Was in Pakistan, Says Former Defense Minister," *Washington Post*, October 14, 2015, https://
www.washingtonpost.com/news/worldviews/wp/2015/10/14/pakistani-leaders
-knew-osama-bin-laden-was-in-pakistan-says-former-defense-minister/.

22.   Elaine Scarry et al., "Destroyer of Worlds," *Harper's*, December 2017, https://harpers.org/archive/2017/12/destroyer-of-worlds/5/.

23.   "The Islamic Society of North America," Investigative Project on Terrorism, accessed April 4, 2018, https://www.investigativeproject.org/profile /178/the-islamic-society-of-north-america; Daniel Pipes, "Is CAIR a Terror Group?," *National Review*, November 28, 2014, http://www.nationalreview.com /article/393614/cair-terror-group-daniel-pipes.

24.   Crawford, "United States Budgetary Costs."

25.   Kimberly Amadeo, "U.S. Debt to China: How Much Does It Own?," The Balance, updated March 22, 2018, https://www.thebalance.com/u-s-debt-to-china-how-much-does-it-own-3306355.

26.   Adam Taylor, "These Are America's 9 Longest Foreign Wars," *Washington Post*, May 29, 2014, https://www.washingtonpost.com/news/worldviews /wp/2014/05/29/these-are-americas-9-longest-foreign-wars/?utm_term= .b78ce1fd5593.

27.   "DHS Budget," Department of Homeland Security, accessed April 4, 2018, https://www.dhs.gov/dhs-budget.

28.   Holly Yan and Joshua Berlinger, "Omar Mateen Timeline: What Led Up to the Gunman's Rampage?," Cable News Network, updated June 23, 2016, http:// www.cnn.com/2016/06/22/us/omar-mateen-timeline/index.html.

29.   Kevin Sullivan et al., "Orlando Shooter Posted Messages on Facebook Pledging Allegiance to the Leader of ISIS and Vowing More Attacks," *Washington Post*, June 15, 2016, https://www.washingtonpost.com/world/national-security /investigation-into-orlando-shooting-continues-no-impending-charges-expected /2016/06/15/c3eccf5e-3333-11e6-8758-d58e76e11b12_story.html?utm_term =.3633fc7e1e33.

30.   Patrick Poole, "A Detailed Look at 'The Purge' of U.S. Counter-Terrorism Training by the Obama Administration," TheBlaze Inc., March 26, 2014, https://www.theblaze.com/news/2014/03/26/a-detailed-look-at-the-purge -of-u-s-counter-terrorism-training-by-the-obama-administration.

31.   "Russia Warned U.S. About Boston Marathon Bomb Suspect Tsarnaev: Report," Reuters, March 25, 2014, https://www.reuters.com/article/us-usa -explosions-boston-congress/russia-warned-u-s-about-boston-marathon-bomb-sus-pect-tsarnaev-report-idUSBREA2P02Q20140326.

32.   Dee Dee Myers, "Is Nidal Hasan a Terrorist or Not?," *Vanity Fair*, November 2009, https://www.vanityfair.com/news/2009/11/is-nidal-hasan-a -terrorist-or-not; Carol Cratty, "FBI Official: Hasan Should Have Been Asked About E-Mails With Radical Cleric," Cable News Network, updated August 2, 2012, https://www.cnn.com/2012/08/01/politics/hasan-fbi/index.html; Scott Wilson, Carrie Johnson, and Spencer S. Hsu, "Inquiry Begins Into Motive of Shootings Suspect Hasan," *Washington Post*, November 7, 2009, http://www .washingtonpost.com/wp-dyn/content/article/2009/11/06/AR2009110604351 .html; Pete Winn, "Pentagon Will Not Classify Fort Hood Shootings as Terrorism—or Anything Else," https://www.cnsnews.com/news/article/pentagon -will-not-classify-fort-hood-shootings-terrorism-or-anything-else; Ned Berkowitz, "DOD: Ft. Hood Massacre Likely 'Criminal Act of Single Individual,' Not

International Terror," May 24, 2013, https://abcnews.go.com/Blotter/dod-ft-hood-massacre-criminal-act-international-terror/story?id=19244244.

33.   Sarah Blaskey, "FBI Apologizes, Says It Failed to Probe Tip on School Shooter Nikolas Cruz," *Miami Herald*, February 16, 2018, http://www.miami herald.com/news/local/community/broward/article200523359.html.

34.   Tom Costello and Alex Johnson, "TSA Chief Out After Agents Fail 95 Percent of Airport Breach Tests," NBC Universal, June 1, 2015, https://www .nbcnews.com/news/us-news/investigation-breaches-us-airports-allowed-weapons-through-n367851; Peter Neffenger, "TSA's 2017 Budget—A Commitment to Security (Part I)," Department of Homeland Security, March 1, 2016, https:// www.tsa.gov/news/testimony/2016/03/01/hearing-fy17-budget-request-transportation-security-administration.

35.   La-Keya Stinchcomb and Dante Renzulli, "Passenger With Gun in Carry-On Goes Unnoticed by TSA," WGCL-TV, updated December 13, 2015, http://www.cbs46.com/story/30523628/passenger-on-plane-with-gun-goes-unnoticed-by-tsa; Martin Gould and Robin Rayne Nelson, "EXCLUSIVE: 'How Could TSA Not Have Spotted It?' Trucker Carried His LOADED Ruger Semi-Automatic Pistol on to Crowded Southwest Flight From Atlanta to Chicago by Accident—And Was Never Stopped," Associated Newspapers Ltd., updated November 14, 2015, http://www.dailymail.co.uk/news/article-3317767/Oh-mother-God-did-Trucker-accidentally-carries-LOADED-Ruger-semi-automatic-flight-Atlanta-Chicago-TSA-fails-stop-him.html.

36.   Jason Clough, "TSA Failed to Catch Man With Loaded Gun on Airplane," Nexstar Broadcasting Inc., updated November 16, 2015, http://www.wfla .com/national/tsa-failed-to-catch-man-with-loaded-gun-on-airplane/1051725914.

37.   Alan Neuhauser, "15 Years After 9/11, TSA Is Still Falling Short," *U.S. News & World Report*, September 9, 2016, https://www.usnews.com/news /articles/2016-09-09/15-years-after-9-11-the-tsa-is-still-falling-short.

38.   Bart Jansem, "TSA Defends Full-Body Scanners at Airport Checkpoints," *USA Today*, March 2, 2016, https://www.usatoday.com/story/news /2016/03/02/tsa-defends-full-body-scanners-airport-checkpoints/81203030/.

39.   Jason Edward Harrington, "Dear America, I Saw You Naked," *Politico*, January 30, 2014, https://www.politico.com/magazine/story/2014/01/tsa-screener-confession-102912.

40.   Harrington, "Dear America."

41.   Harrington, "Dear America."

42.   "TSA Year in Review: Record Amount of Firearms Discovered in 2017," Department of Homeland Security, January 29, 2018, https://www.tsa.gov /blog/2018/01/29/tsa-year-review-record-amount-firearms-discovered-2017.

43.   "The Islamic State's Suspected Inroads Into America," *Washington Post*, updated March 12, 2018, https://www.washingtonpost.com/graphics/national /isis-suspects/.

44.   Catherine Herridge, "FBI Using Elite Surveillance Teams to Track at Least 48 High-Risk ISIS Suspects," FOX News Network LLC, November 27, 2015, https://www.foxnews.com/politics/2015/11/26/fbi-using-elite-surveillance-teams-to-track-at-least-48-high-risk-isis-suspects.html.

CHAPTER 3—THE MYTH AND IRRELEVANCE OF THE PEACEFUL MAJORITY

1.   GLOOG—Get Lawyers Out Of Government, "Brigitte Gabriel Gives FANTASTIC Answer to Muslim Woman Claiming All Muslims Are Portrayed Badly," YouTube, June 18, 2014, https://www.youtube.com/watch?v=Ry3Nzk AOo3s.

2.   "Transcript of Republican Debate in Miami, Full Text," Cable News Network, updated March 15, 2016, http://www.cnn.com/2016/03/10/politics /republican-debate-transcript-full-text/index.html.

3.   "Pres Obama on Fareed Zakaria GPS," Cable News Network, February 1, 2015, http://cnnpressroom.blogs.cnn.com/2015/02/01/pres-obama-on-fareed -zakaria-gps-cnn-exclusive/.

4.   Steven Kull et al., "Public Opinion in the Islamic World on Terrorism, al Qaeda, and US Policies," WorldPublicOpinion.org, February 25, 2009, archived at https://web.archive.org/web/20090325182034/www.worldpublicopinion.org /pipa/pdf/feb09/STARTII_Feb09_rpt.pdf.

5.   "The Nazi Rise to Power," *Holocaust Encyclopedia*, United States Holocaust Memorial Museum, accessed April 6, 2018, https://www.ushmm.org/wlc /en/article.php?ModuleId=10008206.

6.   "The World's Muslims: Religion, Politics and Society," Pew Research Center, April 30, 2013, http://assets.pewresearch.org/wp-content/uploads/sites /11/2013/04/worlds-muslims-religion-politics-society-full-report.pdf.

7.   Jacob Poushter, "In Nations With Significant Muslim Populations, Much Disdain for ISIS," Pew Research Center, November 17, 2015, http://www .pewresearch.org/fact-tank/2015/11/17/in-nations-with-significant-muslim -populations-much-disdain-for-isis/.

8.   Kull et al., "Public Opinion."

9.   "The World's Muslims," Pew Research Center.

10.   "The World Factbook: Egypt," Central Intelligence Agency, accessed April 6, 2018, https://www.cia.gov/library/publications/the-world-factbook/geos /eg.html.

11.   "Egypt Attack: Gunman Targets Coptic Christians in Church and Shop," BBC, December 29, 2017, http://www.bbc.com/news/world-middle-east-42511813.

12.   "The World Factbook: Egypt," Central Intelligence Agency; "The World's Muslims," Pew Research Center.

13.   Neha Sahgal and Tim Townsend, "Four-in-Ten Pakistanis Say Honor Killing of Women Can Be at Least Sometimes Justified," Pew Research Center, May 30, 2014, http://www.pewresearch.org/fact-tank/2014/05/30/four-in-ten -pakistanis-say-honor-killing-of-women-can-be-at-least-sometimes-justified/.

14.   Poushter, "In Nations With Significant Muslim Populations."

15.   "The World's Muslims," Pew Research Center.

16.   "Poll No. 191," PCPO, accessed April 6, 2018, http://www.pcpo.org /index.php/polls/114-poll-no-191.

17.   Associated Press, "Poll: 32% of Palestinians Support Itamar Attack," Ynetnews.com, June 4, 2011, https://www.ynetnews.com/articles/0,7340,L -4053251,00.html.

18.   "The World's Muslims," Pew Research Center.

19.   Michael Lipka, "Muslims and Islam: Key Findings in the U.S. and Around the World," Pew Research Center, August 9, 2017, http://www.pew research.org/fact-tank/2017/08/09/muslims-and-islam-key-findings-in-the-u-s -and-around-the-world/.

20.   "The World's Muslims," Pew Research Center.

21.   "The World's Muslims," Pew Research Center.

22.   "The World's Muslims," Pew Research Center.

23.   "Chapter 1: Beliefs About Sharia," Pew Research Center, April 30, 2013, http://www.pewforum.org/2013/04/30/the-worlds-muslims-religion-politics -society-beliefs-about-sharia/.

24.   "The World's Muslims," Pew Research Center. Statistics for Niger and Senegal were not available.

25.   "The World's Muslims," Pew Research Center. Statistics for Niger and Senegal were not available.

26.   Kull et al., "Public Opinion."

27.   Kull et al., "Public Opinion."

28.   "Muslim Americans: Middle Class and Mostly Mainstream," Pew Research Center, May 22, 2007, http://www.pewresearch.org/files/old-assets/pdf /muslim-americans.pdf.

29.   Madeline Grant, "16% of French Citizens Support ISIS, Poll Finds," *Newsweek*, August 26, 2014, http://www.newsweek.com/16-french-citizens -support-isis-poll-finds-266795.

30.   "Why Do Europe's Muslims Hate the West?," Investor's Business Daily Inc., March 31, 2016, https://www.investors.com/politics/editorials/why-do -europes-muslims-hate-the-west/.

31.   "Attitudes to Living in Britain—A Survey of Muslim Opinion," GfK, April 27, 2006, archived at https://web.archive.org/web/20060830173405/https:// www.imaginate.uk.com/MCC01_SURVEY/Site%20Download.pdf.

32.   "C4/Juniper Survey of Muslims 2015," ICM Unlimited, accessed April 6, 2018, https://www.icmunlimited.com/wp-content/uploads/2016/04/Mulims-full -suite-data-plus-topline.pdf.

33.   Patrick Hennessy and Melissa Kite, "Poll Reveals 40pc of Muslims Want Sharia Law in UK," *Telegraph*, February 19, 2006, https://www.telegraph.co.uk /news/uknews/1510866/Poll-reveals-40pc-of-Muslims-want-sharia-law-in-UK .html.

34.   "U.S. Muslims Concerned About Their Place in Society, but Continue to Believe in the American Dream," Pew Research Center, July 26, 2017, http:// assets.pewresearch.org/wp-content/uploads/sites/11/2017/07/09105631 /U.S.-MUSLIMS-FULL-REPORT-with-population-update-v2.pdf.

35.   "Muslim Americans: No Signs of Growth in Alienation or Support for Extremism," Pew Research Center, August 30, 2011, http://www.people-press

.org/2011/08/30/muslim-americans-no-signs-of-growth-in-alienation-or-support
-for-extremism/.

36.   "Poll of U.S. Muslims Reveals Ominous Levels of Support for Islamic
Supremacists' Doctrine of Shariah, Jihad," Center for Security Policy, June 23,
2015, https://www.centerforsecuritypolicy.org/2015/06/23/nationwide-poll-of-us
-muslims-shows-thousands-support-shariah-jihad/.

37.   "Muslim Americans: Middle Class and Mostly Mainstream," Pew
Research Center.

38.   TruthRevoltOriginals, "Ben Shapiro: The Myth of the Tiny Radical
Muslim Minority," YouTube, October 15, 2014, https://www.youtube.com
/watch?v=g7TAAw3oQvg.

39.   Rebecca Hartmann, "Ben Shapiro Destroys Peter Beinart: 'Hamas Celebrates Every Time You're on Television,'" TruthRevolt.org, August 7, 2014,
https://www.truthrevolt.org/news/ben-shapiro-destroys-peter-beinart-hamas-
celebrates-every-time-youre-television.

40.   Peter Beinart (@PeterBeinart), "hey @ACTBrigitte, I know u think
Koran is uniquely murderous + Jews dislike violent texts. But we just celebrated a
holiday called Purim…," Twitter, March 22, 2017, 7:00 a.m., https://twitter.com
/PeterBeinart/status/844549447946321920.

41.   Brigitte Gabriel (@ACTBrigitte), "We seem to have the Jewish suicide
bomber threat under control," Twitter, March 22, 2017, 7:09 a.m., https://twitter
.com/ACTBrigitte/status/844551680507154432.

42.   Michael Lipka and Conrad Hackett, "Why Muslims Are the World's
Fastest-Growing Religious Group," Pew Research Center, April 6, 2017, http://
www.pewresearch.org/fact-tank/2017/04/06/why-muslims-are-the-worlds-fastest
-growing-religious-group/.

Chapter 4—Weaponizing the Internet

1.   "9/11 Timeline," A&E Television Networks LLC, accessed April 6, 2018,
http://www.history.com/topics/9-11-timeline.

2.   Chris Smith, "ISIS Used Encrypted Communications With Paris
Attackers, Officials Believe," BGR Media LLC, November 17, 2015, http://bgr
.com/2015/11/17/isis-paris-attacks-encryption/.

3.   Tim Lister et al., "ISIS Goes Global: 143 Attacks in 29 Countries Have
Killed 2,043," Cable News Network, updated February 12, 2018, http://www
.cnn.com/2015/12/17/world/mapping-isis-attacks-around-the-world/index.html;
Tim Lister and Paul Cruickshank, "Dead Boston Bomb Suspect Posted Video of
Jihadist, Analysis Shows," Cable News Network, updated April 22, 2013, https://
edition.cnn.com/2013/04/20/us/brother-religious-language.

4.   Nick Schager, "How Islamic Terrorists Are Being Radicalized Online,"
The Daily Beast Company LLC, March 25, 2017, https://www.thedailybeast.com
/how-islamic-terrorists-are-being-radicalized-online.

5.   Schager, "Islamic Terrorists."

6.   Paul Szoldra, "Inside the Hacker Underworld of ISIS," Insider Inc., June
16, 2016, http://uk.businessinsider.com/isis-hacking-division-operates-2016-6?IR=T.

7.   Corey Charlton, "The Devil's Lair," *The Sun*, September 25, 2017, https://www.thesun.co.uk/news/4542748/isis-beatles-gang-of-british-killers-including-jihadi-john-seen-unmasked-together-for-the-first-time-in-chilling-footage/.

8.   "Junaid Hussain," Counter Extremism Project, accessed April 6, 2018, https://www.counterextremism.com/extremists/junaid-hussain.

9.   Eliott C. McLaughlin, "ISIS Jihadi Linked to Garland Attack Has Long History as Hacker," Cable News Network, May 7, 2015, https://www.cnn.com/2015/05/06/us/who-is-junaid-hussain-garland-texas-attack/index.html.

10.   Dipesh Gadher, "British Hacker Is No 3 on Pentagon 'Kill List,'" *The Times*, August 2, 2015, https://www.thetimes.co.uk/article/british-hacker-is-no-3-on-pentagon-kill-list-6g95bfqwfnz.

11.   Matthew Weaver, "Sally Jones: UK Punk Singer Who Became Leading Isis Recruiter," *Guardian*, October 12, 2017, https://www.theguardian.com/world/2017/oct/12/sally-jones-the-uk-punk-singer-who-became-isiss-white-widow.

12.   Paul Sperry, "Meet the American Women Who Are Flocking to Join ISIS," *New York Post*, May 13, 2017, https://nypost.com/2017/05/13/meet-the-western-women-who-are-flocking-to-join-isis/.

13.   Benjamin Soloway and Henry Johnson, "ISIS Is Training Indonesian 'Cubs of the Caliphate' to Kill for the Cause," May 19, 2016, http://foreignpolicy.com/2016/05/19/isis-is-training-indonesian-cubs-of-the-caliphate-to-kill-for-the-cause/.

14.   Soloway and Johnson, "'Cubs of the Caliphate.'"

15.   Soloway and Johnson, "'Cubs of the Caliphate.'"

16.   Tom Westcott, "Revealed—Isis Trained 'Caliphate Cubs' to BEHEAD Their Victims by Practising on a CHILD'S Head Taped Onto Sinister Mannequin in Historic Iraqi Desert City." Associated Newspapers Ltd., May 2, 2017, http://www.dailymail.co.uk/news/article-4464896/Caliphate-Cubs-trained-behead-ISIS-victims.html.

17.   Westcott, "Revealed."

18.   Sperry, "Meet the American Women."

19.   Mina Hamblet, "The Islamic State's Virtual Caliphate," *Middle East Quarterly* 24, no. 4 (Fall 2017), http://www.meforum.org/6894/the-islamic-state-virtual-caliphate.

20.   CNN Wire, "ISIS Has Inspired Over 70 Terrorist Attacks in 20 Countries," WGNO, March 22, 2016, http://wgno.com/2016/03/22/isis-has-inspired-over-70-terrorist-attacks-in-20-countries/.

21.   Elliot Friedland, "New Issue of ISIS Propaganda Magazine Rumiyah," Clarion Project Inc. May 8, 2017, https://clarionproject.org/new-issue-of-isis-propaganda-magazine-rumiyah/.

22.   Lizzie Dearden, "Isis Calls on Supporters to Wage 'All-Out War' on West During Ramadan With New Terror Attacks," *Independent*, March 26, 2017, http://www.independent.co.uk/news/world/middle-east/isis-ramadan-2017-all-out-war-west-new-terror-attacks-manchester-suicide-bombing-islamic-state-a7758121.html.

23.   Evan Bleier and Christopher Brennan, "A Hundred American Soldiers Named on ISIS 'Kill List'—But Servicemen Say They Are 'Unfazed' by Extremists' Threats," Associated Newspapers Ltd., updated March 23, 2015, http://www .dailymail.co.uk/news/article-3007128/Soldiers-names-addresses-photos-published -ISIS-s-kill-list-say-unfazed-threat.html.

24.   Zamawang Almemar, "Cyber Campaign Takes Aim at ISIS Recruiting," The Cipher Brief, September 5, 2017, https://www.thecipherbrief.com/cyber -campaign-takes-aim-isis-recruiting.

25.   Selena Larson, "Twitter Suspends 377,000 Accounts for Pro-Terrorism Content," Cable News Network, March 21, 2017, http://money.cnn.com/2017 /03/21/technology/twitter-bans-terrorism-accounts/index.html.

26.   Larson, "Twitter Suspends 377,000 Accounts."

27.   John Haltiwanger, "Thousands of ISIS Fighters Returning to Western Countries, Including United States," *Newsweek*, November 2, 2017, http://www .newsweek.com/thousands-isis-fighters-returning-western-countries-including -united-states-699658.

28.   Mike Rogers, "How ISIS Uses the Internet to Recruit New Members (Hint: It Involves Kittens)," *New York Daily News*, September 6, 2017, http:// www.nydailynews.com/news/national/isis-Internet-recruit-members-hint-kittens -article-1.3473890.

29.   Simon Cottee, "The Challenge of Jihadi Cool," *The Atlantic*, December 24, 2015, https://www.theatlantic.com/international/archive/2015/12/isis-jihadi -cool/421776/.

30.   German Lopez, "In One Year, Drug Overdoses Killed More Americans Than the Entire Vietnam War Did," Vox Media Inc., updated June 8, 2017, https://www.vox.com/policy-and-politics/2017/6/6/15743986/opioid-epidemic -overdose-deaths-2016.

31.   Josh Katz, "The First Count of Fentanyl Deaths in 2016: Up 540% in Three Years," *New York Times*, September 2, 2017, https://www.nytimes.com /interactive/2017/09/02/upshot/fentanyl-drug-overdose-deaths.html.

32.   Eric Lieberman, "Google's New Fact-Check Feature Almost Exclusively Targets Conservative Sites," The Daily Caller, January 9, 2018, http://dailycaller .com/2018/01/09/googles-new-fact-check-feature-almost-exclusively-targets -conservative-sites/; "PROOF: Google Fact-Checks Only Conservative Websites," Truth Revolt, January 10, 2018, https://www.truthrevolt.org/news/proof-google -fact-checks-only-conservative-websites.

33.   Judson Phillips, "Clamp Down on Big Tech's Media Bias," *Washington Post*, January 16, 2018, https://www.washingtontimes.com/news/2018/jan/16 /social-media-companies-ban-conservative-voices/.

34.   Christopher Hope and Kate McCann, "Google, Facebook and Twitter Told to Take Down Terror Content Within Two Hours or Face Fines," *Telegraph*, September 19, 2017, https://www.telegraph.co.uk/news/2017/09/19/google -facebook-twitter-told-take-terror-content-within-two/.

35.   Doug Mainwaring, "'Shadow Banning': How Twitter Secretly Censors Conservatives Without Them Even Knowing It," LifeSiteNews.com, January 12,

2018, https://www.lifesitenews.com/news/shadow-banning-how-twitter-secretly
-censors-conservatives-without-them-even.

36. Mainwaring, "'Shadow Banning.'"

37. Mainwaring, "'Shadow Banning.'"

38. Marc Geppert, "Facebook Accused of 'Shadowbanning' Page Mapping Migrant Crimes," Breitbart, June 15, 2016, http://www.breitbart.com/tech/2016/06/16/facebook-shadowbans-page-mapping-migrant-refugee-crimes/.

39. Kirk Mitchell, "Arvada Teen Jihadist Wannabe Sentenced to Four Years in Prison," *Denver Post*, updated August 26, 2016, https://www.denverpost.com/2015/01/23/arvada-teen-jihadist-wannabe-sentenced-to-four-years-in-prison/.

40. Michael Martinez, Ana Cabrera, and Sara Weisfeldt, "Colorado Woman Gets 4 Years for Wanting to Join ISIS," Cable News Network, updated January 24, 2015, https://www.cnn.com/2015/01/23/us/colorado-woman-isis-sentencing/index.html.

41. United States of America v. Shannon Maureen Conley, 14-mj-1045-KLM, United States District Court for the District of Colorado (April 9, 2014), https://extremism.gwu.edu/sites/g/files/zaxdzs2191/f/Conley%20Criminal%20Complaint.pdf.

42. TheDenverChannel.com Team, "Shannon Conley, Arvada Teen Who Tried to Join ISIS to Wage Jihad, Sentenced to 4 Years in Prison," TheDenverChannel.com, January 23, 2015, https://www.thedenverchannel.com/news/local-news/sentencing-for-shannon-conley-arvada-teen-who-tried-to-join-isis-to-wage-jihad.

43. United States of America v. Conley.

44. Kirk Mitchell, "Arvada Teen Shannon Conley's Suspicious Activities Prompted Church Security Measures," *Denver Post*, updated April 27, 2016, https://www.denverpost.com/2014/07/03/arvada-teen-shannon-conleys-suspicious-activities-prompted-church-security-measures/.

45. United States of America v. Conley.

46. Haltiwanger, "ISIS Fighters Returning."

47. Haltiwanger, "ISIS Fighters Returning."

Chapter 5—Replacement Civilization

1. Jaweed Kaleem, "Islam in America: Mosques See Dramatic Increase in Just Over a Decade, According to Muslim Survey," HuffPost, February 29, 2012, https://www.huffingtonpost.com/2012/02/29/mosques-in-united-states-study_n_1307851.html.

2. Roya Aziz and Monica Lam, "Profiles: The Lackawanna Cell," *Frontline*, WGBH, October 16, 2003, https://www.pbs.org/wgbh/pages/frontline/shows/sleeper/inside/profiles.html.

3. Dina Temple-Raston, *The Jihad Next Door* (Philadelphia: PublicAffairs, 2007), 153, https://books.google.com/books?id=aK02wJ_6dEcC&pg.

4. "Buffalo Terror Suspect Admits al Qaeda Training," Cable News Network, May 20, 2003, http://www.cnn.com/2003/LAW/05/20/buffalo.terror/.

5.   Associated Press, "Things to Know About Somalis in Minnesota," FOX News Network LLC, September 19, 2016, http://www.foxnews.com/us/2016 /09/19/things-to-know-about-somalis-in-minnesota.html.

6.   Associated Press, "Somalis in Minnesota."

7.   Daniel Greenfield, "Somalia and the Hyena Cure," FrontPageMag.com, October 15, 2013, https://www.frontpagemag.com/fpm/207547/somalia-and -hyena-cure-daniel-greenfield; Richard Hooper, "Where Hyenas Are Used to Treat Mental Illness," BBC, October 17, 2013, http://www.bbc.com/news /magazine-24539989.

8.   Amy Forliti, "Somali Gangs Move Into Sex Trafficking, Fraud," NBC Universal, updated February 7, 2011, http://www.nbcnews.com/id/41446307 /ns/us_news-crime_and_courts/t/somali-gangs-move-sex-trafficking-fraud /#.WsfASYjwYdU.

9.   Ann Coulter, *Adios, America* (Washington, DC: Regnery Publishing, 2015), chapter 6, https://books.google.com/books?id=yJl0AwAAQBAJ&pg.

10.   Forliti, "Somali Gangs."

11.   Associated Press, "As Somali Gangs Evolve, So Does Law Enforcement," CBS Interactive Inc., February 6, 2011, https://www.cbsnews.com/news/as -somali-gangs-evolve-so-does-enforcement/.

12.   United States Census Bureau, "2016 American Community Survey 1-Year Estimates," American FactFinder, https://factfinder.census.gov/faces /tableservices/jsf/pages/productview.xhtml?src=bkmk.

13.   United States Census Bureau, "2016 American Community Survey."

14.   Susan Brower, "Demographic Overview of Minnesota," Minnesota State Demographic Center, September 24, 2015, https://mn.gov/bms-stat/assets/sb-mn -overview-for-foreign-journalists-us-state-dept-sept2015-post.pdf.

15.   Benny Carlson, Karin Magnusson, and Sofia Rönnqvist, "Somalier På Arbetsmarknaden—Har Sverige Något Att Lära?," Regeringskansliet, accessed April 9, 2018, http://www.regeringen.se/contentassets/55f58b2bc8fd4f66842e37f5 4c38fc51/somalier-pa-arbetsmarknaden---har-sverige-nagot-att-lara.

16.   United States Census Bureau, "2016 American Community Survey"; Brower, "Demographic Overview of Minnesota."

17.   "Mental Health in Somalia," WHO, February 2, 2011, http://www.who .int/hac/crises/som/somalia_mental_health/en/.

18.   Christopher Chantrill, "Welfare Spending Analysis," usgovernment spending.com, accessed April 9, 2018, https://www.usgovernmentspending .com/welfare_spending_analysis.

19.   bloody hades, "Betsy Hodges Mayor of Minneapolis Wearing a Hijab Declares Full Support for All Somalis," YouTube, July 24, 2017, https://www .youtube.com/watch?v=VviqpNzJobo.

20.   Libor Jany, "Minneapolis Police Officer Mohamed Noor Turns Himself in on Murder, Manslaughter Charges in Justine Damond Killing," *Star Tribune*, March 21, 2018, http://www.startribune.com/minneapolis-police-officer -mohamed-noor-turns-himself-in-on-charges-in-justine-damond-killing/477405923 /#1; Sahan Journal, "Mohamed Noor is the newest Somali police officer in

Minneapolis," Facebook, May 24, 2016, https://www.facebook.com/sahanjournal /posts/531465303705243.

21.   Katie Strick, "Consultant Is Suspended by Hospital After Confronting Surgeon Who Planned to Operate in Her Hijab Despite It Being Against Safety Regulations," Associated Newspapers Ltd., updated March 7, 2016, http://www .dailymail.co.uk/news/article-3479740/Consultant-suspended-hospital-confronting -surgeon-planned-operate-hijab-despite-against-safety-regulations.html.

22.   Strick, "Consultant Is Suspended."

23.   Strick, "Consultant Is Suspended."

24.   Nick Gutteridge, "Migrants Knock Thousands of Pounds off UK House Prices, Study Says," *Express*, updated September 16, 2015, https://www.express .co.uk/news/uk/605315/migrants-drop-UK-house-prices-Syrian-refugees -Cameron-Britain.

25.   Gutteridge, "UK House Prices."

26.   Sarah O'Grady, "'House Prices Driven Down in Areas Full of Migrants,' Shows New Study," *Express*, September 25, 2013, https://www.express.co.uk /life-style/property/431969/House-prices-driven-down-in-areas-full-of-migrants -shows-new-study.

27.   Gutteridge, "UK House Prices."

28.   Will Worley, "Italy Covers Naked Statues During Iran President Hassan Rouhani's Visit," *Independent*, January 27, 2016, http://www.independent.co.uk /news/world/europe/italy-covers-up-naked-statues-iran-president-hassan-rouhani -visit-nude-a6834836.html.

29.   Patrick Goodenough, "'Submission' to Islam: Critics Slam Cover-Up of Rome's Nude Statues for Iran's President," CNSNews.com, January 27, 2016, https://www.cnsnews.com/news/article/susan-jones/submission-islam-critics-slam -cover-romes-nude-statues-irans-president.

30.   Daniel R. Coats, "Worldwide Threat Assessment of the US Intelligence Community," Office of the Director of National Intelligence, May 11, 2017, https://www.dni.gov/files/documents/Newsroom/Testimonies/SSCI%20 Unclassified%20SFR%20-%20Final.pdf.

31.   Seth J. Frantzman, "Not a Clash of Civilizations; But World Culture vs. Islamist Culture," *Jerusalem Post*, February 1, 2016, http://www.jpost.com/Opinion /Not-a-clash-of-civilizations-but-world-culture-vs-Islamist-culture-443521.

32.   Liam Deacon, "'Multicultural Toilets' for 'Global Defecation' Seek to Stop Migrants Pooping on the Floor," Breitbart, February 4, 2016, http://www .breitbart.com/london/2016/02/04/germany-develops-multicultural-toilets-to-stop -migrants-defecating-on-floor/.

33.   Deacon, "'Multicultural Toilets.'"

34.   Noel Brennan, "Certain Crimes Will Now Have Lighter Sentences in Denver," KUSA-TV, May 23, 2017, http://www.9news.com/article/news/crime /certain-crimes-will-now-have-lighter-sentences-in-denver/442367895.

35.   Jeffrey S. Passel and D'Vera Cohn, "20 Metro Areas Are Home to Six-in-Ten Unauthorized Immigrants in U.S.," Pew Research Center, February 9, 2017, http://www.pewresearch.org/fact-tank/2017/02/09/us-metro-areas-unauthorized -immigrants.

CHAPTER 6—TRANSFORMATION THROUGH IMMIGRATION

1.   Gustavo López and Jynnah Radford, "Facts on U.S. Immigrants, 2015," Pew Research Center, May 3, 2017, http://www.pewhispanic.org/2017/05/03 /facts-on-u-s-immigrants-trend-data/.

2.   "Modern Immigration Wave Brings 59 Million to U.S., Driving Population Growth and Change Through 2065," Pew Research Center, September 28, 2015, http://www.pewhispanic.org/2015/09/28/modern-immigration-wave-brings -59-million-to-u-s-driving-population-growth-and-change-through-2065/.

3.   "Immigration Wave," Pew Research Center.

4.   "Immigration Wave," Pew Research Center.

5.   "Immigration Wave," Pew Research Center.

6.   "Immigration Wave," Pew Research Center.

7.   "The Religious Affiliation of U.S. Immigrants: Majority Christian, Rising Share of Other Faiths," Pew Research Center, May 17, 2013, http://www .pewforum.org/2013/05/17/the-religious-affiliation-of-us-immigrants/#muslim.

8.   "1993 World Trade Center Bombing Fast Facts," Cable News Network, updated February 28, 2018, http://www.cnn.com/2013/11/05/us/1993-world -trade-center-bombing-fast-facts/index.html.

9.   J. Gilmore Childers and Henry J. DePippo, statement before the Senate Judiciary Committee Subcommittee on Technology, Terrorism, and Government Information, "Foreign Terrorists in America: Five Years After the World Trade Center," February 24, 1998, archived at https://web.archive.org/web/200712 27065444/http://judiciary.senate.gov/oldsite/childers.htm.

10.   Besheer Mohamed, "New Estimates Show U.S. Muslim Population Continues to Grow," Pew Research Center, January 3, 2018, http://www.pewresearch .org/fact-tank/2018/01/03/new-estimates-show-u-s-muslim-population-continues -to-grow/.

11.   Phillip Connor, "U.S. Resettles Fewer Refugees, Even as Global Number of Displaced People Grows," Pew Research Center, October 12, 2017, http://www .pewglobal.org/2017/10/12/u-s-resettles-fewer-refugees-even-as-global-number-of -displaced-people-grows/.

12.   Connor, "U.S. Resettles Fewer Refugees."

13.   Associated Press, "Kerry Brings Paris a 'Hug' After Terror Attacks," CBS Interactive Inc., January 16, 2015, https://www.cbsnews.com/news/john -kerry-brings-paris-a-hug-and-james-taylor-after-france-terror-attacks/.

14.   Connor, "U.S. Resettles Fewer Refugees."

15.   Office of Refugee Resettlement, "Annual Report to Congress FY 2014," U.S. Department of Health and Human Services, accessed April 9, 2018, https:// www.acf.hhs.gov/sites/default/files/orr/orr_annual_report_to_congress_fy_2014 _signed.pdf; Ann Corcoran, "Will the Thousands of Syrian Refugees Now Being Admitted to the US Be Christians?," Refugee Resettlement Watch (blog), October 4, 2014, https://refugeeresettlementwatch.wordpress.com/2014/10/04/will-the -thousands-of-syrian-refugees-now-being-admitted-to-the-us-be-christians/.

16.   Jens Manuel Krogstad and Jynnah Radford, "Key Facts About Refugees to the U.S.," Pew Research Center, January 30, 2017, http://www.pewresearch .org/fact-tank/2017/01/30/key-facts-about-refugees-to-the-u-s/.

17.   Marc Thiessen, "How ISIS Smuggles Terrorists Among Syrian Refugees," *Newsweek*, April 27, 2016, http://www.newsweek.com/how-isis-smuggles -terrorists-among-syrian-refugees-453039.

18.   "Hearing Before the Committee on Homeland Security and Governmental Affairs United States Senate One Hundred Fourteenth Congress," First Session, November 19, 2015, https://www.hsdl.org/?view&did=799312, 13.

19.   U.S. Code, Title 8, Chapter 12, Subchapter 1, § 1101, "Definitions," https://www.law.cornell.edu/uscode/text/8/1101#a_42_A.

20.   Jie Zong and Jeanne Batalova, "Refugees and Asylees in the United States," Migration Policy Institute, June 7, 2017, https://www.migrationpolicy.org /article/refugees-and-asylees-united-states.

21.   Cindy Carcamo, "Domestic Violence Ruling May Help Thousands of Immigrants Get Asylum," *Los Angeles Times*, September 5, 2014, http://www .latimes.com/nation/la-na-ff-immig-domestic-20140906-story.html; Lawrence Keketso, "USA: FGM Reason to Get Asylum in US," Female Genital Cutting Education and Networking Project, June 14, 2008, http://www.fgmnetwork.org /gonews.php?subaction=showfull&id=1213476114&ucat=1&; Bryan Robinson, "Unusual Asylum Cases Spark Debate," ABC News, September 25, 2017, http:// abcnews.go.com/US/story?id=95646&page=1.

22.   "Refugee Resettlement Fact Sheet," Refugee Resettlement Watch (blog), June 20, 2013, https://refugeeresettlementwatch.wordpress.com/refugee -resettlement-fact-sheets/.

23.   Associated Press, "First Syrian Refugees Arrive in U.S. Under Faster Program," CBS Interactive Inc., April 7, 2016, https://www.cbsnews.com/news /first-syrian-refugees-arrive-in-us-under-faster-surge-program/.

24.   "Supreme Court Upholds Trump Travel Ban," CBS Interactive Inc., June 26, 2018, https://www.cbsnews.com/news/travel-ban-upheld-supreme-court -decision-tuesday-trump-2018-06-26/.

25.   House of Representatives Judiciary Committee, "Goodlatte: Why Does the President Ignore Concerns About Syrian Refugees?," press release, October 27, 2015, https://judiciary.house.gov/press-release/goodlatte-why-does-the-president -ignore-concerns-about-syrian-refugees/.

26.   "Refugee Resettlement Fact Sheet," Refugee Resettlement Watch.

27.   Chris Alto, "Chattanooga's Refugee Resettlement Contractor Likely to Close Office Under New State Department Guidance," The Tennessee Star, December 23, 2017, https://tennesseestar.com/2017/12/23/chattanoogas-refugee -resettlement-contractor-likely-to-close-office-under-new-state-department-guidance/.

28.   "The Reception and Placement Program," U.S. Department of State, accessed April 11, 2018, https://www.state.gov/j/prm/ra/receptionplacement/.

29.   "Refugee Resettlement Fact Sheet," Refugee Resettlement Watch.

30.   Steven A. Camarota and Karen Zeigler, "The High Cost of Resettling Middle Eastern Refugees," Center for Immigration Studies, November 2015, https://cis.org/sites/default/files/camarota-refugees-15_0.pdf.

31. Alison Siskin, "Noncitizen Eligibility for Federal Public Assistance: Policy Overview," Congressional Research Service, December 12, 2016, https://fas .org/sgp/crs/misc/RL33809.pdf.

32. Paul Bedard, "Refugee Costs: $8.8 Billion, $80,000 Per Immigrant, Free Welfare, Medicaid," *Washington Examiner*, February 5, 2018, https://www .washingtonexaminer.com/refugee-costs-88-billion-80-000-per-immigrant-free -welfare-medicaid.

33. Office of Refugee Resettlement, "Annual Report to Congress FY 2013," U.S. Department of Health and Human Services, accessed April 9, 2018, https:// www.acf.hhs.gov/sites/default/files/orr/arc_2013_508.pdf.

34. Office of Refugee Resettlement, "Annual Report to Congress."

35. Leo Hohmann, "Global Meatpacking Giant Goes All in for Refugee Labor," WND.com, updated October 24, 2017, http://www.wnd.com/2017/10 /global-meatpacking-giant-goes-all-in-for-refugee-labor/.

36. Hohmann, "Global Meatpacking Giant."

37. Thomas Gounley, "Somali Refugees Change Face of Southwest Mo. Town," *USA Today*, February 6, 2017, https://www.usatoday.com/story/news /nation-now/2017/02/06/somali-refugees-missouri/97548508/.

38. Josh Letner, "Somali Workers Back on Job at Tyson Plant," *Joplin Globe*, October 25, 2011, http://www.joplinglobe.com/news/local_news/somali-workers -back-on-job-at-tyson-plant/article_979fde40-57ac-501e-b168-719ebc6bd6c0.html.

39. Hohmann, "Global Meatpacking Giant"; Gounley, "Somali Refugees."

40. Conor Gaffey, "Starbucks to Hire 10,000 Refugees in Response to Trump Immigration Ban," *Newsweek*, January 30, 2017, http://www.newsweek .com/starbucks-hire-10000-refugees-response-trump-immigration-ban-549994.

41. Kate Taylor, "Starbucks' Brand Perception Has Plummeted Since It Announced Plan to Hire Refugees," Insider Inc., February 22, 2017, http://www .businessinsider.com/starbucks-brand-perception-falls-with-refugee-plan-2017-2.

42. Lorna E. Thorpe et al., "Infectious Tuberculosis Among Newly Arrived Refugees in the United States," *New England Journal of Medicine* 350 (May 13, 2004): 2105–2106, https://doi.org/10.1056/NEJM200405133502023.

43. Lewis Sanders IV, "Two Million: Germany Records Largest Influx of Immigrants in 2015," Deutsche Welle, March 21, 2016, http://www.dw.com/en /two-million-germany-records-largest-influx-of-immigrants-in-2015/a-19131436.

44. "Infectious Disease Epidemiology Annual Report—2016," Robert Koch Institute, accessed April 11, 2018, https://www.rki.de/EN/Content/infections /epidemiology/inf_dis_Germany/yearbook/yearbook_summary_2016.html; Soeren Kern, "Germany: Infectious Diseases Spreading as Migrants Settle In," Gatestone Institute, July 14, 2017, https://www.gatestoneinstitute.org/10676 /germany-migrants-infectious.

45. Kristine M. Schmit et al., "Tuberculosis—United States, 2016," *Morbidity and Mortality Weekly Report* 66 (August 1, 2017): 289–294, http://dx.doi .org/10.15585/mmwr.mm6611a2.

46. Schmit et al., "Tuberculosis."

47.   Reuters, "Kansas City High School Finds 27 Positive TB Cases," *Las Vegas Review-Journal,* March 18, 2015, https://www.reviewjournal.com/life /health/kansas-city-high-school-finds-27-positive-tb-cases/.

48.   Michelle Russell, Hope Pogemiller, and Elizabeth D. Barnett, "Newly Arrived Immigrants & Refugees," Centers for Disease Control and Prevention, June 13, 2017, https://wwwnc.cdc.gov/travel/yellowbook/2018/advising-travelers -with-specific-needs/newly-arrived-immigrants-refugees.

49.   Bedard, "Refugee Costs."

CHAPTER 7—TERROR AT THE GATES

1.   Catherine Herridge, "300 Refugees Subjects of FBI Terror Investigations, U.S. Officials Say," FOX News Network LLC, March 6, 2017, http://www .foxnews.com/us/2017/03/06/300-refugees-subjects-fbi-terror-investigations -u-s-officials-say.html.

2.   Fernanda Santos, "Border Agents: 'We're Not Going to Apologize for What We Believe In," *New York Times,* March 28, 2017, https://www.nytimes .com/2017/03/28/us/border-patrol-agents-trump-green-line-podcast.html.

3.   "Supreme Court Upholds Trump Travel Ban," CBS Interactive Inc.

4.   Herridge, "300 Refugees."

5.   Adam Shaw, "Trump Signs Proclamation Sending National Guard to Mexico Border Immediately," FOX News Network LLC, April 4, 2018, http:// www.foxnews.com/politics/2018/04/04/trump-to-sign-proclamation-sending -national-guard-to-border-immediately.html.

6.   Aaron Brown, "'Just Wait...' Islamic State Reveals It Has Smuggled THOUSANDS of Extremists Into Europe," *Express,* updated November 19, 2015, https://www.express.co.uk/news/world/555434/Islamic-State-ISIS -Smuggler-THOUSANDS-Extremists-into-Europe-Refugees.

7.   Christiane Amanpour and Thom Patterson, "Passport Linked to Terrorist Complicates Syrian Refugee Crisis," Cable News Network, updated November 15, 2015, https://www.cnn.com/2015/11/15/europe/paris-attacks -passports/index.html.

8.   Amanpour and Patterson, "Passport Linked to Terrorist."

9.   Amanpour and Patterson, "Passport Linked to Terrorist."

10.   Sebastian Rotella, "How Europe Left Itself Open to Terrorism," *Frontline,* WGBH, October 18, 2016, https://www.pbs.org/wgbh/frontline/article/how -europe-left-itself-open-to-terrorism/.

11.   Kenneth L. Lasoen, "Indications and Warning in Belgium: Brussels Is Not Delphi," *Journal of Strategic Studies* 40 (March 2017): 927–962, https://doi .org/10.1080/01402390.2017.1288111.

12.   Bojan Pancevski, "Paris Attackers Posed as Refugees," *Australian,* October 3, 2016, https://www.pressreader.com/australia/the-australian /20161003/281934542444445.

13.   Melissa Eddy, "Germany Seeks Tunisian Tied to Berlin Christmas Market Attack," *New York Times,* December 21, 2016, https://www.nytimes .com/2016/12/21/world/europe/berlin-christmas-market-attack.html.

14.   Andy Eckardt and Carlo Angerer, "Wuerzburg Train Attack: ISIS Flag Found in Teen Attacker's Room in Germany," NBC Universal, July 19, 2016, https://www.nbcnews.com/news/world/wuerzburg-train-attack-isis-flag-found -teen-attacker-s-room-n612156.

15.   "German Police: Syrian Asylum Seeker Arrested in Machete Slaying," RFE/RL Inc., July 24, 2016, https://www.rferl.org/a/germany-man-kills-woman -machete/27877747.html.

16.   "Ansbach Explosion: Bomber Pledged Allegiance to IS," BBC, July 25, 2016, http://www.bbc.com/news/world-europe-36882831.

17.   Amanda Devlin and David Hughes, "KILLER UNMASKED: Who Was Salman Abedi? Manchester Bombing Terrorist Whose Brother Hashem Faces Arrest in the UK," *The Sun*, March 27, 2018, https://www.thesun.co.uk /news/3626664/salman-abedi-manchester-bombing-terror-attacker/.

18.   Chiara Palazzo and Emily Allen, "Manchester Terror Attack: Everything We Know," *Telegraph*, May 26, 2017, https://www.telegraph.co.uk/news/0 /manchester-terror-attack-everything-know-far/.

19.   CNN Wire Staff, "Somali-American Accused of Plotting to Bomb Oregon Tree-Lighting Event," Cable News Network, November 27, 2010, http:// www.cnn.com/2010/CRIME/11/27/oregon.bomb.plot/index.html; Lynne Terry, "Family of Portland's Bomb Suspect, Mohamed Mohamud, Fled Chaos in Somalia for New Life in America," Oregon Live LLC, updated December 5, 2010, http:// www.oregonlive.com/portland/index.ssf/2010/12/suspect_in_portland_bomb _plot.html.

20.   Jana Winter, "Portland Terror Suspect a Self-Proclaimed Moral Authority Online," FOX News Network LLC, December 3, 2010, http://www .foxnews.com/us/2010/12/03/oregon-alleged-tree-bomber-online-moral-authority .html.

21.   CNN Wire Staff, "Oregon Tree-Lighting Event."

22.   Jason Ryan, "Kentucky Terror Case: Two Iraqis Charged With Sup- porting Al Qaeda in Iraq," ABC News, May 31, 2011, http://abcnews.go.com /Politics/kentucky-terror-case-waad-ramadan-alwan-mohanad-shareef/story?id =13727518.

23.   Matthew Hendley, "Abdullatif Aldosary, Alleged Casa Grande Bomber, Now a Murder Suspect?," Phoenix New Times, May 6, 2013, http://www .phoenixnewtimes.com/news/abdullatif-aldosary-alleged-casa-grande-bomber-now -a-murder-suspect-6653777.

24.   Anthony Kimery, "UPDATED: Iraqi Refugee Charged in Ariz. IED Bombing had Arms Cache, Bomb Materials in Home; ICE Didn't Deport After Earlier Felony, But Said Reassessing Under Terrorism Statutes," Homeland Secu- rity Today, December 5, 2012, https://www.hstoday.us/kimery-report /updated-iraqi-refugee-charged-in-ariz-ied-bombing-had-arms-cache-bomb -materials-in-home-ice-didn-t-deport-after-earlier-felony-but-said-reassessing -under-terrorism-statutes/.

25.   "Boston Marathon Bombing," A&E Television Networks LLC, accessed April 12, 2018, https://www.history.com/topics/boston-marathon-bombings.

26.   Associated Press, "Report: Uzbek Man Convicted of Terror Charges Drops Appeal," FOX News Network LLC, June 24, 2016, http://www.foxnews .com/us/2016/06/24/report-uzbek-man-convicted-terror-charges-drops-appeal .html.

27.   John Sowell, "Kurbanov Sent to Prison for 25 Years in Boise Terror Plot," *Idaho Statesman*, January 7, 2016, http://www.idahostatesman.com/news /local/crime/article53610300.html.

28.   Brittny Mejia, "Man Serving 25 Years in Terrorism Case Pleads Guilty to Attempted Murder of Victorville Prison Warden," *Los Angeles Times*, March 13, 2018, http://www.latimes.com/local/lanow/la-me-ln-prisoner-attempted -murder-20180313-story.html.

29.   Associated Press, "Iraqi Refugee Living in Houston Pleads Guilty to Trying to Help ISIS," CBS Interactive Inc., October 17, 2016, https://www .cbsnews.com/news/iraqi-refugee-living-in-houston-pleads-guilty-to-trying-to -help-isis/.

30.   Department of Justice, "Iraqi Refugee Convicted of Attempting to Provide Material Support to ISIL," press release, October 17, 2016, https://www .investigativeproject.org/documents/case_docs/3107.pdf.

31.   Department of Justice, "Iraqi Refugee."

32.   Kristine Phillips, Jessica Contrera, and Brian Murphy, "Minnesota Stabbing Survivor: 'He Looked Me Dead in the Eyes,'" *Washington Post*, September 19, 2016, https://www.washingtonpost.com/news/post-nation/wp/2016/09/18 /man-shot-dead-after-stabbing-8-people-in-a-minnesota-mall/?utm_term= .a4958c876653.

33.   Mike Levine and Emily Shapiro, "Chilling Video Shows Minnesota Mall Stabbing Suspect Attack Clerk," ABC News, October 6, 2016, http://abcnews .go.com/US/chilling-video-shows-minnesota-mall-stabbing-suspect-attack /story?id=42619413.

34.   Associated Press, "FBI: Minnesota Mall Attack Likely Premeditated," CBS Broadcasting Inc., October 6, 2016, http://baltimore.cbslocal.com/2016 /10/06/fbi-minnesota-mall-attack-likely-premeditated/.

35.   Dustin Volz and Alex Dobuzinskis, "Islamic State Claims Responsibility for Minnesota Mall Attack," Reuters, September 18, 2016, https://www.reuters .com/article/us-minnesota-mall-stabbings/islamic-state-claims-responsibility-for -minnesota-mall-attack-idUSKCN11O04S.

36.   Pete Williams et al., "Suspect Identified in Ohio State Attack as Abdul Razak Ali Artan," NBC Universal, November 28, 2016, https://www.nbcnews .com/news/us-news/suspect-dead-after-ohio-state-university-car-knife-attack -n689076.

37.   Kevin Stankiewicz, "Humans of Ohio State," *The Lantern* 136, no. 40 (August 25, 2016), 5, https://issuu.com/thelantern/docs/082516.

38.   Dan Barry et al., "'Always Agitated, Always Mad': Omar Mateen, According to Those Who Knew Him," *New York Times*, June 18, 2016, https:// www.nytimes.com/2016/06/19/us/omar-mateen-gunman-orlando-shooting.html.

39.   David French, "It's Time We Faced the Facts about the Muslim World," *National Review*, September 19, 2016, https://www.nationalreview.com/2016/09 /chelsea-bombing-minnesota-stabbing-jihadist-threat-america-grows/.

40.   "The 9/11 Commission Report," NPR, accessed April 12, 2018, https:// www.npr.org/documents/2004/9-11/911reportexec.pdf.

Chapter 8—Targeting the Innocent

1.   Alvin Schmidt, *How Christianity Changed the World* (Grand Rapids, MI: Zondervan, 2004).

2.   Lori Palatnik, "Eishet Chayil," Aish.com, accessed April 13, 2018, http:// www.aish.com/sh/ht/fn/48966686.html.

3.   Palatnik, "Eishet Chayil."

4.   Rachel Avraham, "Muslim Doctor: Israel Is an Inspiration to the Islamic World," United With Israel, July 8, 2013, https://unitedwithisrael.org/muslim -physician-israel-is-an-inspiration-to-the-islamic-world/.

5.   "Myths & Facts—Human Rights in Arab Countries," American-Israeli Cooperative Enterprise, accessed April 13, 2018, http://www.jewishvirtuallibrary .org/myths-and-facts-human-rights-in-arab-countries.

6.   Aaron Bandler, "7 Things You Need To Know About Women's March Organizer Linda Sarsour," *Daily Wire*, July 7, 2017, https://www.dailywire.com /news/18368/7-things-you-need-know-about-womens-march-aaron-bandler; Brett T., "Tweets from 2017: Women Allowed to Drive in Saudi Arabia Soon Per Royal Decree," Twitchy.com, September 26, 2017, https://twitchy.com/brettt-3136 /2017/09/26/tweets-from-2017-women-allowed-to-drive-in-saudi-arabia-soon -per-royal-decree/.

7.   "Sex Trafficking Fact Sheet," Equality Now, accessed May 10, 2018, https://www.equalitynow.org/sex-trafficking-fact-sheet.

8.   "Trafficking in Persons Report," United States Department of State, June 2017, https://www.state.gov/documents/organization/271339.pdf.

9.   Jessica Durando, "Report: 1,200 Women Assaulted on New Year's Eve in German Cities," *USA Today*, July 11, 2016, https://www.usatoday.com/story /news/world/2016/07/11/cologne-germany-sexual-assaults/86939142/.

10.   Von Georg Mascolo and Britta von der Heide, "1200 Frauen Wurden Opfer von Silvester-Gewalt," trans. Google, *Süddeutsche Zeitung*, July 10, 2016, http://www.sueddeutsche.de/politik/uebergriffe-in-koeln-frauen-wurden-opfer -von-silvester-gewalt-1.3072064.

11.   Nick Hallett, "More Than 200 Charged in One Day Over Cologne Sex Attacks," Breitbart, January 10, 2016, http://www.breitbart.com/london /2016/01/10/more-than-200-charged-in-one-day-over-cologne-sex-attacks/.

12.   Michael Sheils McNamee, "Dozens of Sexual Assaults in German City on New Year's Eve," Journal Media Ltd., January 5, 2016, http://www.thejournal .ie/sexual-assaults-german-city-new-years-eve-2532129-Jan2016/.

13.   Asifa Quaraishi, "Her Honor: An Islamic Critique of the Rape Laws of Pakistan From a Woman-Sensitive Perspective," *Michigan Journal of International Law* 18, no. 2 (1997): 287, https://repository.law.umich.edu/cgi/viewcontent .cgi?referer=https://www.google.com/&httpsredir=1&article=1467&context=mjil.

14.   Mais Haddad, "Victims of Rape and Law: How the Laws of the Arab World Protect Rapists, Not Victims," JURIST Legal News and Research Services Inc., May 9, 2017, http://www.jurist.org/dateline/2017/05/Mais-Haddad-arab-world-laws-protect-the-rapist-not-the-victim.php.

15.   "Saudi: Why We Punished Rape Victim," Cable News Network, updated November 20, 2007, http://www.cnn.com/2007/WORLD/meast/11/20/saudi.rape.victim/index.html; Haddad, "Victims of Rape and Law."

16.   Diana West, "From US Helpers in Iraq to Sex Criminals in Colorado," Townhall.com, January 24, 2014, https://townhall.com/columnists/dianawest/2014/01/24/from-us-helpers-in-iraq-to-sex-criminals-in-colorado-n1783901.

17.   West, "Sex Criminals."

18.   West, "Sex Criminals."

19.   West, "Sex Criminals."

20.   "Terror and Death at Home Are Caught in F.B.I. Tape," *New York Times*, October 28, 1991, https://www.nytimes.com/1991/10/28/us/terror-and-death-at-home-are-caught-in-fbi-tape.html.

21.   Joe Treen, "'Die, My Daughter, Die!,'" *People* 37, no. 2 (January 20, 1992), http://people.com/archive/die-my-daughter-die-vol-37-no-2/.

22.   "Terror and Death," *New York Times*.

23.   "Terror and Death," *New York Times*.

24.   Treen, "'Die, My Daughter, Die!'"; Associated Press, "St. Louis Woman Serving Life for Daughter's Murder Dies in Prison," *St. Louis Post-Dispatch*, April 30, 2014, http://www.stltoday.com/news/local/crime-and-courts/st-louis-woman-serving-life-for-daughter-s-murder-dies/article_c0a85a29-2826-5b3f-ade5-f0199f557aaa.html.

25.   Divya Talwar and Athar Ahmad, "'Honour Crime': 11,000 UK Cases Recorded in Five Years," BBC, July 9, 2015, http://www.bbc.com/news/uk-33424644.

26.   Cynthia Helba et al., "Report on Exploratory Study Into Honor Violence Measurement Methods," National Criminal Justice Reference Service, May 2015, https://www.ncjrs.gov/pdffiles1/bjs/grants/248879.pdf.

27.   Helba et al., "Honor Violence."

28.   Helba et al., "Honor Violence."

29.   "Executive Order 13780: *Protecting the Nation From Foreign Terrorist Entry Into the United States* Initial Section 11 Report," press release, United States Department of Justice, January 2018, https://www.justice.gov/opa/press-release/file/1026436/download.

30.   Mark Mather and Charlotte Feldman-Jacobs, "Women and Girls at Risk of Female Genital Mutilation/Cutting in the United States," Population Reference Bureau, February 5, 2016, http://www.prb.org/Publications/Articles/2015/us-fgmc.aspx.

31.   "Female Genital Mutilation (FGM)," WHO, accessed April 13, 2018, http://www.who.int/reproductivehealth/topics/fgm/prevalence/en/.

32.   Stephanie Chen, "Pediatricians Now Reject all Female Genital Cutting," Cable News Network, May 27, 2010, http://www.cnn.com/2010/HEALTH/05/27/AAP.retracts.female.genital.cutting/index.html.

33.   Howard Goldberg et al., "Female Genital Mutilation/Cutting in the United States: Updated Estimates of Women and Girls at Risk, 2012," *Public Health Reports* 131, no. 2 (March 1, 2016): 340–347, https://doi.org/10.1177 /0033354916131100218.

34.   Janice Williams, "Nearly 100 Girls May Have Had Genitals Cut by Doctors in Michigan, Prosecutor Says," *Newsweek*, June 8, 2017, http://www.newsweek .com/genital-mutilation-girls-michigan-doctor-623295.

35.   Williams, "100 Girls."

36.   Williams, "100 Girls."

37.   Abigail Hauslohner, "A Virginia Imam Said Female Genital Mutilation Prevents 'Hypersexuality,' Leading to Calls for His Dismissal," *Washington Post*, June 5, 2017, https://www.washingtonpost.com/news/acts-of-faith/wp/2017 /06/05/virginia-mosque-embattled-after-imam-said-female-genital-mutilation -prevents-hypersexuality/?utm_term=.dbf74dd53753.

38.   Williams, "100 Girls."

39.   Williams, "100 Girls."

40.   Williams, "100 Girls."

41.   Williams, "100 Girls."

42.   Associated Press, "Jury Convicts New York TV Executive of Beheading Wife," FOX News Network LLC, February 7, 2011, http://www.foxnews.com /us/2011/02/07/closing-arguments-begin-new-york-beheading-murder-trial.html; Liz Robbins, "Upstate Man Charged With Beheading His Estranged Wife," *New York Times*, February 17, 2009, http://www.nytimes.com/2009/02/18/nyregion /18behead.html.

43.   Associated Press, "Man Accused of Beheading Wife Called 'Gentle,'" NBC Universal, updated February 17, 2009, http://www.nbcnews.com/id /29245206/ns/us_news-crime_and_courts/t/man-accused-beheading-wife -called-gentle/.

44.   Associated Press, "Brutal Irony in New York Woman's Beheading," CBS Interactive Inc., February 18, 2009, https://www.cbsnews.com/news/brutal-irony -in-new-york-womans-beheading/.

45.   Associated Press, "Brutal Irony."

46.   Bill Meyer, "Police: TV Exec, Who Tried to Debunk Stereotypes of Islam, Beheads Wife After She Files for Divorce," Advance Ohio, updated February 18, 2009, http://www.cleveland.com/nation/index.ssf/2009/02/police_tv _exec_who_tried_to_de.html.

47.   Office of Refugee Resettlement, "Report to Congress FY 2008," United States Department of Health and Human Services, April 20, 2011, https:// www.acf.hhs.gov/sites/default/files/orr/annual_orr_report_to_congress_2008 .pdf; "Refugee Admission Statistics," United States Department of State, accessed April 13, 2018, https://2009-2017.state.gov/j/prm/releases/statistics/index.htm; Jens Manuel Krogstad and Jynnah Radford, "Key Facts About Refugees to the U.S.," Pew Research, January 30, 2017, http://www.pewresearch.org/fact-tank /2017/01/30/key-facts-about-refugees-to-the-u-s/.

48.   Common Sense, "Muslim 'Refugees' Threaten Minnesota Community With Rape," YouTube, January 31, 2017, https://www.youtube.com/watch?v =w6fdDOJLVcA.

49.   Dan Debaun, "Governor Dayton Speaks Out Against Discrimination in St. Cloud," WJON, October 13, 2015, http://wjon.com/governor-dayton-speaks -out-against-discrimination-in-st-cloud-video/.

50.   Jay Akbar, "Migrant Who Admitted Raping a 10-Year-Old Boy at an Austrian Swimming Pool Because of a 'Sexual Emergency' Has His Sentence Cut and Will Soon Be Free," Associated Newspapers Ltd., May 24, 2017, http://www .dailymail.co.uk/news/article-4536856/Migrant-raped-10-year-old-boy-swimming -pool-sentence-cut.html.

51.   Akbar, "Raping a 10-Year-Old Boy."

52.   Akbar, "Raping a 10-Year-Old Boy."

53.   Michelle Malkin, "Yes, Our Troops Were Ordered to Ignore Afghan Pedophiles," *New York Post*, September 15, 2015, https://nypost.com/2015/09/25 /yes-our-troops-were-ordered-to-ignore-afghan-pedophiles/.

54.   Joseph Goldstein, "U.S. Soldiers Told to Ignore Sexual Abuse of Boys by Afghan Allies," *New York Times*, September 20, 2015, http://www.nytimes.com /2015/09/21/world/asia/us-soldiers-told-to-ignore-afghan-allies-abuse-of-boys .html.

55.   Malkin, "Afghan Pedophiles."

56.   Dan Lamothe, "Family of Slain Marine Sues Marine Corps, Alleging Cover-Up," *Washington Post*, October 16, 2014, https://www.washingtonpost.com /news/checkpoint/wp/2014/10/16/family-of-slain-marine-sues-marine-corps -alleging-cover-up/?utm_term=.f3b900ec400c.

57.   Malkin, "Afghan Pedophiles."

58.   Malkin, "Afghan Pedophiles."

59.   Will Roscoe and Stephen O. Murray, *Islamic Homosexualities: Culture, History and Literature* (New York: New York University Press, 1997), 90, https:// books.google.com/books?id=6Zw-AAAAQBAJ&.

60.   Jane Wardell, "Islamic Scholar in Homosexuality Comments Row Leaves Australia," Reuters, June 14, 2016, https://www.reuters.com/article /us-australia-preacher-visa/islamic-scholar-in-homosexuality-comments-row-leaves -australia-idUSKCN0Z00F1.

CHAPTER 9—LAMESTREAM MEDIA

1.   "Top 100 Followers in Musician/Band," TwitterCounter, accessed May 10, 2018, https://twittercounter.com/pages/100/musician-band.

2.   Kanye West (@kanyewest), "You don't have to agree with trump but the mob can't make me not love him….," Twitter, April 25, 2018, 11:30 a.m., https:// twitter.com/kanyewest/status/989179757651574784.

3.   Kumail Nanjiani (@kumailn), "This was the worst twitter day in twitter history.," Twitter, April 25, 2018, 7:47 p.m., https://twitter.com/kumailn /status/989304967067455488.

4.   Kanye West (@kanyewest), "we got love," Twitter, April 25, 2018, 2:19 p.m., https://twitter.com/kanyewest/status/989222392630202368?lang=en;

Kanye West (@kanyewest), "Obama was in office for eight years and nothing in Chicago changed.," Twitter, April 25, 2018, 5:38 p.m., https://twitter.com /kanyewest/status/989272340432240641.

5.   Ben Shapiro, "HYPOCRITES: Leftists Tell Kanye to Shut Up and Rap," The Daily Wire, April 26, 2018, https://www.dailywire.com/news/29933 /hypocrites-leftists-tell-kanye-shut-and-rap-ben-shapiro.

6.   "Trevor Noah Net Worth (House Cars Income Salary Wealth)," FinApp, accessed May 14, 2015, https://finapp.co.in/trevor-noah-net-worth/.

7.   *People* (@people), "Kanye West 'Seems to Be on the Edge' and 'Is Very Hard to Deal with Right Now'," Twitter, April 24, 2018, 8:02 p.m., https:// twitter.com/people/status/988946399747338240.

8.   Emily Zanotti, "The Kardashians Run to Kanye West's Rescue as He's Under Assault by the Left," The Daily Wire, April 25, 2018, https://www.daily wire.com/news/29896/kardashians-run-kanye-wests-rescue-hes-under-emily -zanotti.

9.   Ben Shapiro, "DRAGON ENERGY: John Legend Tries to Intimidate Kanye West Into Rescinding Trump Support. Kanye Flattens Him.," The Daily Wire, April 26, 2018, https://www.dailywire.com/news/29931/dragon-energy -john-legend-tries-intimidate-kanye-ben-shapiro.

10.   Shapiro, "DRAGON ENERGY."

11.   Trey Sanchez, "BBC Hides Islam in Report on Muslim Stabbing Attack," TruthRevolt.org, June 9, 2017, https://www.truthrevolt.org/news/bbc -hides-islam-report-muslim-stabbing-attack.

12.   Michael Heaver (@Michael_Heaver), "It's a fact that attack victim's boss (who BBC have quoted and interviewed) has said attackers shouted about Koran and Allah.," Twitter, June 8, 2017, 3:14 a.m., https://twitter.com/Michael_Heaver /status/872758610614530048.

13.   Judith Berman, "Sweden's War on Free Speech," Gatestone Institute, April 14, 2018, https://www.gatestoneinstitute.org/12078/sweden-free-speech.

14.   Berman, "Sweden's War."

15.   Richard Eskow, "Let's Nationalize Fox News: Imagining a Very Different Media," Salon.com, July 8, 2014, https://www.salon.com/2014/07/08/lets _nationalize_amazon_and_google_publicly_funded_technology_built_big_tech/.

16.   Daniel Burke, "The Secret Costs of Islamophobia," Cable News Network, updated November 15, 2016, https://www.cnn.com/2016/09/23/us/islamerica -secret-costs-islamophobia/index.html.

17.   "2016 Hate Crime Statistics," Federal Bureau of Investigation, accessed April 17, 2016, https://ucr.fbi.gov/hate-crime/2016/tables/table-1.

18.   "2016 Hate Crime Statistics," Federal Bureau of Investigation

19.   Justin Trudeau (@JustinTrudeau), "My heart goes out to Khawlah Noman following this morning's cowardly attack on her in Toronto. Canada is an open and welcoming country, and incidents like this cannot be tolerated.," Twitter, January 12, 2018, 12:57 p.m., https://twitter.com/justintrudeau/status/951921098 341445634?lang=en.

20.   Ralph Ellis, "Hijab Cutting Incident Did Not Happen, Toronto Police Say," Cable News Network, updated January 15, 2018, https://www.cnn.com /2018/01/15/us/toronto-girl-hijab-cutting-update/index.html.

21.   Caleb Parke, "Hate Crimes and Hoaxes: 10 Campus Stories Debunked in 2017," FOX News Network LLC, December 27, 2017, http://www.foxnews .com/us/2017/12/27/hate-crimes-and-hoaxes-10-campus-stories-debunked-in-2017 .html.

22.   Derek Hawkins, "She Claimed She Was Attacked by Men Who Yelled 'Trump' and Grabbed Her Hijab. Police Say She Lied.," *Washington Post,* December 15, 2016, https://www.washingtonpost.com/news/morning-mix /wp/2016/12/15/she-claimed-she-was-attacked-by-men-who-yelled-trump-and -grabbed-her-hijab-police-say-she-lied/?utm_term=.32f5853997e0.

23.   David Mack and Talal Ansari, "Woman Arrested for Allegedly Making Up Story of NY Subway Attack by Trump Supporters," BuzzFeedNews, updated December 15, 2016, https://www.buzzfeed.com/davidmack/nyc-subway-false -report?utm_term=.jwlENMlyX#.au1m9gnZ5.

24.   "Muslim Woman 'Made Up NY Subway Hate Attack' by Trump Fans," BBC, December 15, 2016, http://www.bbc.com/news/world-us-canada-38328242.

25.   William Hicks, "NYPD Arrests Muslim Girl Who Claimed Attack by Trump Supporters," FOX News Network LLC, December 14, 2016, http://www .foxnews.com/us/2016/12/14/nypd-arrests-muslim-girl-who-claimed-attack-by -trump-supporters.html.

26.   Jonathan Adelman, "The Israeli Arabs: Trailblazers of a Better Middle East," HuffPost, updated August 19, 2016, https://www.huffingtonpost.com /jonathan-adelman/the-israeli-arabs-trailbl_b_8010020.html.

27.   "Five Palestinians Killed 'After Attacking Israelis,'" BBC, February 14, 2016, http://www.bbc.com/news/world-middle-east-35574604.

28.   Associated Press, "Three Palestinian Teenagers Shot Dead on West Bank," *Guardian,* February 14, 2016, https://www.theguardian.com/world/2016 /feb/14/three-palestinian-teenagers-shot-dead-on-west-bank.

29.   Dan Gainor, "Media Goes Crazy Over Trump Announcement on Jerusalem, CNN's Sloppy Mistake, and Other Journalism Disasters," FOX News Network LLC, December 9, 2017, http://www.foxnews.com/opinion/2017/12/09 /media-goes-crazy-over-trump-announcement-on-jerusalem-cnn-s-sloppy-mistake -and-other-journalism-disasters.html; "CBS This Morning," December 6, 2017, archived at https://archive.org/details/KPIX_20171206_150000_CBS_This _Morning/start/540/end/600.

30.   Tea Partier, "CNN's Aaron David Miller Likens Embassy Move to Hitting Palestinians on the Head With Hammer," YouTube, December 8, 2017, https://www.youtube.com/watch?v=VNrqe_wM7Oc.

31.   Yaniv Kubovich, Jack Khoury, and Yotam Berger, "Five Palestinians Reported Seriously Hurt in Clashes With Israeli Troops in West Bank, Gaza," *Haaretz,* December 29, 2017, https://www.haaretz.com/israel-news/5-palestinians -reported-seriously-hurt-in-clashes-with-idf-1.5629973.

32.   "Trump Recognizes Jerusalem as the Capital of Israel and Plans to Move US Embassy From Tel Aviv," ABC News, December 6, 2017, http://abcnews

.go.com/WNT/video/trump-recognizes-jerusalem-capital-israel-plans-move
-us-51629103.

33.   "Morning Joe," MSNBC, December 6, 2017, archived at https://archive
.org/details/MSNBCW_20171206_110000_Morning_Joe/start/5160/end/5220.

34.   Mark Ruffalo (@MarkRufffalo), "Isreal, please show restraint in the face
of these protests….," Twitter, December 7, 2017, 8:36 a.m., https://twitter.com
/markruffalo/status/938764197944528897?lang=en.

35.   Tim Graham, "Election in the Streets," Media Research Center, August
28, 2006, http://archive.mrc.org/SpecialReports/2006/report082806_p1.asp.

36.   Brad Wilmouth, "CBS Evening News Ignores Jury Acquitting Illegal
Immigrant in Kate Steinle Killing," Media Research Center, December 2, 2017,
https://www.newsbusters.org/blogs/nb/brad-wilmouth/2017/12/02/cbs-en
-ignores-jury-acquitting-illegal-immigrant-kate-steinle.

37.   Ann Coulter, *Adios, America: The Left's Plan to Turn Our Country Into a
Third World Hellhole* (Washington, DC: Regnery Publishing, 2016).

38.   Coulter, *Adios, America*; "Alleged Ringleader Convicted in 2008 Gang
Rape of Lesbian Woman in Richmond," CBS Broadcasting Inc., December 18,
2013, http://sanfrancisco.cbslocal.com/2013/12/18/alleged-ringleader-convicted
-in-2008-gang-rape-of-lesbian-woman-in-richmond/.

39.   Associated Press, "Richmond Man Convicted in Gang Rape of Lesbian,"
San Diego Union-Tribune, December 18, 2013, http://www.sandiegouniontribune
.com/sdut-richmond-man-convicted-in-gang-rape-of-lesbian-2013dec18-story.html.

40.   Gary Peterson, "Richmond Man Sentenced to 411 Years, Four Months
for Gang Rape," *Mercury News*, May 16, 2014, https://www.mercurynews.com
/2014/05/16/richmond-man-sentenced-to-411-years-four-months-for-gang-rape/.

41.   Henry K. Lee, "400-Plus Years for Gang Rape of Targeted Lesbian," *San
Francisco Chronicle*, May 19, 2014, https://www.sfchronicle.com/crime/article/400
-plus-years-for-gang-rape-of-targeted-lesbian-5489586.php.

42.   Associated Press, "Man Sentenced in California Gang Rape of Lesbian,"
San Diego Union-Tribune, May 20, 2014, http://www.sandiegouniontribune.com
/sdut-man-sentenced-in-california-gang-rape-of-lesbian-2014may20-story.html.

43.   Rich Noyes, "Bias: 1,000 Minutes for Trump/Russia 'Collusion' vs. 20
Seconds for Hillary/Russia Scandal," Media Research Center, October 25, 2017,
https://www.newsbusters.org/blogs/nb/rich-noyes/2017/10/25/bias-1000
-minutes-trumprussia-collusion-vs-20-seconds-hillaryrussia.

44.   Noyes, "Bias."

45.   Dan Gainor, "Soros Spends Over $48 Million Funding Media Organiza-
tions," Media Research Center, accessed April 17, 2018, https://www.mrc.org
/commentary/soros-spends-over-48-million-funding-media-organizations.

46.   JackofSpades, "WE FOUND IT! The 60 Minutes Interview George
Soros Tried To Bury!," YouTube, February 2, 2017, https://www.youtube.com
/watch?v=zVmQ05J9tHs.

47.   Dan Gainor, "Over 30 Major News Organizations Linked to George
Soros," Media Research Center, accessed April 17, 2018, https://www.mrc.org
/commentary/over-30-major-news-organizations-linked-george-soros.

48.   Gainor, "Soros Spends Over $48 Million."

49. "Mission Statement," Columbia Journalism Review, accessed May 15, 2018, https://www.cjr.org/about_us/mission_statement.php.

50. Gainor, "Soros Spends Over $48 Million."

51. CNN, "Amanpour Receives Press Freedom Award," YouTube, November 23, 2016, https://www.youtube.com/watch?v=NawMb9ia0F4.

52. CNN, "Amanpour Receives Press Freedom Award."

53. Paul Farhi, "Brian Williams Admits That His Story of Coming Under Fire While in Iraq Was False," *Washington Post*, February 4, 2015, https://www.washingtonpost.com/lifestyle/style/brian-williams-admits-that-his-story-of-coming-under-fire-while-in-iraq-was-false/2015/02/04/d7fe32d0-acc0-11e4-9c91-e9d2f9fde644_story.html?utm_term=.51a36431f649.

54. Michael Beckman, "Christiane Amanpour Calls the Islamic Terrorists 'Activists,'" YouTube, January 9, 2015, https://www.youtube.com/watch?v=F7YIi7O0XKg; Matthew Balan, "CNN's Amanpour: 'Republican Candidates…Decided to Make A War On Moslems,'" Media Research Center, September 24, 2015, https://www.newsbusters.org/blogs/nb/matthew-balan/2015/09/24/cnns-amanpour-republican-candidatesdecided-make-war-moslems; CNN, "Amanpour Receives Press Freedom Award."

55. CNN, "Amanpour Receives Press Freedom Award."

56. Wajahat Ali et al., "Fear, Inc.," Center for American Progress, April 2011, https://cdn.americanprogress.org/wp-content/uploads/issues/2011/08/pdf/islamophobia.pdf.

Chapter 10—CAIR and the Terrorist Front-Scheme

1. Ayaan Hirsi Ali, "'The Quran Is Our Law; Jihad Is Our Way,'" *Wall Street Journal*, updated February 18, 2011, https://www.wsj.com/articles/SB10001424052748704132204576136590964621006.

2. Stephane Lacroix, "Osama bin Laden and the Saudi Muslim Brotherhood," *Foreign Policy*, October 3, 2012, http://foreignpolicy.com/2012/10/03/osama-bin-laden-and-the-saudi-muslim-brotherhood/; "Inside the Terror Network," *Frontline*, WGBH, January 17, 2002, https://www.pbs.org/wgbh/pages/frontline/shows/network/personal/whowere.html; "Profile: Ayman al-Zawahiri," BBC, August 13, 2015, http://www.bbc.com/news/world-middle-east-13789286; William McCants, "Who is Islamic State Leader Abu Bakr al-Baghdadi?," BBC, March 8, 2016, http://www.bbc.com/news/world-middle-east-35694311.

3. "The Muslim Brotherhood 'Project,'" trans. Scott Burgess, Investigative Project on Terrorism, December 1, 1982, https://www.investigativeproject.org/documents/misc/687.pdf.

4. "An Explanatory Memorandum on the General Strategic Goal for the Group in North America," Investigative Project on Terrorism, May 22, 1991, http://www.investigativeproject.org/documents/misc/20.pdf.

5. "An Explanatory Memorandum on the General Strategic Goal for the Group in North America."

6. Adam Taylor, "Why the U.A.E. Is Calling 2 American Groups Terrorists," *Washington Post*, November 17, 2014, https://www.washingtonpost.com

/news/worldviews/wp/2014/11/17/why-the-u-a-e-is-calling-2-american-groups
-terrorists/?utm_term=.6e65d52390e9.

7.   Andrew C. McCarthy, "The Roots of CAIR's Intimidation Campaign,"
National Review, April 12, 2014, http://www.nationalreview.com/article/375620
/roots-cairs-intimidation-campaign-andrew-c-mccarthy.

8.   Steven Emerson, "Part 1: CAIR Exposed," IPT News, March 24, 2008,
https://www.investigativeproject.org/621/cair-exposed.

9.   United States v. Holy Land Foundation, et al., Government Exhibit
Philly Meeting 16, (N.D. Texas 2008), http://coop.txnd.uscourts.gov/judges
/hlf2/09-29-08/Philly%20Meeting%2016.pdf.

10.   Daniel Pipes and Sharon Chadha, "CAIR: Islamists Fooling the Establishment," *Middle East Quarterly* 13, no. 2 (Spring 2006), http://www.meforum
.org/916/cair-islamists-fooling-the-establishment.

11.   Deny Islam, "The Truth About CAIR: Read It, Memorize It, Broadcast
It," The Counter Jihad Report, November 25, 2011, https://counterjihadreport
.com/2011/11/25/the-truth-about-cair-read-it-memorize-it-broadcast-it/.

12.   Council on American-Islamic Relations, "Vision, Mission, Core Principles," updated October 1, 2015, https://www.cair.com/about-us/vision-mission
-core-principles.html.

13.   Emerson, "Part 1: CAIR Exposed."

14.   United States v. Holy Land Foundation, et al., Government Exhibit
Elbarasse Search 3, (N.D. Texas 2008), http://coop.txnd.uscourts.gov/judges
/hlf2/09-25-08/Elbarasse%20Search%203.pdf.

15.   "CAIR's Funding," Investigative Project on Terrorism, accessed April 25,
2018, https://www.investigativeproject.org/documents/misc/110.pdf.

16.   "CAIR's Funding," Investigative Project on Terrorism.

17.   "CAIR's Funding," Investigative Project on Terrorism.

18.   Council on American-Islamic Relations, "Help for Victims," accessed
April 25, 2018, archived at http://web.archive.org/web/20010917013636/http://
cair-net.org/.

19.   "IDB Approves New Projects Worldwide," press release, Embassy of the
Kingdom of Saudi Arabia, August 15, 1999, archived at http://web.archive.org
/web/20000417093241/http://saudiembassy.net/press_release/99_spa/08_15_aid
.html; Associated Press, "U.S. Muslims Split Over Saudi Donations," *Intelligencer*,
November 30, 2002, https://www.theintelligencer.com/news/article/U-S
-Muslims-Split-Over-Saudi-Donations-10568764.php.

20.   "CAIR's Funding," Investigative Project on Terrorism.

21.   "CAIR's Funding," Investigative Project on Terrorism.

22.   Greg Palast and David Pallister, "FBI Claims Bin Laden Inquiry Was
Frustrated," *Guardian*, November 7, 2001, https://www.theguardian.com/world
/2001/nov/07/afghanistan.september11.

23.   "CAIR's Awad: In Support of the Hamas Movement," Investigative
Project on Terrorism, March 22, 1994, https://www.investigativeproject.org/223
/cairs-awad-in-support-of-the-hamas-movement.

24.   Itamar Marcus and Nan Jacques Zilberdik, "PA TV Honors Murderer by Joining Family's Birthday Party," Palestinian Media Watch, April 25, 2017, http://palwatch.org/main.aspx?fi=157&doc_id=20768.

25.   "Hamas: 'Glory Record' (1988–1994)," American-Israeli Cooperative Enterprise, accessed April 25, 2018, http://www.jewishvirtuallibrary.org/hamas -quot-glory-record-quot.

26.   "Patterns of Global Terrorism: 1992—Appendix B: Background Information on Terrorist Groups," Federation of American Scientists, accessed April 25, 2018, https://fas.org/irp/threat/terror_92/backg.html.

27.   "The Council on American-Islamic Relations (CAIR): CAIR Exposed," Investigative Project on Terrorism, accessed April 25, 2018, http://www .investigativeproject.org/documents/misc/122.pdf.

28.   "The Council on American-Islamic Relations (CAIR)," Investigative Project on Terrorism.

29.   Steven Emerson, "Part 4: CAIR Remains Apologist for Terrorist Hamas, Seeks To Silence Critics," Investigative Project on Terrorism, March 27, 2008, https://www.investigativeproject.org/627/cair-remains-apologist-for-terrorist -hamas-seeks-to-silence.

30.   "The Council on American-Islamic Relations (CAIR)," Investigative Project on Terrorism.

31.   Jake Tapper, "Islam's Flawed Spokesmen," Salon Media Group Inc., September 26, 2001, https://www.salon.com/2001/09/26/muslims_2/.

32.   "CAIR's True Colors," Investigative Project on Terrorism, January 30, 2009, https://www.investigativeproject.org/986/cairs-true-colors.

33.   "Prepared Testimony of Steven Emerson Before the Senate Foreign Relations Committee Subcommittee on African Affairs Terrorism, Sudan and Us Counter-Terrorist Policy May 15, 1997," Investigative Project on Terrorism, accessed May 22, 2018, https://www.investigativeproject.org/documents /testimony/7.pdf.

34.   Emerson, "Part 4."

35.   "'Global War on Christians' Smears Islam," Council on American-Islamic Relations, updated March 11, 2015, http://www.cair.com/action-alerts/168 -global-war-on-christians-smears-islam.html.

36.   Art Moore, "Muslims Try to Quash Bush Nominee," WND.com, April 22, 2003, http://www.wnd.com/2003/04/18400/.

37.   "Slavery and Stereotypes," *Washington Post*, January 17, 1998, https:// www.washingtonpost.com/archive/opinions/1998/01/17/slavery-and-stereotypes /cba815a3-1657-4356-8480-5182c6020b56/?utm_term=.a66b06df5d6a.

38.   Pat Nason, "Analysis: Ethnicity of Movie Villains at Issue," UPI, January 29, 2001, https://www.upi.com/Archives/2001/01/29/Analysis-Ethnicity-of -movie-villains-at-issue/2246980744400/.

39.   CAIR, "#AmericanSniper—The real American Sniper was a hate-filled killer," Facebook, January 19, 2015, https://www.facebook.com/CAIRNational /posts/10152698528137695.

40.   Caleb Downs, "FBI Interviewing Muslims in Texas Over Alleged Al-Qaeda Terrorist Threat, Community Leader Says," *Dallas Morning News*,

November 6, 2016, https://www.dallasnews.com/news/texas/2016/11/06/fbi
-interviewingmuslims-texas-alleged-al-qaeda-terrorthreat-community-leader-says.

41. Downs, "FBI Interviewing Muslims."
42. Downs, "FBI Interviewing Muslims."
43. Council on American-Islamic Relations, "CAIR Open Letter to 2016 Republican Presidential Candidates: Engage Muslim Voters, Reject Islamophobia," January 26, 2015, https://www.cair.com/images/pdf/Open-Letter-to-2016 -Republican-Presidential-Candidates.pdf.
44. Council on American-Islamic Relations, "CAIR Open Letter."
45. Council on American-Islamic Relations, "CAIR Open Letter."
46. Council on American-Islamic Relations, *Legislating Fear*, accessed April 25, 2018, https://www.cair.com/images/islamophobia/Legislating-Fear.pdf.
47. Council on American-Islamic Relations, *Legislating Fear*.
48. Council on American-Islamic Relations, *Legislating Fear*.
49. Daniel Cox et al., "What it Means to Be American: Attitudes Towards Increasing Diversity in America Ten Years After 9/11," PRRI, September 6, 2011, https://www.prri.org/research/what-it-means-to-be-american/; Council on American-Islamic Relations, *Legislating Fear*.
50. Joe Kimball, "Islamic Group Says Speaker With Anti-Muslim Views Shouldn't Speak at Tea Party Event in Little Falls Public School," MinnPost, July 24, 2013, https://www.minnpost.com/political-agenda/2013/07/islamic-group -says-speaker-anti-muslim-views-shouldnt-speak-tea-party-event.
51. Kimball, "Speaker With Anti-Muslim Views."
52. "CAIR: June 10 Anti-Islam Hate Rallies Show Convergence of White Supremacism, Islamophobia," Council on American-Islamic Relations, updated June 7, 2017, https://www.cair.com/press-center/press-releases/14389-cair-june -10-anti-islam-hate-rallies-show-convergence-of-white-supremacism-islamophobia .html.
53. Shelia Poole, "CAIR-Ga to Hold 'No to Extremism' Rally to Counter Anti-Sharia Event," *Atlanta Journal-Constitution*, updated August 23, 2017, https://www.ajc.com/events/cair-hold-extremism-rally-counter-anti-sharia-event /VBAIFBpUPkOpZKHRhunkhM/.
54. "Russia Special Counsel Mueller Worked with Radical Islamist Groups to Purge Anti-Terrorism Training Material Offensive to Muslims," Judicial Watch Inc., May 18, 2017, https://www.judicialwatch.org/blog/2017/05/russia-special -counsel-mueller-conspired-radical-islamic-groups-fbi-chief/; "U.S. Government Purges of Law Enforcement Training Material Deemed 'Offensive' to Muslims," Judicial Watch Inc., December 5, 2013, http://www.judicialwatch.org/wp-content /uploads/2013/12/JWSRGovtPurgeAndActiveMeasures5Dec2013.pdf?V=1.
55. "Government Purges," Judicial Watch Inc.
56. "MPAC & Interfaith Leaders Meet with FBI Director Mueller to Address Concerns Regarding Training Materials," Muslim Public Affairs Council, February 15, 2012, https://www.mpac.org/programs/government-relations /mpac-interfaith-leaders-meet-with-fbi-director-mueller-to-address-concerns -regarding-training-materials.php#.Um6wLpGG71o.

57.　John H. Cushman Jr., "General Orders Review of Military Schools After Class Is Told U.S. Is at War With Islam," *New York Times*, April 25, 2012, https://www.nytimes.com/2012/04/26/us/new-review-ordered-on-anti-islamic -themes-in-military-courses.html.

58.　"Enough Is Enough: The Anti-Muslim Training Tide Must Turn," Muslim Public Affairs Council, May 18, 2012, https://www.mpac.org/programs /government-relations/dc-news-and-views/enough-is-enough-the-anti-muslim -training-tide-must-turn.php.

59.　"International Security Threats," House Intelligence Committee Hearing, February 10, 2011, https://www.c-span.org/video/?297949-1 /international-security-threats.

60.　Paul Sperry, "Boston Bombers' Mosque Tied to ISIS," *New York Post*, September 7, 2014, https://nypost.com/2014/09/07/jihadi-behind-beheading -videos-linked-to-notorious-us-mosque/.

61.　TPNNVideos, "Rep Gohmert Blasts Obama FBI Director: 'Sir, if you're going to call me a liar…,'" YouTube, June 13, 2013, https://www.youtube.com /watch?feature=player_embedded&v=I3ZdJtIxmP8.

62.　Hussein Ibish, "The UAE's Evolving National Security Strategy," Arab Gulf States in Washington, April 6, 2017, http://www.agsiw.org/wp-content /uploads/2017/04/UAE-Security_ONLINE.pdf; Bureau of Counterterrorism and Countering Violent Extremism, "Country Reports on Terrorism 2016: Middle East and North Africa," United States Department of State, accessed April 25, 2018, https://www.state.gov/j/ct/rls/crt/2016/272232.htm.

63.　"CAIR Gets Police to Cancel 'Anti-Muslim' Terrorism Training," Judicial Watch Inc., August 21, 2013, https://www.judicialwatch.org/blog/2013/08 /cair-gets-police-to-cancel-anti-muslim-terrorism-training/.

64.　"NYPD to Purge Anti-Terrorism Material Offensive to Muslims," Judicial Watch Inc., January 19, 2016, https://www.judicialwatch.org/blog/2016/01 /nypd-to-purge-anti-terrorism-material-offensive-to-muslims/.

Chapter 11—The Leftist-Islamist Coalition

1.　CAIR, "#CAIR-WA: ACLU to Honor Washington State Office of the Council on American-Islamic Relations," Facebook, November 7, 2013, https:// www.facebook.com/CAIRNational/posts/10151791145462695.

2.　"Appeal to Ninth Circuit Filed After Federal Court in Seattle Upholds Censorship of Anti-Terrorism Advertisement," The Counter Jihad Report, March 12, 2014, https://counterjihadreport.com/tag/faces-of-global-terrorism/.

3.　Nina Shapiro, "A Mystery of Violence," Sound Publishing Inc., December 15, 2009, http://archive.seattleweekly.com/2009-12-16/news/a-mystery -of-violence.

4.　Abdirizak Bihi, "The Extent of Radicalization in the American Muslim Community and That Community's Response," Committee on Homeland Security, US House of Representatives, March 10, 2011, https://homeland.house.gov /files/Testimony%20Bihi.pdf.

5.　Charles C. Johnson, "Somali-American Leader: 'I Tried to Warn America' About Homegrown Radicalization," The Daily Caller, September 23,

2013, http://dailycaller.com/2013/09/23/somali-american-leader-i-tried-to-warn
-america-about-homegrown-radicalization/.

6.   Abdur-Rahman Muhammad, "Whether or Not Ground Zero Mosque Is
Built, U.S. Muslims Have Access to the American Dream," *New York Daily News*,
September 5, 2010, http://www.nydailynews.com/opinion/not-ground-zero
-mosque-built-u-s-muslims-access-american-dream-article-1.440737.

7.   Adil James, "CAIR Fundraiser Grosses $130K," MuslimObserver.com,
March 26, 2009, http://muslimobserver.com/cair-fundraiser-grosses-130k/; "Illinois Imam Misrepresented Role With Hamas Front Under Oath," Investigative
Project on Terrorism, October 7, 2010, https://www.investigativeproject.org/2229
/illinois-imam-misrepresented-role-with-hamas.

8.   ACLU, "Group Asks Court to Clear Names of Two Organizations
Unconstitutionally Labeled 'Unindicted Co-Conspirators,'" press release, June 18,
2008, https://www.aclu.org/news/aclu-challenges-governments-stigmatizing
-mainstream-muslim-groups-holy-land-case.

9.   ACLU, "New Comprehensive Report Details Effects of Flawed Policies
on Muslim Charitable Giving," press release, June 16, 2009, https://www.aclu.org/
news/terrorism-finance-laws-undermine-american-muslims-religious-freedom-says
-aclu.

10.   "Secular Coalition to House Reps: Loyalty of Americans Not Based on
Religious Affiliations," Secular Coalition for America, July 26, 2012, https://www
.secular.org/news/secular-coalition-house-reps-loyalty-americans-not-based
-religious-affiliations.

11.   "Letter to Michele Bachmann, Trent Franks, Louie Gohmert, Thomas
Rooney, and Lynn Westmoreland," Interfaith Alliance, July 26, 2012, archived at
https://web.archive.org/web/20121018080618/http://interfaithalliance.org
/images/PDF_DOCS/letter_to_reps_bachmann_franks_gohmert_rooney_and
_westmoreland_from_42_organizations.pdf.

12.   "Coalition Asks DOJ to Open Civil Rights Investigation Into the
NYPD's Surveillance of American Muslims," ACLU, October 24, 2013, https://
www.aclu.org/other/coalition-asks-doj-open-civil-rights-investigation-nypds
-surveillance-american-muslims?redirect=national-security/coalition-asks-doj
-open-civil-rights-investigation-nypd-surveillance-muslims; "Factsheet: The NYPD
Muslim Surveillance Program," ACLU, accessed April 25, 2018, https://www.aclu
.org/other/factsheet-nypd-muslim-surveillance-program.

13.   Matt Apuzzo and Adam Goldman, "After Spying on Muslims, New
York Police Agree to Greater Oversight," *New York Times*, March 6, 2017, https://
www.nytimes.com/2017/03/06/nyregion/nypd-spying-muslims-surveillance
-lawsuit.html.

14.   Reuven Blau et al., "Terrorist Sayfullo Saipov Celebrates Deadly Manhattan Truck Attack While at Hospital: 'He Feels Accomplished,'" *New York
Daily News*, November 2, 2017, http://www.nydailynews.com/new-york
/manhattan/terrorist-sayfullo-saipov-feels-accomplished-nyc-attack-article
-1.3603698.

15.   Hannah Adely and William Lamb, "Mosque Where NYC Terror Suspect Worshipped Was Target of Controversial NYPD Surveillance Effort,"

northjersey.com, updated November 1, 2017, https://www.northjersey.com/story
/news/passaic/paterson/2017/10/31/nyc-terror-suspects-mosque-target
-controversial-nypd-surveillance-effort/819826001/.

16. "Linda Sarsour," ACLU, accessed April 25, 2018, https://www.aclu.org
/issues/immigrants-rights/linda-sarsour.

17. Southern Poverty Law Center (@splcenter), "Islamophobes have been
attacking #WomensMarch organizer @lsarsour. We stand with her against this
type of hate and bigotry. #IMarchWithLinda," Twitter, January 23, 2017, 1:11
p.m., https://twitter.com/splcenter/status/823639309240729601.

18. Alexander Nazaryan, "Linda Sarsour, Feminist Movement Leader, Too
Extreme for CUNY Graduation Speech, Critics Argue," *Newsweek*, May 24, 2017,
http://www.newsweek.com/linda-sarsour-feminist-movement-leader-too
-extreme-cuny-graduation-speech-615031.

19. Glamour, "Meet the 2017 'Glamour' Women of the Year," *Glamour*,
October 30, 2017, https://www.glamour.com/story/women-of-the-year-2017
-winners.

20. Meredith Clark, "Women's March Organizer Linda Sarsour: 'We Need
to Translate the Emotions and Frustrations of Right Now,'" *Glamour*, February 2,
2017, https://www.glamour.com/story/womens-march-organizer-linda-sarsour-we
-need-to-translate-the-emotions-and-frustrations-of-right-now.

21. Linda Sarsour (@lsarsour), "Donate to the #Harvey Hurricane Relief
Fund," Twitter, August 28, 2017, 9:42 p.m., https://twitter.com/lsarsour
/status/902391077046452224.

22. "Donate to the Hurricane Harvey Community Relief Fund," Texas Organizing Project Education Fund, accessed April 25, 2018, https://act.myngp.com
/Forms/-3833118145683060992.

23. Texas Organizing Project, accessed April 25, 2018, http://organizetexas
.org/; Christine Rousselle, "Linda Sarsour Criticized for Grifting for Fake Hurricane Harvey Charity," Townhall.com, August 30, 2017, https://townhall.com
/tipsheet/christinerousselle/2017/08/30/linda-sarsour-grifter-n2375106.

24. Linda Sarsour (@lsarsour), "TOP is one of many organizations on this
list you can choose to support. Grassroots orgs on ground.Long term needed.,"
Twitter, August 30, 2017, 7:20 a.m., https://twitter.com/lsarsour/status
/902898902797574146.

25. Linda Sarsour, "In context of what's happening in Palestine in response
to the announcement about Jerusalem and in general living under the longest
and most brutal military occupation - we have to get a few things straight.," Facebook, December 9, 2017, https://www.facebook.com/linda.sarsour/posts
/10156134842730572.

26. Daniel Greenfield, "Linda Sarsour Blasts 'Jewish Media', Defends Farrakhan, at Antisemitism Panel," FrontPageMag.com, November 30, 2017, https://
www.frontpagemag.com/point/268568/linda-sarsour-blasts-jewish-media-defends
-daniel-greenfield; Petra Marquardt-Bigman, "How 'Woke' Are Feminist Farrakhan Fans Like Linda Sarsour?," *Algemeiner*, May 24, 2017, https://www
.algemeiner.com/2017/05/24/how-woke-are-feminist-farrakhan-fans-like-linda
-sarsour/.

27.   Ian Schwartz, "Linda Sarsour Asks Muslims To Form 'Jihad' Against Trump, Not To Assimilate," RealClearHoldings LLC, July 6, 2017, https://www .realclearpolitics.com/video/2017/07/06/linda_sarsour_asks_muslims_to_form _jihad_against_trump_not_to_assimilate.html.

28.   Islamic Society of North America (ISNA), "Linda Sarsour Gives the Keynote Address at the Community Service Recognition Luncheon. #ISNA54," Facebook, July 1, 2017, https://www.facebook.com/isnahq/videos/1015453 8687786105/.

29.   Brooke Singman, "Muslim Activist Suggests Resisting Trump Is a 'Form of Jihad,'" FOX News Network LLC, July 7, 2017, http://www.foxnews.com /politics/2017/07/07/muslim-activist-suggests-resisting-trump-is-form-jihad.html; David M. Swindle, "Siraj Wahhaj on Jihad," The Middle East Forum, January 30, 2017, https://www.meforum.org/islamist-watch/blog/january-2017/siraj-wahhaj -on-jihad.

30.   Linda Sarsour, "54th Annual ISNA Conference—July 3, 2017," Iowa State University of Science and Technology, July 3, 2017, https://awpc.cattcenter .iastate.edu/2017/08/30/54th-annual-isna-conference-july-3-2017/.

31.   Islamic Society of North America (ISNA), "Linda Sarsour Gives the Keynote Address at the Community Service Recognition Luncheon."

32.   Ben Shapiro, "The Jihad-Loving Left Loves Linda Sarsour," *National Review,* July 12, 2017, https://www.nationalreview.com/2017/07/democrats-revere -linda-sarsour-terrorist-apologist-trump-hatred-unites/; Souad Mekhennet, "Under Attack as Muslims in the U.S.," *New York Times,* August 7, 2012, https://www .nytimes.com/2012/08/08/us/08iht-letter08.html.

33.   Sarmad S. Ali, "Kerry Drew Disenchanted Arabs in Bay Ridge," Columbia Graduate School of Journalism, 2004, archived at http://web.archive .org/web/20041115120337/http:/www.jrn.columbia.edu/studentwork/election /2004/minority_ali01.asp.

34.   Linda Sarsour (@lsarsour), "Nothing is creepier than Zionism.Challenge racism, #NormalizeJustice. Check out this video by @remroum," Twitter, October 31, 2012, 7:39 a.m., https://twitter.com/lsarsour/status/263651398250545152 ?lang=en; Collier Meyerson, "Can You Be a Zionist Feminist? Linda Sarsour Says No," *The Nation,* March 13, 2017, https://www.thenation.com/article/can-you-be -a-zionist-feminist-linda-sarsour-says-no/.

35.   Danielle Tcholaklan, "Muslim Community Groups Respond To NYPD 'Terrorism Enterprise Investigations,'" Metro.US, August 28, 2013, archived at https://web.archive.org/web/20130828222618/https://www.metro.us/newyork /news/local/2013/08/28/muslim-community-groups-respond-to-nypd-terrorism -enterprise-investigations.

36.   David Rutz, "Sarsour in 2012: NYPD Informants 'Manufacture' Terrorism Cases Against American Muslims," Washington Free Beacon, April 18, 2016, http://freebeacon.com/national-security/sarsour-nypd-informants-have -manufactured-terrorism-charges-against-american-muslims/.

37.   Khaled A. Beydoun and Linda Sarsour, "Trayvon Martin: The Myth of US Post-Racialism," Al Jazeera Media Network, March 22, 2012, https://www .aljazeera.com/indepth/opinion/2012/03/2012321910466650.html.

38.   Linda Sarsour (@lsarsour), "Underwear bomber was the #CIA all along. Why did I already know that?! Shame on us - scaring the American people.," Twitter, May 8, 2012, 7:40 p.m., https://twitter.com/lsarsour/status/20005271917 8883073?lang=en.

39.   Bari Weiss, "When Progressives Embrace Hate," *New York Times*, August 1, 2017, https://www.nytimes.com/2017/08/01/opinion/womens-march -progressives-hate.html; "Farrakhan's Saviour's Day Sermon (Part 2) Loaded With Anti-Semitism," Anti-Defamation League, March 3, 2015, https://www.adl.org /blog/farrakhans-saviours-day-sermon-part-2-loaded-with-anti-semitism.

CHAPTER 12—THE BUSINESS OF FAKE HATE

1.   James Barrett, "'Red Flag' Report: Media's Favorite 'Hate Group' Watchdog SPLC Transfers MILLIONS To Offshore Investments," August 31, 2017, Daily Wire, https://www.dailywire.com/news/20484/red-flag-report -southern-poverty-law-center-james-barrett; Eric Rozenman, "The Southern Poverty Law Center—A Reliably Dubious Source," Jewish Policy Center, December 17, 2017, https://www.jewishpolicycenter.org/2017/12/17/18072/; Sarah Begley, "Read the List of the 917 Hate Groups Identified by the Southern Poverty Law Center," *Time*, February 15, 2017, http://time.com/4671800/hate-groups-on -the-rise/.

2.   Ben Schreckinger, "Has a Civil Rights Stalwart Lost Its Way?," *Politico*, July/August 2017, https://www.politico.com/magazine/story/2017/06/28/morris -dees-splc-trump-southern-poverty-law-center-215312.

3.   "Hate Map," Southern Poverty Law Center, accessed April 25, 2018, https://www.splcenter.org/hate-map.

4.   "About Us," Southern Poverty Law Center, accessed April 25, 2018, https://www.splcenter.org/about.

5.   Ken Blackwell, "The Hypocrisy of the Black Lives Matter Movement & the Southern Poverty Law Center," The Daily Caller, August 22, 2016, http:// dailycaller.com/2016/08/22/the-hypocrisy-of-the-black-lives-matter-movement -the-southern-poverty-law-center; Darren Boyle, "'White People to the Back of the March': Black Lives Matter Protest Leader Calls for Racial Segregation of Her Supporters During Demonstration Outside the DNC," Associated Newspapers Ltd., updated October 27, 2016, http://www.dailymail.co.uk/news/article -3710701/White-people-march-Black-Lives-Matter-protest-leader-calls-racial -segregation-demonstration-outside-DNC-Philadelphia.html.

6.   J. Richard Cohen, "Black Lives Matter Is Not a Hate Group," *Time*, July 19, 2016, http://time.com/4413786/splc-black-lives-matter/.

7.   Cohen, "Black Lives Matter."

8.   Andrew Desiderio, "Southern Poverty Law Center Puts Ben Carson on Its 'Extremist Watch List,'" Mediaite LLC, February 8, 2015, https://www .mediaite.com/online/southern-poverty-law-center-puts-ben-carson-on-its -extremist-watch-list/.

9.   "SPLC Statement on Dr. Ben Carson," Southern Poverty Law Center, February 11, 2015, https://www.splcenter.org/sites/default/files/d6_legacy_files /downloads/publication/splc_statement_carson_feb2015.pdf.

10.   "Ben Carson," Southern Poverty Law Center.

11.   "Hate Map," Southern Poverty Law Center.

12.   David A. Graham, "How Did Maajid Nawaz End Up on a List of 'Anti-Muslim Extremists'?," *The Atlantic*, October 29, 2016 https://www.theatlantic.com/international/archive/2016/10/maajid-nawaz-splc-anti-muslim-extremist/505685/.

13.   Chris Tomlinson, "U.S. Far-Left Group SPLC To Pay Counter-Extremist Maajid Nawaz $3.3M Settlement Over Anti-Muslim 'Hate List,'" Breitbart, June 18, 2018, http://www.breitbart.com/london/2018/06/18/u-s-far-left-anti-hate-group-to-pay-maajid-nawaz-3-3-million-dollar-settlement-for-including-him-on-hate-list/.

14.   Ian Schwartz, "Muslim Anti-Extremist Maajid Nawaz on Maher; Talks Lawsuit Against Southern Poverty Law Center," RealClearHoldings LLC, June 24, 2017, https://www.realclearpolitics.com/video/2017/06/24/muslim_anti-extremist_maajid_nawaz_on_maher_talks_lawsuit_against_southern_poverty_law_center.html.

15.   Schwartz, "Maajid Nawaz."

16.   Schwartz, "Maajid Nawaz."

17.   "Ayaan Hirsi Ali: My Life Under a Fatwa," *Independent*, November 27, 2007, https://www.independent.co.uk/news/people/profiles/ayaan-hirsi-ali-my-life-under-a-fatwa-760666.html.

18.   "Ayaan Hirsi Ali," *Independent*.

19.   Ayaan Hirsi Ali, "Why Is the Southern Poverty Law Center Targeting Liberals?," *New York Times*, August 24, 2017, https://www.nytimes.com/2017/08/24/opinion/southern-poverty-law-center-liberals-islam.html.

20.   "Southern Poverty Law Center," CharityWatch Report, May 9, 2017, http://www.alreporter.com/wp-content/uploads/2017/05/Charity-Watch.pdf.

21.   Joe Schoffstall, "Southern Poverty Law Center Transfers Millions in Cash to Offshore Entities," Washington Free Beacon, August 31, 2017, http://freebeacon.com/issues/southern-poverty-law-center-transfers-millions-in-cash-to-offshore-entities/; Southern Poverty Law Center, Form 8879-EO, 2015, https://www.splcenter.org/sites/default/files/990_103116.pdf

22.   Kimberly Kindy, Sari Horowitz, and Devlin Barrett, "Federal Government Has Long Ignored White Supremacist Threats, Critics Say," *Washington Post*, September 2, 2017, https://www.washingtonpost.com/national/federal-government-has-long-ignored-white-supremacist-threats-critics-say/2017/09/02/bf2ed00c-8698-11e7-961d-2f373b3977ee_story.html?utm_term=.dbee81517b5c.

23.   "917 Hate Groups," *Time*.

24.   "Hate Groups Increase for Second Consecutive Year as Trump Electrifies Radical Right," Southern Poverty Law Center, February 15, 2017, https://www.splcenter.org/news/2017/02/15/hate-groups-increase-second-consecutive-year-trump-electrifies-radical-right.

25.   "Active Anti-Muslim Groups," Southern Poverty Law Center, March 2, 2015, https://www.splcenter.org/fighting-hate/intelligence-report/2015/active-anti-muslim-groups.

26.   "Hate Groups Increase," Southern Poverty Law Center.

27.   "Anti-Muslim," Southern Poverty Law Center, accessed April 25, 2018, https://www.splcenter.org/fighting-hate/extremist-files/ideology/anti-muslim.

28.   "Active Hate Groups in the United States in 2015," Southern Poverty Law Center, February 17, 2016, https://www.splcenter.org/fighting-hate/intelligence-report/2016/active-hate-groups-united-states-2015.

29.   Maria Puente, "George, Amal Clooney Donate $1M to Southern Poverty Law Center to Combat Hate Groups," *USA Today*, August 22, 2017, https://www.usatoday.com/story/life/2017/08/22/george-amal-clooney-donate-1-m-southern-poverty-law-center-combat-hate-groups/590033001/.

30.   Zameena Mejia, "Apple Is Giving $2 Million to Aid Charlottesville. Here's How Much Tim Cook Has Already Donated to Human Rights," CNBC LLC, August 17, 2017, https://www.cnbc.com/2017/08/17/tim-cook-apple-will-donate-2-million-to-aid-charlottesville.html.

31.   Associated Press, "MGM to Match Employee Donations to Civil Rights Groups," *U.S. News & World Report*, August 19, 2017, https://www.usnews.com/news/best-states/nevada/articles/2017-08-19/mgm-to-match-employee-donations-to-civil-rights-groups.

32.   Jack Rosenthal, "A Terrible Thing to Waste," *New York Times*, July 31, 2009, https://www.nytimes.com/2009/08/02/magazine/02FOB-onlanguage-t.html.

33.   Gage Cohen, "Alexandria Shooter 'Liked' Southern Poverty Law Center on Facebook," CNSNews.com, June 14, 2017, https://www.cnsnews.com/news/article/gage-cohen/alexandria-shooter-liked-southern-poverty-law-center-facebook.

34.   Paul Bedard, "Support for Southern Poverty Law Center Links Scalise, Family Research Council Shooters," Washington Examiner, June 14, 2017, http://www.washingtonexaminer.com/support-for-southern-poverty-law-center-links-scalise-family-research-council-shooters/article/2625982.

Chapter 13—The Death of Free Speech

1.   "History," Organisation of Islamic Cooperation, accessed April 27, 2018, https://www.oic-oci.org/page/?p_id=52&p_ref=26&lan=en.

2.   "Freedom in the World: Aggregate and Subcategory Scores," Freedom House, accessed April 27, 2018, https://freedomhouse.org/report/freedom-world-aggregate-and-subcategory-scores; "Human Rights Risk Index 2016—Q4," Vensk Maplecroft, 2016, https://reliefweb.int/sites/reliefweb.int/files/resources/2016_ITF_Human_Rights_Index_2016-01.pdf.

3.   "Freedom in the World," Freedom House.

4.   Louis Doré, "The Countries Where Apostasy Is Punishable by Death," Indy100, May 7, 2017, https://www.indy100.com/article/the-countries-where-apostasy-is-punishable-by-death--Z110j2Uwxb.

5.   "Strengthening Respect for Human Rights Key for Preventing Conflict, Stabilizing Post-Conflict Situations, Third Committee Told," United Nations, press release, November 3, 2008, https://www.un.org/press/en/2008/gashc3933.doc.htm.

6.   "Racism, Racial Discrimination, Xenophobia and All Forms of Discrimination," United Nations Economic and Social Council, April 20, 1999, http://repository.un.org/bitstream/handle/11176/224178/E_CN.4_1999_L.40-EN.pdf?sequence=3&isAllowed=y.

7.   "Resolution Adopted by the Human Rights Council 16/18," United Nations General Assembly, April 12, 2011, http://www2.ohchr.org/english/bodies/hrcouncil/docs/16session/A.HRC.RES.16.18_en.pdf.

8.   Clare M. Lopez, "Free Speech Champions Fight Back Against OSCE 'Islamophobia' Industry," Center for Security Policy, October 11, 2016, https://www.centerforsecuritypolicy.org/2016/10/11/free-speech-champions-fight-back-against-osce-islamophobia-industry/.

9.   Jon Greenberg, "Has the WH Supported the Spread of Blasphemy Laws?," Poynter Institute, January 14, 2015, http://www.politifact.com/punditfact/statements/2015/jan/14/jonathan-turley/gw-law-prof-white-house-supported-muslim-allies-tr/.

10.   Lopez, "Free Speech Champions."

11.   Jason Burke, "The Murder That Shattered Holland's Liberal Dream," *Guardian*, November 7, 2004, https://www.theguardian.com/world/2004/nov/07/terrorism.religion.

12.   *Telegraph* Foreign Staff, "Prophet Mohammed Cartoons Controversy: Timeline," *Telegraph*, May 4, 2015, http://www.telegraph.co.uk/news/worldnews/europe/france/11341599/Prophet-Muhammad-cartoons-controversy-timeline.html.

13.   CNN Library, "2015 Charlie Hebdo Attacks Fast Facts," Cable News Network, updated December 25, 2017, https://www.cnn.com/2015/01/21/europe/2015-paris-terror-attacks-fast-facts/index.html.

14.   Morgan Jones, "How the LDS Church's Response to 'The Book of Mormon' Musical Is Actually Working," Deseret News Publishing Company, November 16, 2016, https://www.deseretnews.com/article/865667313/How-the-LDS-Churchs-response-to-The-Book-of-Mormon-musical-is-actually-working.html.

15.   Charles Hurt, "Susan Rice Somehow Manages to Make Banghazi Cover-Up Seem Minor," *Washington Times*, April 4, 2017, https://www.washingtontimes.com/news/2017/apr/4/susan-rice-somehow-manages-to-make-benghazi-cover-/.

16.   Jonathan Rauch, "In Hindsight, the War on Terror Began With Salman Rushdie," *The Atlantic*, March 2005, https://www.theatlantic.com/magazine/archive/2005/03/in-hindsight-the-war-on-terror-began-with-salman-rushdie/303854/.

17.   Tara John, "Iranian Hardliners Raise Bounty on Salman Rushdie to Almost $4 Million," *Time*, February 23, 2016, http://time.com/4233580/fatwa-salman-rushdie-iran/.

18.   David Harris, "Nima Rashedan: The Magic Is in the Hands of the People," Clarion Project Inc., January 28, 2015, https://clarionproject.org/nima-rashedan-magic-hands-people/.

19.   Greg Myre, "From Threats Against Salman Rushdie to Attacks on 'Charlie Hebdo,'" NPR, January 8, 2015, https://www.npr.org/sections/parallels

/2015/01/08/375662895/from-threats-against-salman-rushdie-to-attacks-on
-charlie-hebdo.

20. "2 Bookstores in Berkeley Are Firebombed; Rushdie Tie Is Explored,"
New York Times, March 1, 1989, http://www.nytimes.com/1989/03/01/world
/2-bookstores-in-berkeley-are-firebombed-rushdie-tie-is-explored.html.

21. David E. Pitt, "Office of Weekly Paper in Riverdale Is Firebombed," *New
York Times*, March 1, 1989, http://www.nytimes.com/1989/03/01/nyregion/office
-of-weekly-paper-in-riverdale-is-firebombed.html.

22. Reuters, "London Bookshop Bombings Are Tied to 'Satanic Verses,'"
New York Times, April 11, 1989, http://www.nytimes.com/1989/04/11/world
/london-bookshop-bombings-are-tied-to-satanic-verses.html; United Press
International, "Bookstore Bombed," United Press International Inc. September 14, 1989, https://www.upi.com/Archives/1989/09/14/Bookstore-
bombed/3380621748800/.

23. Sanjoy Hazarika, "12 Die in Bombay in Anti-Rushdie Riot," *New York
Times*, February 25, 1989, http://www.nytimes.com/books/99/04/18/specials
/rushdie-riot.html.

24. Hazarika, "Anti-Rushdie Riot."

25. Robert Fulford, "How Salim Mansur Is Trying to Clarify the Theories
and Inner Conflicts That Have Shaped Islam," *National Post*, February 8, 2018,
http://nationalpost.com/entertainment/books/how-salim-mansur-is-trying-to
-clarify-the-theories-and-inner-conflicts-that-have-shaped-islam.

26. Daniel Pipes, "The Clash to End All Clashes?," February 7, 2006, http://
www.danielpipes.org/3361/the-clash-to-end-all-clashes.

27. Pipes, "The Clash to End All Clashes?"

28. Jimmy Carter, "Rushdie's Book Is an Insult," *New York Times*, March 5,
1989, https://www.nytimes.com/1989/03/05/opinion/rushdie-s-book-is-an-insult
.html.

29. Bradford Richardson, "Dave Rubin, Lapsed Progressive, Explains Why
He Left the Left: Video," *Washington Times*, February 6, 2017, https://www
.washingtontimes.com/news/2017/feb/6/dave-rubin-lapsed-progressive-explains
-why-he-left/.

30. Richardson, "Dave Rubin."

31. Stipoon, "Christopher Hitchens Responds to a Jihad Sympathizer,"
YouTube, August 20, 2009, https://www.youtube.com/watch?v=axHR8AOxxkc.

32. Patrick Poole, "The Muslim Brotherhood 'Project,'" FrontPageMagazine,
May 11, 2006, http://www.onthewing.org/user/Islam%20-%20Muslim%20
Brotherhood%20Project.pdf.

33. "An Explanatory Memorandum on the General Strategic Goal for the
Group in North America."

34. "An Explanatory Memorandum on the General Strategic Goal for the
Group in North America."

35. Indicrat, "David Horowitz Brilliantly Exposes Muslim Student's True
Intentions—UC San Diego," YouTube, February 16, 2017, https://www.youtube
.com/watch?v=pmlIJ0mUXKU.

36.   Michael Bodley, "At Berkeley Yiannopoulos Protest, $100,000 in Damage, 1 Arrest," *San Francisco Chronicle*, updated February 2, 2017, https://www.sfgate.com/crime/article/At-Berkeley-Yiannopoulos-protest-100-000 -in-10905217.php.

37.   Bay City News, "Protest Against 'Troll' Milo Yiannopoulos Causes Over $100K in Damage to UC Campus," *San Francisco Examiner*, February 2, 2017, http://www.sfexaminer.com/protest-troll-milo-yiannopoulos-causes-100k-damage -uc-campus/.

38.   Wayne Freedman, "VIDEO: Trump Supporter Pepper Sprayed at Milo Protest," ABC Inc., February 1, 2017, http://abc7news.com/news/video-trump -supporter-pepper-sprayed-at-milo-protest/1733004/.

39.   Madison Park and Kyung Lah, "Berkeley Protests of Yiannopoulos Caused $100,000 in Damage," Cable News Network, February 2, 2017, https://www.cnn.com/2017/02/01/us/milo-yiannopoulos-berkeley/index.html.

40.   Park and Lah, "Berkeley Protests."

41.   Chris De Benedetti, "Comedian Bill Maher Speaks Amid Handful of Protesters at UC Berkeley Commencement," *Mercury News*, updated August 12, 2016, https://www.mercurynews.com/2014/12/20/comedian-bill-maher-speaks -amid-handful-of-protesters-at-uc-berkeley-commencement/.

42.   Khwaja Ahmed, "Stop Bill Maher From Speaking at UC Berkeley's December Graduation," Change.org Inc., accessed April 27, 2018, https://www .change.org/p/university-of-california-berkeley-stop-bill-maher-from-speaking-at -uc-berkeley-s-december-graduation.

43.   Sam Frizell, "Watch Bill Maher Take Down the Students Protesting His Berkeley Commencement Address," *Time*, November 1, 2014, http://time .com/3552583/bill-maher-islam-berkeley-commencement/.

44.   Real Time with Bill Maher, "Bill Maher Responds to Berkeley Petition," YouTube, October 31, 2014, https://www.youtube.com/watch?v=wcB-zvsRslY.

45.   Joe Concha, "Bill Maher: Berkeley Is 'Cradle for F------ Babies,'" The Hill, April 22, 2017, http://thehill.com/homenews/media/330042-bill-maher -berkley-is-cradle-for-f-babies.

46.   Hallie Jackson, Elizabeth Chuck, and Ali Vitali, "Secret Service Rushes Stage to Protect Donald Trump at Ohio Rally," NBC Universal, March 12, 2016, https://www.nbcnews.com/politics/2016-election/secret-service-rushes-stage -protect-donald-trump-ohio-rally-n537181.

47.   Alex Shephard, "A Donald Trump Rally in Chicago Has Been Canceled for 'Safety Reasons,'" *The New Republic*, 2016, https://newrepublic.com/minutes /131493/donald-trump-rally-chicago-canceled-safety-reasons.

48.   *Time* Staff, "Linda Sarsour Gives CUNY Commencement Speech: 'Commit to Never Being Bystanders,'" *Time*, June 2, 2017, http://time.com /4802373/linda-sarsour-cuny-commencement-address-transcript/; William F. Jasper, "Radicalism 101: Why Do Our Universities Hire Terrorists as Professors?," *The New American*, April 10, 2013, https://www.thenewamerican.com/culture /education/item/15068-radicalism-101-why-do-our-universities-hire-terrorists -as-professors.

49.　Becket Adams, "CNN's Cuomo Clarifies His 'Clumsy' Claim About First Amendment," *Washington Examiner*, May 7, 2015, http://www.washington examiner.com/cnns-cuomo-clarifies-his-clumsy-claim-about-first-amendment /article/2564175.

50.　Adams, "Cuomo Clarifies."

51.　Adams, "Cuomo Clarifies."

52.　"Chris Cuomo," A&E Television Networks LLC, accessed April 27, 2018, https://www.biography.com/people/chris-cuomo-5606.

53.　Howard Dean (@GovHowardDean), "Hate speech is not protected by the first amendment.," Twitter, April 20, 2017, 5:13 p.m., https://twitter.com /govhowarddean/status/855212805506703361?lang=en.

54.　Daniel Greenfield, "Why Did Marco Rubio Submit an Islamist MPAC Resolution Against Islamophobia?," FrontPageMag.com, June 20, 2017, https:// www.frontpagemag.com/point/267051/why-did-marco-rubio-submit-islamist -mpac-daniel-greenfield.

55.　Andrew C. McCarthy, "In Initially Airbrushing Orlando Jihadist's Calls, DOJ Followed Obama-Clinton U.N. Resolution Against Negative Speech About Islam," *National Review*, June 20, 2016, http://www.nationalreview.com/corner /436854/doj-followed-obama-clinton-un-resolution-against-negative-speech-about -islam.

56.　"Asking Congress to Respond to Hate Crimes," Muslim Public Affairs Council, May 2, 2017, https://www.mpac.org/publications/policy-papers/asking -congress-to-respond-to-hate-crimes.php.

57.　"Behind the Façade: The Muslim Public Affairs Council," Investigative Project on Terrorism, accessed April 27, 2018, http://www.investigativeproject .org/documents/misc/358.pdf; Judith Bergman, "Marco Rubio Helps Muslims Pass Senate Resolution to Criminalize Free Speech (Updated)," Creeping Sharia (blog), June 21, 2017, https://creepingsharia.wordpress.com/2017/06/21/rubio -helps-pass-muslims-resolution-to-criminalize-free-speech/.

58.　Julie Carey and David Culver, "Virginia Republicans Visit Mosque to Address Concerns," NBCUniversal Media LLC, November 11, 2016, https://www .nbcwashington.com/news/local/Virginia-Republicans-Visit-Mosque-to-Address -Concerns-400892091.html.

59.　Chuck Ross, "Loretta Lynch Plans to Visit Mosque Once Raided in Counterterrorism Probe," The Daily Caller, December 9, 2016, http://dailycaller .com/2016/12/09/loretta-lynch-plans-to-visit-mosque-once-raided-in -counterterrorism-probe/; Ayesha Ahmad, "Muslim Community Members Encourage Coalition-Building," Islam Online, March 26, 2002, archived at http:// web.archive.org/web/20020804061344/http:/www.islamonline.net/English /News/2002-04/10/article08.shtml.

60.　"In the Matter of Searches Involving 555 Grove Street, Herndon, Virginia, and Related Locations," Investigative Project on Terrorism, March 2002, https://www.investigativeproject.org/documents/case_docs/891.pdf.

61.　Robert Spencer, "The New York Times Finds Some Moderate Muslims," FrontPageMag.com, August 4, 2010, https://www.frontpagemag.com/fpm/67814 /new-york-times-finds-some-moderate-muslims-robert-spencer.

62.　　John Rossomando, "DHS Denies Grant to Islamic Radicalization Enabler MPAC," Investigative Project on Terrorism, June 23, 2017, https://www.investigativeproject.org/6333/dhs-denies-grant-to-islamic-radicalization.

63.　　Michael Mayo, "Mayo: At Local Mosque, Cleric Calls for War on ISIS," *Sun-Sentinel*, November 20, 2015, http://www.sun-sentinel.com/news/fl-muslims-mayocol-b112215-20151120-column.html; "Politicians Attend Iftaar at Darul Uloom Institute," *Al-Hikmat*, July/August 2015, 16, http://alhikmat.com/images/JULY-AUG_2015_MAGAZINE_INSHAA_ALLAAH_AMEEN_MA.pdf.

64.　　Judith Bergman, "U.S. Trying to Criminalize Free Speech—Again," Gatestone Institute, June 20, 2017, https://www.gatestoneinstitute.org/10544/criminalize-free-speech.

CHAPTER 14—OPERATION INDOCTRINATION

1.　　Ashe Schow, "Student Group Sues After Members Arrested for Handing Out Copies of Constitution," The Daily Signal, January 19, 2017, http://dailysignal.com/2017/01/19/student-group-sues-after-members-arrested-for-handing-out-copies-of-constitution/.

2.　　Donna Brazile, "Inside Hillary Clinton's Secret Takeover of the DNC," *Politico*, November 2, 2017, https://www.politico.com/magazine/story/2017/11/02/clinton-brazile-hacks-2016-215774.

3.　　Marc Bodnick, "Why Are College Students So Obsessed With Che Guevara?," Quora, updated July 28, 2010, https://www.quora.com/Why-are-college-students-so-obsessed-with-Che-Guevara.

4.　　Young America's Foundation, "Murdered by Ché," TheRealCuba.com, accessed April 27, 2018, http://www.therealcuba.com/?page_id=32.

5.　　George Diaz, "Colin Kaepernick Castro T-Shirt Is Ignorant of Facts, Insulting," *Orlando Sentinel*, August 30, 2016, http://www.orlandosentinel.com/sports/george-diaz-en-fuego/os-colin-kaepernick-castro-t-shirt-20160830-story.html.

6.　　Glenn Garvin, "Red Ink: The High Human Cost of the Cuban Revolution," *Miami Herald*, December 1, 2016, http://www.miamiherald.com/news/nation-world/world/americas/cuba/article118282148.html.

7.　　Seth Rosenthal, "Colin Kaepernick Wore Some Police Pig Socks at 49ers Camp," Vox Media Inc., September 1, 2016, https://www.sbnation.com/lookit/2016/9/1/12751038/colin-kaepernick-wore-some-police-pig-socks-49ers-camp.

8.　　Asma Uddin and Firdaus Arasfu, "What the 'March Against Sharia' Protests Teach Us About Countering Hateful Speech," *Teen Vogue*, June 11, 2017, https://www.teenvogue.com/story/march-against-sharia-countering-hateful-speech.

9.　　"Adolf Hitler Quotes," BrainyQuote, accessed April 27, 2018, https://www.brainyquote.com/quotes/adolf_hitler_378177.

10.　　Bernard Goldberg, "Left-Wing Fools in the High Church of American Liberalism," BernardGoldberg.com, April 25, 2018, https://bernardgoldberg.com/70201-2/.

11.　　Goldberg, "Left-Wing Fools."

12.　　Goldberg, "Left-Wing Fools."

13.　　Goldberg, "Left-Wing Fools."

14.   Goldberg, "Left-Wing Fools."

15.   Paul C. Grzella and Cheryl Makin, "Rutgers Professor's Comments Called Anti-Semitic, Homophobic," October 26, 2017, My Central Jersey, https://www.mycentraljersey.com/story/news/local/2017/10/26/rutgers-michael-chikindas-anti-semitic/801989001/; Shiri Moshe, "Rutgers Professor Calls Judaism 'Most Racist Religion,' Blames Jews for Armenian Genocide, in Flurry of Antisemitic, Homophobic and Sexist Posts," *Algemeiner*, October 24, 2017, http://www.algemeiner.com/2017/10/24/rutgers-professor-calls-judaism-most-racist-religion-blames-jews-for-armenian-genocide-in-flurry-of-antisemitic-homophobic-and-sexist-posts/.

16.   George Ciccariello-Maher, "Which Way Out of the Venezuelan Crisis?," *Jacobin*, accessed April 27, 2018, https://www.jacobinmag.com/2017/07/venezuela-elections-chavez-maduro-bolivarianism; Theodore Kupfer, "No, George Ciccariello-Maher Doesn't Believe in Academic Freedom," *National Review*, October 12, 2017, https://www.nationalreview.com/2017/10/george-ciccariello-maher-academic-freedom-plea/; George Ciccariello-Maher (@ciccmaher), "Some guy gave up his first class seat for a uniformed soldier. People are thanking him. I'm trying not to vomit or yell about Mosul.," Twitter, March 26, 2017, 10:22 a.m., https://twitter.com/ciccmaher/status/846019558515359745?lang=en.

17.   Melissa Gray, "Drexel Professor Resigns Amid Threats Over Controversial Tweets," Cable News Network, December 29, 2017, https://www.cnn.com/2017/12/28/us/drexel-university-professor-resigns/index.html.

18.   Gray, "Drexel Professor Resigns."

19.   "George Orwell Quotes," Goodreads, accessed April 27, 2018, https://www.goodreads.com/quotes/7076-the-most-effective-way-to-destroy-people-is-to-deny.

20.   Daniel J. Flynn, "Howard Zinn's Biased History," History News Network, June 9, 2003, http://historynewsnetwork.org/article/1493.

21.   Patricia Sullivan, "Howard Zinn, 87; Wrote Best-Selling 'People's History of the United States,'" *Washington Post*, January 29, 2010, http://www.washingtonpost.com/wp-dyn/content/article/2010/01/28/AR2010012803804.html.

22.   Mark Tapson, "Matt Damon Brings Howard Zinn to Life," FrontPageMag.com, February 7, 2012, https://www.frontpagemag.com/fpm/121750/matt-damon-brings-howard-zinn-life-mark-tapson.

23.   Ron Radosh, "The Influence of Howard Zinn on the Loss of Patriotism, and the Antidote to Zinn, Dinesh D'Souza's *America*," PJ Media, July 4, 2014, https://pjmedia.com/ronradosh/2014/7/4/the-influence-of-howard-zinn-on-the-loss-of-patriotism-and-the-antidote-to-zinn-dinesh-dsouzas-movie-america/.

24.   "People's History Project," Trustees of Dartmouth College, accessed April 27, 2018, http://neukom.dartmouth.edu/projects/peopleshistoryproject.html.

25.   "Howard Zinn," United States Government Memorandum, June 20, 1969, https://web.archive.org/web/20110119015249/http://foia.fbi.gov/zinn_howard/1142983_000s2.pdf.

26. Cliff Kincaid, "Leftist 'Historian' Howard Zinn Lied About Red Ties," Accuracy in Media, July 30, 2010, https://www.aim.org/aim-column/leftist -%E2%80%9Chistorian%E2%80%9D-howard-zinn-lied-about-red-ties/.

27. Kincaid, "Zinn Lied About Red Ties"; "Howard Zinn," United States Government Memorandum.

28. Michael Kazin, "Howard Zinn's History Lessons," *Dissent*, Spring 2004, https://www.dissentmagazine.org/article/howard-zinns-history-lessons.

29. Greg Piper, "Arizona Banned From Enforcing Law Against Public School Courses That 'Promote Resentment Toward a Race,'" The College Fix, December 29, 2017, https://www.thecollegefix.com/post/40500/.

30. Phyllis Schlafly, "Un-American American History Courses," Townhall .com, August 10, 2010, https://townhall.com/columnists/phyllisschlafly /2010/08/10/un-american-american-history-courses-n1402051.

31. Schlafly, "Un-American American History."

32. Brown v. Board of Education of Topeka, United States Supreme Court, May 17, 1954, https://www.oyez.org/cases/1940-1955/347us483.

33. Martin Luther King Jr., "I Have a Dream...," March on Washington, 1963, https://www.archives.gov/files/press/exhibits/dream-speech.pdf.

34. "Why One Former Ariz. Teacher Supports the Ethnic Studies Law," FOX News Network LLC, May 17, 2010, http://www.foxnews.com/story /2010/05/18/why-one-former-ariz-teacher-supports-ethnic-studies-law.html.

35. Schlafly, "Un-American American History."

36. Schlafly, "Un-American American History."

37. John A. Ward, "Guest Opinion: Raza Studies Gives Rise to Racial Hostility," *Tucson Citizen*, May 21, 2008, http://tucsoncitizen.com/morgue /2008/05/21/85853-guest-opinion-raza-studies-gives-rise-to-racial-hostility/.

38. Schlafly, "Un-American American History."

39. Gilbert T. Sewall, "Islam in the Classroom," American Textbook Council, June 2008, http://historytextbooks.net/ED501724.pdf.

40. Sewall, "Islam in the Classroom."

41. Schlafly, "Un-American American History."

42. William J. Bennetta, "How a Public School in Scottsdale, Arizona, Subjected Students to Islamic Indoctrination," Textbook League, accessed April 27, 2018, http://www.textbookleague.org/tci-az.htm.

43. Bennetta, "Islamic Indoctrination."

44. Chris Alto, "Council on Islamic Education Worked with Textbook Publishers, Educational Organizations and Teachers to Erase 'Misconceptions,'" The Tennessee Star, December 1, 2017, https://tennesseestar.com/2017/12/01/council -on-islamic-education-worked-with-textbook-publishers-educational-organizations -and-teachers-to-erase-miconceptions/.

45. "CFNS Research and Intervention at the Brevard County, Florida School Board Meeting," Citizens for National Security, July 23, 2013, https://cfns.us /CFNS-School-Board.php.

46. World Hijab Day Organization Inc., accessed April 27, 2018, https:// worldhijabday.com/.

47. Sewall, "Islam in the Classroom."

48.   Sewall, "Islam in the Classroom."
49.   Sewall, "Islam in the Classroom."
50.   Sewall, "Islam in the Classroom."
51.   Sewall, "Islam in the Classroom."
52.   Tony Blankley, "A Disturbing Book Worth Reading," Eagle Publishing Inc., December 24, 2008, http://humanevents.com/2008/12/24/a-disturbing-book-worth-reading/.
53.   Blankley, "Disturbing Book."
54.   Sewall, "Islam in the Classroom."
55.   Paul Sperry, "Look Who's Teaching Johnny About Islam," WND.com, May 3, 2004, http://www.wnd.com/2004/05/24442/.
56.   Sperry, "Look Who's Teaching."
57.   Eklund v. Byron Union School District, United States District Court Northern District of California San Francisco Division, First Supplemental Complaint, April 22, 2003, https://www.scribd.com/document/266923198/Eklund-v-Byron-Union-School-District
58.   Eklund v. Byron Union School District; Sperry, "Look Who's Teaching."
59.   Eklund v. Byron Union School District.
60.   Sperry, "Look Who's Teaching"; Winfield Myers, "From the Mailbag: Yousef Salem Attacks Israel," Middle East Forum, October 27, 2006, https://www.meforum.org/campus-watch/campus-news/blog/october-2006/from-the-mailbag-yousef-salem-attacks-israel.
61.   "Course: Islam, A Simulation of Islamic History and Culture" (Interraction Publishers, 1991).
62.   "Course: Islam."
63.   Katie Zavadski, "School District Renames Christmas Break 'Winter Break' Instead of Accommodating Muslim Holidays," New York, November 12, 2014, http://nymag.com/daily/intelligencer/2014/11/school-district-bans-religious-holiday-names.html.
64.   Bob Unruh, "Texas Warns Book Publishers: 'No More White-Washing Islam," WND.com, September 24, 2010, http://www.wnd.com/2010/09/207577/; Texas State Board of Education, "Summary of Action Items," Mother Jones and the Foundation for National Progress, September 24, 2010, https://www.motherjones.com/files/texassboeresolution.pdf.
65.   Bob Unruh, "Texas Children Roped Into Islamic Training," WND.com, May 30, 2008, http://www.wnd.com/2008/05/65659.
66.   Unruh, "Texas Children."
67.   Unruh, "Texas Children."
68.   "'Open Tent' at Amherst Middle School," Cabinet, May 31, 2007, archived at https://web.archive.org/web/20070606205049/http://www.cabinet.com/apps/pbcs.dll/article?Date=20070531&Category=MILFORD01&ArtNo=70531004&SectionCat=Milford01.
69.   "'Open Tent,'" Cabinet.
70.   Jay Rey, "On Wearing a Hijab for a Day: 'People Look at You Differently," Buffalo News, updated February 2, 2018, http://buffalonews.com/2018/02/01/on-wearing-a-hijab-for-a-day-people-look-at-you-differently/.

71.   Rey, "Wearing a Hijab."

72.   Rey, "Wearing a Hijab."

73.   Caleb Parke, "High School Assignment Had Kids Simulate Islamic Pilgrimage to Mecca," FOX News Network LLC, October 17, 2017, http://www
.foxnews.com/us/2017/10/17/high-school-assignment-had-kids-simulate-islamic
-pilgrimage-to-mecca.html.

74.   Parke, "Pilgrimage to Mecca."

75.   Allison Pries, "Chatham Mother Sues School District for Allegedly Trying to Convert Her Son to Islam," NJ.com, January 27, 2018, http://www
.nj.com/morris/index.ssf/2018/01/chatham_mother_sues_school_district_saying
_that_tr.html.

76.   Pries, "Chatham Mother Sues."

77.   Ed Barmakian, "Chatham Mom Files Federal Lawsuit Against Chatham School District, BOE for Promotion of Islam," TAP Into LLC, January 24, 2018, https://www.tapinto.net/towns/chatham/articles/chatham-mom-files-federal
-lawsuit-against-chatham.

78.   "FCDF Files Motion for Preliminary Injunction to Stop San Diego Unified School District's 'Anti-Islamophobia' Initiative," Freedom of Conscience Fund, February 20, 2018, https://www.fcdflegal.org/fcdf-files-motion-for-preliminary
-injunction-to-stop-san-diego-unified-school-districts-anti-islamophobia-initiative/.

79.   "FCDF Files Motion," Freedom of Conscience Fund.

80.   Michael F. Haverluck, "Schools' 'Anti-Bullying' Agenda Teams w/
'Muslim Mafia,'" American Family News Network, February 22, 2018, https://
www.onenewsnow.com/education/2018/02/22/schools-anti-bullying-agenda
-teams-wmuslim-mafia.

81.   Ashley Stahl, "Why Democrats Should Be Losing Sleep Over Generation Z," *Forbes*, August 11, 2017, https://www.forbes.com/sites/ashleystahl
/2017/08/11/why-democrats-should-be-losing-sleep-over-generation-z
/#6d2893667878.

82.   Stahl, "Democrats Should Be Losing Sleep."

83.   Jim Edwards, "Goldman Sachs Has Made a Chart of the Generations … and It Will Make the Millennials Shudder," Business Insider, December 5, 2015, http://www.businessinsider.com/goldman-sachs-chart-of-the-generations-and-gen
-z-2015-12?r=UK&IR=T.

84.   Max Daly, "Gen Z Is Too Busy to Drink or Do Drugs," VICE, February 2, 2017, https://www.vice.com/en_us/article/wnzg3y/this-is-why-gen-z-takes-fewer
-drugs-than-you.

85.   Daly, "Gen Z Is Too Busy."

86.   Joan Hope, "Get Your Campus Ready for Generation Z," *Dean & Provost* 17, no. 8 (April 2016), https://doi.org/10.1002/dap.30174.

87.   Salena Zito, "Why the Generation After Millennials Will Vote Republican," *New York Post*, July 1, 2017, https://nypost.com/2017/07/01/why-the-next
-generation-after-millennials-will-vote-republican/.

Chapter 15—Activism for Our Nation

1.   David Harsanyi, "Why Does the Left Get a Pass on Anti-Semitism?," The Federalist, April 6, 2018, http://thefederalist.com/2018/04/06/why-does-the -left-get-a-pass-on-anti-semitism/.

2.   Matt Vespa, "ICYMI: Progressives Want Slave Reparations Included In Democratic Party Platform," Townhall.com, April 25, 2018, https://townhall .com/tipsheet/mattvespa/2018/04/25/icymi-progressives-want-slave-reparations -included-in-democratic-party-platform-n2474369.

3.   Thomas Fuller, "Immigration Agency Rails Against Oakland Mayor's Warning of Raids," New York Times, February 28, 2018, https://www.nytimes .com/2018/02/28/us/oakland-mayor-ice-warning.html.

4.   Adam Shaw, "'Angel Families' Want to See Oakland Mayor Prosecuted for Thwarting ICE Raids," FOX News Network LLC, March 14, 2018, http:// www.foxnews.com/politics/2018/03/14/angel-families-want-to-see-oakland-mayor -prosecuted-for-thwarting-ice-raids.html.

5.   Robert Spencer, "Maine: House Democrats Vote to Allow Female Genital Mutilation," Jihad Watch, April 23, 2018, https://www.jihadwatch.org /2018/04/maine-house-democrats-vote-to-allow-female-genital-mutilation.

INDEX

A **FREE GIFT** FOR YOU

★ ★ ★ ★ ★

Our world is really distracted. There are lots of books you can choose, yet you chose to read mine. Not only did you choose to read it, but you made it all the way through, which I really appreciate.

As my way of saying **THANK YOU** *for choosing to read this book, I am offering you a gift:*

★ Video: 1,400 years of Islamic history

★ A Wake-Up Call: Video with vital refugee information

★ E-book download: *A Quick-Start Guide to Rise: Easy Tips, Tricks, and Encouragement to Support American Values and Freedom*

To claim this **FREE GIFT**, *please go to* ***RisetoAct.com/gift.***

Thanks again, and see you on the front lines,

Brigitte Gabriel